THE LIFE OF
ST. CATHERINE
OF SIENA

*"Know, sweetest daughter," He said, 'that in
the time to come your earthly pilgrimage will be
distinguished by such marvellous new gifts from
me that the hearts of ignorant carnal men will be
amazed and incredulous . . . But you must not be
anxious or afraid, for I shall be always with you, and
I shall free your soul from the evil tongues and the
lips that utter lies. Carry out undauntedly whatever
the Spirit prompts you to do, for through you I shall
snatch many souls from the jaws of hell and by my
grace transport them to the kingdom of heaven."*
—*Our Lord to St. Catherine, pages 150–151*

THE LIFE OF
ST. CATHERINE
OF SIENA

BLESSED RAYMOND OF CAPUA
Confessor to the Saint

Translated by
George Lamb

TAN Books
Charlotte, North Carolina

TAN Books
Charlotte, North Carolina
www.TANBooks.com
2011

CONTENTS

PART TWO

CONTENTS

INTRODUCTION

T HOUGH saints have sometimes been at loggerheads and, for instance, you would trust St. Jerome on St. Augustine no more than you would Manning on Newman, a special authority invests one saint when he does bring himself to write the life of another. Not that literary skill is guaranteed, but that, in the first place, informed sympathy with the heart of the matter can be expected, a response to what holiness is about, some account of the essential business which does not reduce it to the terms of a psychological case-history or substitute for it merely a natural, if unusual, reaction to the conditions of environment. Next, when the two have lived and prayed closely together, have followed the same daily round and undergone the same weather, have shared friends, acquaintances, and critics, have belonged to the same religious family and engaged in common enterprises, and, finally, have kept no secrets from each other, then you rightly look for an appreciation of the individual embodiment of holiness, together with the moods, the cast of countenance, and even the quirks that went with this falling and remaining in love with God.

Such is the recommendation for this biography, the translation of the *Legend* of Blessed Raymond of Capua (1330–1399), which is the main source for what we know about St. Catherine of Siena (1347–1380). He sprang from the nobility of the *Regno*, being descended from Peter delle Vigne, the famous chancellor of Frederick II, and was reader in theology at Siena when he took over from Thomas della Fonte, a fellow-member of the Dominican community there, the direction of Catherine Benincasa, the dyer's daughter, a woman of twenty-seven already remarkable for her religious devotion and independent ways. Thomas, who may have felt that she was proving too much of a handful for him to manage, was self-effacing and made no fuss; later he supplied many of the recollections which were worked into the story Raymond had to be pressed to compose. Catherine herself was convinced that it was Our Lady who had sent this well-trained priest to be her confessor.

Presently he found that she was almost a full-time job, not only because of the spiritual questions she opened out, but also because she was a public figure, soon to move at the centre of international politics: her fame spread to England, and a century later Caxton printed the *Lyf of St. Katherin of Senis*. She had a profoundly theological habit of mind, and could not find enough time to dwell on the mystery of the Blessed Trinity. Always while she was acting as a welfare-worker at everybody's beck and call, fighting corruption, civil and ecclesiastical, pleading for peace, bringing back the Pope to Rome from his exile at Avignon, she yearned for the solitude where she could have occupied herself with meditation. It would have been an escape, for on taxing him whom she loved above all, "Oh where were you, Lord," for seeming so terribly distant when she was disturbed by what she regarded as worse than distractions, his answer came, "There was I, daughter, in the midst of them."

Raymond was to Catherine both father and son. Always obedient to him as a priest, sometimes impatient with him as a man, she might scold him and he in revenge might take advantage of his status and rap out orders like a pettish drill-sergeant. But she valued his advice and usually he was gentle with her and defended even her gaucheries. "Oh Lord God," she once burst out, "what kind of spiritual father is this you have given me, who finds excuses even for my sins!" They were devoted to one another.

Their temperaments were very different. For she was like the Sienese wine—very red. High-spirited and fearless, used to getting her own way where others were concerned, not one of a family of twenty-five with a bustling mother for nothing, devoid of human respect, generous in her loving and sometimes tart in its expression, it was remarked of her that she looked everybody in the face. One of the redoubtable women of history, she can be compared to St. Teresa among the yogis and Catherine of Russia among the commissars. Whereas one fancies that Raymond in appearance was a mousy little man. He suffered from ill-health, was constitutionally timid, somewhat prim and sensitive to scandal; occasionally he was puzzled by her behaviour and her projects could catch him lagging behind. Yet he was a reliable man of affairs, circumspect, a good negotiator, and he grew in stature from his friendship with her, and was ready to beard the fierce John Hawkwood, the Essex man turned condottiere, or to undertake risky journeys through the enemy lines. Prior of the Minerva at Rome when she died, he was afterwards elected Master General of his Order, in which office he died at Nuremberg during a visitation of the Germanies: some of his brethren judged that his reforming provisions neglected academic standards.

One endearing characteristic was a sense of humour about himself. Ingenuous and not given to self-esteem, he does not hesitate to tell a story against himself. Thus when he was Catherine's impresario at Avignon he confesses how the affectation of piety by the ladies of that sophisticated court hoodwinked him because of their fine dresses and good looks. He leaves the impression of having been a truthful man, incapable of inventing stories or straining the evidence. On the other hand, he was no critical and detached observer. The dear reader he still takes into his confidence will be aware that his memories come stamped with conventions and clichés many of which have passed with the late Middle Ages. No doubt they were shared by his heroine, nevertheless one feels they are stiffened and stylized in his editing. He was no Boswell, and perhaps in portraying the saint he forgot the woman. As, after her death, he dismembered the loved body in accordance with the piety of the time, sending the head to Siena where it might be venerated, but discreetly for fear of the Roman populace, so also he seems to have tried to cut her personality to the cloth of the virtues. He did not succeed, for she speaks out of turn and, like a character in Shakespeare, breaks out of the part assigned to her; shedding the panoply, she gives a lift and a lilt to the lines of his catalogue.

This can scarcely be called prosaic, for it is full of odd happenings; Catherine's own poise was not that which a humdrum psychologist would ascribe to a well-balanced personality—she was too extravagant a giver for that. Here it is well to keep in mind the classical distinction drawn by theologians between sanctifying grace, the friendship with God taken to the pitch of holiness, and the miraculous gifts, *gratiae gratis datae*, which may or may not accompany it. These do not make a saint, though they may help towards canonization. They are given for the sake of others, for profit, *ad utilitatem* says the Vulgate, a means to an end says St. Thomas Aquinas; they are meant to draw attention to something else that really matters, the loving union of human beings with God. (*1 Cor.* 12:7).[1] Since few hagiographers can feel that they have the knack of making holiness itself look interesting on paper, it is not surprising that they turn to the preternatural. Raymond does better than most, for the wonders he narrates always remain tributary to the main stream of his discourse.

The miracles worked by Our Lord himself did not appeal to people not prepared to welcome his message; they led on those who were ready to follow, as the miraculous feeding of the crowd in the desert prepared them for the revelation of the *living bread which came down from heaven, which if any man eat he shall live for ever.* (*John* 6:51) Similarly any prodigies in the lives of the saints are subsidiary to their principal witness. Moreover, although Christ's Church endures in faith in his resurrection, and divine interventions above the course of nature are perennial, individual miracles in the main are manifestations of God's tender and particular providence and are accommodated to circumstances. If, then, they are meant to commend themselves to men of the time rather than to future students of the curious, is it not likely that many of them will be period pieces or examples of regional style?

---

1. See *Summa Theologica*, 1a–2ae.CXI, 1, 3, 4.

Charity itself begins at home, and is racy of its immediate scenes and occasions. Grace makes nobody an anachronism, and it can seize on current imaginations, emotions, manners and fashions. Catherine and Raymond were children of a culture where spiritual forces could be readily materialized in the odour of sanctity and the stink of sin. The truths of faith were vividly pictured, the following of Christ was a challenge to a temper at once chivalrous and evangelical, the impact of his humanity was empirically real, and the Devil was your adversary on the prowl and no mere generalized heading for evil. The stage was better set than now for such phenomena as levitation and the stigmata.

It may be that we take to Catherine despite some of the signs and wonders her contemporaries thought so admirable. We may believe them, without finding them attractive, and have to remind ourselves that she is our model for the general design of her desire, not all the details. But if we cannot applaud—we are under no obligation—let us at least be civil and tolerant, if only from a sense of history and anthropology. Take, for instance, her vow of virginity: was it so precocious when girls of twelve were of a marriageable age? When we treat the saints with flat utilitarianism, it is not they but we who look absurd, and priggish too. Take the self-inflicted punishments: are they not a hatred of selfish indulgence put in very concrete form, the effort to be purged of the dross and to be conformed to Our Saviour? What generous heart waits for suffering to come, but instead goes out to meet it? Catherine may not be everybody's favourite saint; all the same the receptive reader of this work will exemplify the truth of what the Pope who knew her remarked, "that none ever approached her without going away better."

Thomas Gilby, O.P.
Blackfriars Cambridge Ascension Day, 1960

PART ONE

CHAPTER ONE

Catherine's Parents

———————•———————

I N TUSCANY, in the city of Siena, there once lived a man called
Giacomo, whose father, according to the custom in those parts,
was commonly known as Benincasa.

Giacomo was a man honest in all things, without deceit or guile,
free from evil, fearing God. Having lost both his parents, he had taken
to wife a girl of his own city, a certain Lapa, who, though she may have
lacked the shrewdness of the people of today, was quite capable of looking after a home and family. Lapa is still alive, and those who know her
can vouch for this. This couple, joined in matrimony and united in the
simplicity of their life, were of the people; nevertheless they belonged to
a highly respectable class and enjoyed a considerable degree of comfort.

The Lord blessed Lapa and made her fruitful, and she was as an
abounding vine in the house of her husband Giacomo; for almost every
year she gave birth to a son or a daughter, and sometimes even to twins.

I should consider myself guilty of an injustice if I kept silent about
Giacomo's exceptional qualities, all the more so as by now, as is piously
to be believed, he has already arrived at the gates of eternal bliss.

Lapa has told me that his character was so strong and his speech so
moderate that whenever he was faced with any trouble or disturbance
he would never break out into unseemly language, and whenever the

people in his house were annoyed and expressed themselves violently he would at once say to them, with a smile on his lips, "Now then, God bless you, don't get excited, and don't start using words that are unfitting on human lips!" Lapa also told me that one of his fellow citizens once tried quite unjustly to extort a sum of money from him which he falsely claimed was owing to him, and with the help of friends and calumny he caused so much harm to the good man that he brought him to the brink of ruin; but despite all this Giacomo could never bear to hear any complaints made against his calumniator or any evil to be said against him; and when Lapa herself began to do this he gently reproved her, saying, "God bless you, dearest, let be! God will show him the error of his ways and be our defender." Which subsequently happened, for the truth came out as though by a miracle, and this man learned to his cost how much he had erred in his unjust persecution.

This Lapa has recounted to me in all seriousness, and I believe it absolutely, for, as is known by everyone acquainted with her, despite her eighty years she is so far from being capable of duplicity that she could never manage to tell a lie even if she wanted to. Moreover, all who came into contact with Giacomo say that he was a man of the utmost integrity, upright and free from human vices.

Finally I must add that the restraint shown in his manner of speech by this husband and father was so great that no one who lived in his house and was brought up by him could ever use indecent or unseemly talk or bear to hear it spoken, especially if they were girls.

It came about that one of his daughters, whose name was Bonaventura (about whom we shall have more to say later), married a young man of her own city called Niccolo. This young man was an orphan and he fell into the company of young men of his own age who were not merely loose in their language but sometimes absolutely foul-mouthed. Bonaventura was so upset by this that it made her ill; indeed, she lost weight before his very eyes and became quite weak. After a few days, on being asked by her husband what was the cause of her illness, she said stoutly, "In my father's house we never used to hear some of the words that I hear being used here every day; my parents did not bring me up in that way. And you must realize that if you do not stop using these words you will soon see me dead." Niccolo was struck with admiration at this and was so edified by such behaviour on the part of his wife and her family that he forbade his companions to use unseemly language in her presence; and they obeyed him. Thus the modesty and decency that were to be found in Giacomo's house drove licence and indecency from the house of his son-in-law Niccolo.

Giacomo practised the art of making and mixing dyes for dyeing linen or woollen cloth, and both he and his sons were by reason of their trade known throughout the city as "the dyers". This led to the marvel, as we shall show later, that the daughter of a dyer should have been deemed worthy to become the bride of the King of Heaven, he himself helping her, as will be shown below.

Of the information given in this chapter, part is known to the whole city, or at least to most of the citizens; part I have learned from the holy virgin herself and from her mother Lapa; and the rest I have gleaned from religious and lay folk living in the neighbourhood, friends or relatives of Giacomo.

CHAPTER TWO

Catherine's Birth and Infancy

———————•———————

WHILE Lapa, as the result of her frequent confinements, was filling Giacomo's house with sons and daughters like a fruitful bee, heaven willed that towards the end of her productive period she should conceive and bring into the world twins, who by eternal predestination were to be presented before the eyes of the Lord; as in fact happened.

Lapa gave birth, then, to two daughters. Though meek in their physical constitution, they were strong in the sight of the Lord. Looking lovingly upon the creatures she had brought to birth, she realized that she would be unable to feed them both herself and decided to put one of them out to nurse, keeping the other to herself and bringing it up on her own milk. It was the will of God that the one she kept to herself should be the one whom from eternity the Lord had chosen as His bride.

When they received the grace of holy baptism, although they were both to be numbered among the elect, the favoured one was called Catherine and the other Giovanna. Giovanna, who with the grace of baptism had also received the name "of grace", in that same grace ascended into heaven; for in fact she was in a short space of time taken out of this world, Catherine herself remaining at the breast of her own mother to draw subsequently a whole chain of souls to heaven.

Lapa fed the child with great care and diligence, especially in view of the fact that she had chosen her in preference to the one who had died; and for this reason, as she has often told me, she was more fond of Catherine than of any other of her children.

She also told me that because of her continual pregnancies she had never been able to bring up any of her children on her own milk, but that in this case she was able to do so right to the end because she did not become pregnant again until it was time for the child to be weaned; as though it had been appointed that there should be a pause in her childbearing and that she should approach the end of childbirth with one who was to strive after and achieve the end of all perfections. It is clear indeed that what was intended from the beginning by the Prime Mover was ultimately realized in fact.

Lapa produced one more child after Catherine, and the new arrival was given the name of Giovanna in memory of the dead sister. She was Lapa's twenty-fifth child and her last.

When the time came, the child dedicated to the Lord was weaned. She was taken off the milk and began to eat bread, and when she began to walk everyone found her so pleasing and so sensible in the things she said that her mother had difficulty in keeping her at home, because all the friends and neighbours used to carry her off to their own homes so that they could enjoy her wise little sayings and the comfort of her delightful childish gaiety.

It came about that in one such burst of delight they changed her name from Catherine to Euphrosyne, but how I cannot say. In the course of time, as we shall see, she herself discovered the hidden significance of this name—when she proposed to imitate Saint Euphrosyne. But I rather like to imagine that in her childish prattle she tried to imitate other people's words, and that when she tried to join them up together they sounded like the word "Euphrosyne", and the grown-ups delightedly repeated these early stammerings and finally gave her that name.

However that may be, it is quite clear that there was already germinating within her that which was to bear its fruit when she was fully grown up. But no tongue or pen could ever adequately describe the wisdom and sense of what she was to say or the sweetness of her holy company; only those who were ever with her can have any idea of it.

And here I feel compelled by the love I bear her to say that when she spoke she communicated something by which in a way beyond all description the minds of those who heard her were so strongly drawn to good and took such delight in God that every trace of unhappiness disappeared from their hearts. All their private troubles vanished, all their burdens were forgotten, and so great and unusual a tranquillity of mind fell upon them that, amazed within themselves and delighted with the new kind of pleasure they were enjoying, they would think to themselves, "It is good for us to be here . . . let us make here three tabernacles." (*Matt.* 17:4). Nor is this to be wondered at, for without doubt there was hidden invisibly within the breast of this His bride One who when He was transfigured upon the mountain constrained Peter to utter those words.

Let us return to our story.

Catherine was meanwhile growing up and becoming more and more robust, and she was soon to be filled with the Holy Spirit and Divine Wisdom.

When she was about five she learned the Hail Mary, and repeated it over and over again as often as she could, and, as she frequently told me in confession[1] when she had occasion to speak of the matter, she was inspired by heaven to address the Blessed Virgin in this way whenever she went up and down stairs, stopping to kneel on each step as she did so. And so, as she had offered words pleasing to men, she now began to proffer devout words pleasing to God, endeavouring thereby to rise from the things that are seen to the things that are unseen.

---

1. "The virtues and graces of the penitent *are not matters for the seal* [of Confession], provided they are not manifested in order more clearly to declare the sins themselves, e.g., the gravity of ingratitude towards God." (Emphasis in original). (Jone, *Moral Theology*, no. 618, Imprimatur 1961; TAN reprint 1993).—*Publisher*, 2003.

Now that she had embarked upon these acts of devotion and was increasing them every day, the Lord in His Mercy willed to reward her for them with an astonishing vision of grace, to encourage her to receive greater graces and at the same time to intimate to her how, like a little plant tended and watered by the Holy Spirit, she was to grow into the tallest of cedars.

One day—she must have been about six at the time—she had to go with her brother Stefano, who was a little older than she was, to see her sister Bonaventura, who, as has been explained, was married to Niccolo. She may have been going on some errand from her mother, for mothers often go and see their married daughters or get someone else to go, to make sure that they are getting on all right. Having accomplished their mission, the two were coming back down a certain lane (commonly called the Valle Piatta), when the holy little girl happened to look up, and there, hanging in the air in front of her over the roof of the church of the Friars Preachers, she saw a most beautiful bridal chamber decked out in regal splendour, in which, on an imperial throne, dressed in pontifical attire and with the tiara on His head (that is to say, the monarchical papal mitre), sat the Lord Jesus Christ, the Saviour of the world. With him were the Princes of the Apostles Peter and Paul and the holy Evangelist John. At the sight of all this the little girl remained rooted to the ground, gazing lovingly with unblinking eyes upon her Lord and Saviour, who was revealing Himself to her in this way in order to captivate her love. Then, gazing straight at her with eyes full of majesty, and smiling most lovingly, He raised His right hand over her, made the sign of the cross of salvation like a priest, and graciously gave her His eternal benediction.

The grace of this gift was so immediately effective upon the little girl that she was taken right out of herself and entirely into Him she lovingly looked upon, and although she was very timid by nature she stood there in the middle of the street, filled as it was with men and animals, looking upwards with her head quite motionless, forgetting not only her journey but all her other concerns; and she would have remained there as long as the vision lasted if she had not had her attention distracted and been interrupted.

While the Lord was performing these marvels, with Catherine standing there motionless, brother Stefano had wandered on by himself, imagining that his sister was still with him. After a little while he realized that he was alone, and when he turned round and saw his sister standing there gazing up to heaven he began to shout to her, but when he saw that she made no reply and paid no attention to him he had to go back, shouting all the way; and as all this achieved nothing he got hold of her hand and pulled her, saying, "What are you doing? Why don't you come along?" Catherine seemed to come out of a deep sleep; lowering her eyes she said, "If you could see what I can you would not be so cruel and disturb me out of this lovely vision." With these words she raised her eyes again, but the vision had vanished, He thus willing it who had appeared to her; whereupon Catherine, unable to endure this without feeling a sharp sting of sorrow, burst into tears, upbraiding herself bitterly for having allowed her eyes to stop looking up towards heaven.

From that moment it became clear from Catherine's virtues, the gravity of her behaviour, and her extraordinary wisdom, that under her girlish appearance there was hidden a fully formed woman. Her actions, indeed, had nothing childish, nothing girlish, about them, but showed all the signs of a most venerable maturity. From now onwards the fire of Divine love burned within her, enlightening her mind, kindling her will, strengthening her power of thought, and enabling her external acts to conform to the laws of God.

To me, unworthy as I was, she revealed in all humility in confession that at this time, without the aid of teachers or books and taught entirely by the Holy Spirit, she had come to know and value the lives and way of life of the holy Fathers of Egypt and the great deeds of other saints, especially Blessed Dominic, and had felt such a strong desire to do what they did that she had been unable to think about anything else.

This knowledge was the cause of certain innovations in the young girl's life which filled all who witnessed it with amazement. She would seek out hidden places and scourge her young body in secret with a special rope. She gave up all childish games and devoted her time to prayer and meditation instead; unlike most children, she became increasingly silent, and took less and less food to sustain her—a thing unheard-of in the case of growing children.

Inspired by her example, a number of other little girls of her own age gathered round her, eager to hear her talk about salvation and to imitate her as best they could. They began to meet secretly in a corner of the house and scourge themselves with her, repeating the Our Father and the Hail Mary as often as she told them to. These things, as we shall see, were a sign of things to come.

Special graces from God often accompanied these acts of virtue. In fact, as her mother has often told me, and as Catherine herself was unable to deny when I asked her for confirmation of it in secret, frequently, indeed more often than not, when she was going up and down stairs she felt herself being lifted up into the air and her feet no longer touched the stairs. Her mother assured me that she used to go up the stairs so quickly that it made her quite frightened. This generally happened when Catherine wanted to avoid other people, especially men. I rather think that the repeated miracle of going up and down stairs in this way was due to the habit she had formed of saying the Hail Mary on each step.

To bring this chapter to an end, I must add that Catherine, having, as has already been explained, come to know by pure revelation the lives and deeds of the holy Fathers in Egypt, felt a strong inclination to imitate them. She confessed to me that when she was small she had felt a burning desire to become a solitary, but she had never found the way to do this. It was not, in fact, the will of heaven that she should lock herself away in solitude, but on this point she was for some time to remain in her illusion.

Being unable to restrain her desire any longer, in fact, she decided one morning to go in search of solitude. With true childish forethought she armed herself with a loaf of bread, and went off on her own in the direction of her married sister's house near the St. Ansano gate. Having gone through the gate (a thing she had never done before), she went down a steep lane, and finding that there were no houses decided that she had come to the edge of a desert. She went on until at last she found a cave under a crag; this suited her, and into it she went delightedly, convinced that she had found at last the solitude of her dreams.

God, who accepts all good and holy desires, and whom she had already seen from afar smiling at her and giving her his benediction, had not ordained that His bride should lead this kind of life; nevertheless He was not going to let this action of hers go unrewarded, and so, no sooner had she set herself to fervent prayer than she gradually began to rise into the air, as high as the cave would allow, and there she remained until the end of None.[2] Catherine imagined that this was all the Devil's work and that he was using these tricks to try to stop her from praying and from wanting to be a solitary; so she tried to pray more firmly and fervently than ever; but it was not until the time was approaching at which the Son of God completed the work of our salvation upon the cross that as she had risen so she came down again. Then by divine inspiration she realized that this was not the time for afflicting her little body for the Lord or for leaving the paternal roof, and in the same spirit as she had set off she turned back towards home. When she came out of the cave she found herself all alone, and there was all the way back to go—too far for a child of her age. Afraid that her mother and father would think she was lost, she once again commended herself to the Lord and suddenly (as she told her sister-in-law, Lisa, afterwards) she felt herself raised aloft by the Lord, to be deposited a few minutes later near the city gate, none the worse for the experience.

She hurried home, and her mother and father thought that she was simply coming back from her married sister's; and what had really happened was never known until she was grown up and revealed it to her

---

2. None lasted from midday until three in the afternoon.

confessors, amongst whom, though unworthy and the lowest of them all both by election and in merit, am I.

The episodes contained in this chapter have for the most part been related to me by Catherine's mother, Lapa; the others, especially the later ones, I learned from Lisa and the holy virgin herself. But of all that I have said, with the exception of the final episode, I have had further confirmation either from her first confessor, who was brought up as a child in her house, or from absolutely reliable women who were relatives or neighbours of the holy virgin's own parents.

CHAPTER THREE

Catherine Makes a Vow of Virginity

———————•———————

T HE power and efficacy of the vision described in the previous
chapter were such that they soon entirely uprooted all worldly
affections from the young girl's mind, to make way for a holy, single-
minded love for the Son of God and the glorious Virgin, his Mother,
Catherine despising all other things as impure that she might entirely
win the Saviour to herself.

Guided by the Holy Spirit, she began to realize that it was necessary to be perfectly pure in body and soul if she was to do this, and it
became her one desire to preserve her own virginal purity. Then she
was inspired by heaven to ponder the fact that the most holy Mother
of God had herself instituted the life of virginity, and had dedicated
her virginity to the Lord by vow. And so to her she turned. At the age
of seven Catherine was able to meditate on this vow as profoundly as
a woman of seventy. Continuously she besought the Queen of Virgins
and Angels to mercifully help her, and to deign to obtain for her from
the Lord a perfect directing of her spirit, which would enable her to
perform that which was most acceptable to Him and most profitable
for the salvation of her own soul; and she kept telling her of her ardent
desire to live a virginal, angelic life.

The love of her Eternal Bridegroom was in fact burning more

brightly every day in the heart of this wise virgin, ardently urging her mind and taking her towards a life that was heavenly and endless. Being a very sensible girl, she gave these matters a great deal of thought; she was determined not to alienate the Holy Spirit, who by kindling the desire for these things within her was so kindly granting her what she asked.

One day she went off to a secret place, where, since no one could hear her, she could speak aloud, and there, falling on her knees in a spirit of devout humility, she addressed the Blessed Virgin as follows: "O most blessed and holy Virgin, who were the first amongst all women to consecrate your Virginity for ever to the Lord, who then graciously made you the Mother of His only Son, I pray to you that out of your ineffable goodness, ignoring my deserts and all my insufficiencies, you will deign to grant me this great grace—to give me as Husband Him whom I desire with all the power of my soul, your most holy Son, our one Lord Jesus Christ; and I promise Him and you that I will never choose myself any other husband, and will always do all I can to keep my virginity unspotted."

Reader, have you noticed how the gifts granted to this holy virgin, and all her doings, were regulated in an ordered way by that Wisdom which disposes all things by its own gentle power? When Catherine is six she sees her Bridegroom with her own bodily eyes and receives His glorious benediction; when she is seven she makes a vow of virginity. Now the first of these numbers is the most perfect of all numbers and the second is held by all the theologians to signify universality. What are we to understand from this if not that this virgin was to receive from God the universal perfection of all the virtues, and thus arrive at the highest state of glory? If the first number signifies perfection and the second universality, put together they can only mean universal perfection. Therefore it was right that Catherine should be given the name of Catherine, for that too signifies universality.

Reader, you must also consider attentively the order she observed in making this vow. First she endeavours to have as her Bridegroom

Him whom her soul desires, and then she renounces the thought of any other husband and resolves to keep her promise all her life. Could she possibly be denied her desire?

Consider to whom she is turning, what she is asking, and the manner of her asking.

She turns to one who distributes her graces most generously, who, being unable to refuse even sinners, can never reject anyone, who gives to wise and foolish alike, despising no one, opening her hand unceasingly to every needy soul and to all who are poor—to one, in fact, who is an inexhaustible fountain. How can such a one fail to hear an ardent innocent young girl, when even adults full of sin are not beyond the scope of her grace? How can she refuse to accept a vow of virginity, when she was herself the first to institute the life of virginity? How deny her Son to a virgin who asks her for Him with such love, when it was she who brought Him down from heaven to earth to give Him to all who believe?

Now that you have seen how Catherine prayed, consider for what end she prayed. She wants to obtain something that she has been taught to ask for by the very Person of whom she is asking it, seeks what the Person sought has himself invited her to seek. If the Truth cannot deceive, her request cannot be refused, nor can the desire for a thing so solemnly promised ever turn out to be fruitless. Incarnate Truth said, "Ask and it shall be given you; seek and you shall find," (*Matt.* 7:7; *Luke* 11:9) and in another place, "Seek ye therefore first the Kingdom of God and His justice." (*Matt.* 6:33; *Luke* 12:31). And so, small though she is, she asks and seeks anxiously for the Son of God, who is Himself the kingdom of God: how then can she fail to find what she seeks and receive what she asks for?

But if you attend to the manner of her asking, you will see clearly that, the divine law being what it is, her prayer cannot possibly remain unanswered. For in fact she is preparing herself to receive what she wills to obtain, removing every obstacle not only in the present but in the future too, clothing herself for ever in the mantle of purity, a thing dear to the Lord from whom she is asking it. She assumes a solemn obligation before God, so that neither Satan nor the world will be able to break her determination. What conditions are lacking, that her prayer should not perforce be heard? True, she is asking for something for herself, but humbly, insistently; she is asking for something salutary, her own salvation, and to manifest her determination in one single act she makes a perpetual vow, by which she removes all possible obstacles to the fulfilment of her wish.

Good reader, if you are acquainted with the Sacred Scriptures must you not perhaps conclude that, granted the divine law, this prayer must necessarily be answered by the Lord? Be assured, then, that so it was, and that as she asked for the Eternal Bridegroom so she received Him from His most sweet Mother and joined herself to Him in a vow of perpetual virginity, the Mother of God herself acting as mediator.

In the last chapter of Part One of this book I hope with the help of heaven to prove all this with an account of a wonderful miracle.

Having made her vow, the holy maid grew holier every day. The little disciple of Christ began to fight against the flesh before the flesh had begun to rebel. She determined to give up eating meat, as far as she could, at least, and when she was obliged to sit down at table she usually either passed any meat on to her brother Stefano or threw it to the cats on the sly. As regards the discipline she practised upon herself, either alone or with the other children of her own age, she now endeavoured to increase its severity; and, believe it or not, she began to glow with a zeal for souls and with a specially strong love for saints who had laboured for the salvation of their fellow-men.

About this time it was revealed to her by the Lord that holy Father Dominic had formed the Order of Preaching Friars out of a zeal for the Faith and the salvation of souls, and she suddenly developed such a high idea of this Order that whenever she saw any of the Preaching Friars going past the house she would watch where they put their feet and then as soon as they had gone by go and kiss their footprints in a spirit of great humility and devotion. Hence arose within her

17

an unquenchable longing to become a member of the Order and to join in the work of helping souls. Then, remembering that she was a woman, she many times (as she confessed to me) thought of imitating St. Euphrosyne, whose name she had been given, who had gone into a monastery dressed in men's clothing, so that she could go into distant parts where no one knew her, pretending to be a man, and so enter the Order of Preaching Friars and help towards the salvation of souls. But Almighty God had infused this zeal into her soul for other ends and intended to satisfy her desire in quite a different way, and He did not will that this scheme, which she had in mind for a long time, should ever be put into practice.

Meanwhile the holy maiden was growing up in body and especially in spirit. Her humility was strong, her devotion was increasing, her faith was growing more enlightened, hope was strengthening, charity becoming increasingly ardent, and with all these virtues her wisdom was plain to all eyes. Her parents were full of amazement, and her brothers full of admiration; at home they would all look at each other in wonder at finding so much wisdom in so young a child.

In confirmation of this I will repeat something solemnly told me by her mother.

Round about this time, when Catherine was between seven and ten, Lapa wanted to have a Mass said in honour of St. Anthony; so she called her daughter and said, "Go to the parish church and ask the priest to say a Mass in honour of St. Anthony, or get some other priest to say one, and leave the offering of so many candles and this money on the altar." When she heard this, the young girl, always delighted to do anything to honour God, went running off to the church as fast as she could go, found the priest, did what her mother had told her to do, and was so delighted with any celebration of Mass that she stayed in the church until it was all over.

Meanwhile Lapa, who had wanted her to return home as soon as she had left the offering, had begun to worry, and she no sooner set eyes on the girl than she started scolding her, saying, as was the custom in those parts, "Cursed be the chatterers who said you would never come back!" (This is a way some people have of describing people who are a long time turning up.) When she heard her mother say this the wise little maiden was silent for a while, then, taking her aside, she said, humbly, "Lady mother, when I don't do what you tell me to do, or go too far, beat me as much as you like so that next time I shall take more care, because this is meet and just; but I beg you not to let my failings make your tongue run away with you and make you start cursing the neighbours, whoever they may be, because this doesn't suit anyone of your age and it causes me very great pain."

Her mother was rather taken aback by this sage reproof from her little daughter and for a while she hardly knew how to answer, seeing such great wisdom in such a tiny person, but, determined not to show her real feelings, she simply said, "Why have you been so long?" "Because I stayed to hear the Mass you had told me you wanted said," Catherine replied; "as soon as it was over I came straight home."

Her mother was even more highly edified by this, and when Giacomo came in she told him all about it in great detail, saying, "That daughter of yours said this to me, and this." And her father, giving thanks to God in his heart, pondered on what had happened.

From this little incident, unimportant as it is amongst so many others, you can see, reader, how the grace of God went on increasing in the holy virgin during her marriageable years, of which the next chapter is to speak.

And here I stop. The facts I have described in this chapter I learned for the most part from Catherine herself; the rest I got from her mother and others who were at home with her at the time.

CHAPTER FOUR

Bitter Struggles

———————————•———————————

TOWARDS the end of these early years, years that so far as Catherine was concerned were full of marvels and virtue, Almighty God willed that the vine which he had so recently planted in the vineyards of Engaddi should grow still higher and rise to "the height of the cedars of Lebanon", and that the grapes of Cyprus should "put forth on the heights". He therefore caused it to be hidden under the ground for a while to deepen its roots, so that it could spread its branches higher in the sky and bear fruit at the topmost point of perfection. As water which desires to shoot up high first descends into the depths, so is it usually with plants, which reach higher up into the sky the deeper their roots go.

It is not to be wondered at then if sometimes Uncreated Wisdom, the artificer of all things, allows its saints to fall into some fault, so that rising re-invigorated, and living thenceforth more wisely, they strive more ardently to reach the highest state of perfection and to bring off a glorious victory against the Enemy of man.

I say this because when this virgin dedicated to the Lord reached the marriageable age of about twelve she began to be kept at home—according to the local custom, for in Siena it is not usual for unmarried girls of that age to be allowed out of the house.

Besides this, her mother and father and brothers, not knowing her intentions, were already thinking of getting her married, and were trying to find a suitable match for her. Her mother especially, with her daughter's goodness and wisdom in mind, had dreams of rejoicing in some distinguished son-in-law—though her daughter had in fact already obtained a greater son-in-law than she could possibly have imagined!

Lapa began to bother about her daughter's appearance, teaching her how to behave, making her wash her face and neck properly, keeping her hair combed and tidy—in short, doing all she could to make her attractive so that if anyone should come along to ask for her they should find her pretty. But Catherine had quite different ideas, however much, out of respect, she kept quiet about the vow she had made, and she refused to do any of these things: she was fully occupied trying to please, not men, but God.

Her mother anxiously watched the way she was behaving and one day she summoned her married daughter Bonaventura and told her to get Catherine to follow her mother's advice and make herself beautiful like everyone else. Lapa knew that Catherine was very fond of Bonaventura and that she would listen to her more than to anyone else, as in fact she did; and as a result of Bonaventura's determined efforts the Lord permitted the young girl to agree to pay more attention to her dress, though at the same time keeping firmly to her vow not to take a husband.

Later, in confession, she used to acknowledge this fault with so many sobs and tears that one would have thought she had committed heaven knows what sin.[1] Now that she has ascended into heaven I can reveal these things which redound so much to her glory, though in the first place they were meant to be kept secret, and I may mention the argument that arose between us during one of the many general confessions she made to me, when arriving at this point she turned on herself, sobbing and crying and harshly upbraiding herself.

---

1. A confessor is, in certain circumstances, permitted to reveal his penitent's virtues.

Though experience has taught me that pious souls can find sins where there are no sins, and turn quite small ones into big ones, nevertheless, since Catherine was upbraiding herself as though she had committed some fault worthy of everlasting punishment I was constrained to ask her whether she had thought of breaking her vow of virginity. She answered that no such thought had ever come into her head. I next asked her whether, apart from this matter of her virginity, she had dressed up to please any particular man or men in general, and she said that nothing had so upset her as to see or be seen by men or to find herself in their company. Whenever the apprentices in her father's dye works, who lived with the family, came near her, she would rush off as though there were serpents after her—much to everyone's amazement. Nor would she ever stand at the window or the front door to see who was passing. So I asked her, "Why ever should you have deserved eternal punishment for trying to make yourself look pretty, if you didn't carry it to excess?" Catherine replied that the real trouble was that she had loved her sister more than she should have done, and in fact seemed to have loved her more than God; and that that was what made her cry and why she had to do such severe penance for it. And when I said that although there may have been some slight excess, nevertheless it had been very slight indeed and free from any vain intention in itself and so had contained nothing against the law of God, she raised her eyes and her voice to God and exclaimed, "Oh, Lord God, what kind of a spiritual father is this you have given me, who finds excuses for my sins!" Then, growing angry with herself, she turned to me and went on, "Father, is this vile miserable creature who has received so many graces from her Creator without any labour or merit on her own part supposed to spend her time beautifying her putrid flesh to deceive some poor mortal? I don't believe," she went on, "that hell itself would have been a sufficient punishment for me if the divine pity had not had mercy on me." I could not but be silent.

But the real purpose of this discussion had been to find out whether her soul had always remained unstained by mortal sin and whether she had preserved her virginity of mind and body perfectly free not only from the sin of incontinence but from any other consummated sin, and before God and Holy Church I can render this testimony to her: I heard innumerable of her confessions, some of a general kind, and I never once discovered that she had failed to fulfil the divine commandments, unless it be in the case I have just described. But I do not believe that that was a sin, nor do I think that anyone else will think it was, either.

I may add, that I always found her so free from venial sin that in her daily confessions I had difficulty in finding anything to find fault with; for the rest, it is well known to her confessors and to those who were constantly with her that she never, or hardly ever, said anything she shouldn't. She spent all her time in prayer and contemplation and in the edification of her neighbour. Of all the twenty-four hours of the day she slept for hardly one quarter of one hour. While she was eating—if it can be called eating—in her own peculiar way, she would pray and meditate, her mind revolving incessantly around the things she had been taught by the Lord.

I know of a truth and hereby testify before the whole Church of Christ that during all the time I knew her she suffered more from having to eat than a famished man does from being unable to; at such times her body experienced greater torment than a sick man usually feels from being ill. And this was one of the reasons why, as with the grace of God I shall show later, she accepted the matter of eating as a bodily affliction and a torment. But with what offences could her mind be involved, if it was entirely concentrated on God? Nevertheless, Catherine upbraided herself with such severity, and took on the burden of guilt so cunningly, that if her confessor had not been used to her violent way of treating herself he would have believed her to be at fault where there was no fault, and where indeed there was if anything merit in what she had done.

Dear reader, I have made this digression so that you may see how much perfection came through the medium of divine grace from one of the holy virgin's few faults.

And now let us return to our story.

Bonaventura went on trying to cajole the holy girl into imitating her example and dressing up in her best clothes, but she could never get her to feel an inclination for any man or even to be voluntarily seen by men, even though her prayers and assiduity in meditating were gradually losing their fervour. But Almighty God, unable to bear the sight of His chosen bride being drawn even the slightest bit further away from Him, Himself removed the obstacle that was preventing her from uniting herself with Him; for Bonaventura, having led her holy sister into the ways of vanity, shortly afterwards found herself about to give birth, and, young as she was, died in doing so.

And here, reader, note how hateful and displeasing to God are people who do anything to interfere with those who desire to serve Him. Bonaventura was in herself a perfectly good woman from every point of view, but because she had tried to draw one who wished to serve Him towards the world, God came down heavily upon her and punished her with death. She obtained mercy, however, for, as was subsequently revealed to the virgin, after finding herself in purgatory and undergoing severe punishment she ascended to heaven as a result of her sister's prayers; this the latter told me in confidence.

On her sister's death the holy virgin, now seeing clearly the vanity of the world, turned to her Eternal Bridegroom with greater fervour and desire, and acknowledging her culpability and upbraiding herself, prostrate with Mary Magdalene at the feet of her Lord, she gave herself to tears, imploring Him to have mercy on her, praying and pondering on her sin, hoping to hear the words once addressed to Mary herself, "Thy sins are forgiven thee." (*Luke* 7:48). She began to develop a particular devotion towards the Magdalene, doing everything she could to imitate her to obtain forgiveness. This devotion grew and grew until, as with the Lord's help I shall explain in detail later, the Bridegroom of all holy souls and His glorious Mother assigned the Magdalene to the holy virgin as her own mistress and mother.

Things had reached such a state, in fact, that the age-long Enemy,

seeing the virgin now running with the utmost speed to the safe refuge
of the tabernacle of all mercy (her Bridegroom), found to his dismay
that the prey which he had hoped gradually to make his own was escap-
ing out of his hands, and to prevent this from happening he determined
to set a trap for her through her own people at home, hoping that
opposition and persecution would in the end draw her to the things of
this world.

He put it into their heads, in fact, to find Catherine a husband
somehow or other and so get themselves a new member of the family.
They were further encouraged to do this because of the loss of their
other daughter Bonaventura and hoped that Catherine would make up
for the bereavement they had suffered. And so especially after Bonaventura's death they did all they could to find the holy maiden a husband.

When the virgin began to realize this, and, under the Lord's inspiration, saw what the Devil was up to, she began to pray more than ever,
devoting herself entirely to meditation and penance and eschewing all
masculine society, thereby making it quite clear to her family that she
had absolutely no desire for a mortal corruptible husband—because
from her earliest years she had been betrothed in grace to the immortal
King of all the ages.

The holy maiden kept on making this quite clear in every way she
could, but her parents decided to force her and went to see one of the
Order of Preaching Friars, a friend of the family, who is still alive. They
implored him to try to persuade her to give way and this he promised
to do; and in fact he went to see the virgin, and, finding her firm in her
holy intention, felt bound in conscience to give her this sensible advice:
"Since there seems to be absolutely no doubt that you wish to serve the
Lord," he said, "and these people keep pestering you to do the opposite,
show them you mean what you say—cut your hair off, and then perhaps they'll keep quiet!" Accepting this advice as though it came from
heaven, Catherine seized a pair of scissors and joyfully cut her hair off
to the roots, hating it as the cause of her grievous sin. Then she covered
her head with a cap. From then on, in fact, unlike other girls, but in

accordance with the teaching of the Apostle, (*1 Cor.* 11:4–7) she began to go about in a veiled cap.

When her mother Lapa noticed this she asked her why she was wearing this strange kind of headgear, but she could not get any precise answer out of her, for Catherine did not want to lie or prevaricate, and so she mumbled instead of replying openly; whereupon her mother went up to her, snatched the cap off her head, and found her head close-cropped. This gave her a big shock, for Catherine had had very beautiful hair. "Whatever have you done, daughter?" she wailed. Catherine simply put the cap back on her head and walked away, but Lapa's shrieks had brought her husband and sons running up, and when they discovered what had happened they were furious with the girl.

This was the beginning of Catherine's second battle, a fiercer one even than the first; but with the help of heaven it resulted in a victory so complete that the very things that had seemed as though they were bound to act against her worked miraculously to her advantage and united her more closely with the Lord.

In the house they started persecuting her openly, threatening and abusing her. "You wretched girl," they said, "You may have cut off your hair, but don't imagine that you have succeeded in your purpose. Your hair is bound to grow again, and we will force you to take a husband, even if it breaks your heart; you will have no rest until you do what we want you to."

It was decided that from now on Catherine was not to have a room of her own and was to be kept busy doing housework so that she would have no opportunity for praying and uniting herself with her Bridegroom. So that she would realize she was in disgrace the maid was given a rest, and she was made to do all the dirty work in the kitchen in her place, and every day she was deluged with insults, taunts and jeers of a kind especially designed to hurt her feelings as a girl. Finally they managed to find her a young man, whom, according to what I have been told, they would have been very glad to have in the family, and then they attacked her even more fiercely to force her to give her consent to him.

The age-old Adversary, whose guile and malignancy had started all this, imagined that he was triumphing over the girl, but in fact he was only making Catherine stronger, for she was quite unperturbed by all these upsets and under the inspiration of the Holy Spirit she began to build up in her mind a secret cell which she vowed she would never leave for anything in the world. She had begun by having a room in a house, which she could go out of and come into at will; now, having made herself an inner cell which no one could take away from her, she had no need ever to come out of it again.

These were heavenly victories that could never be taken away from her, and they chained Satan down; for Truth itself has declared that the Kingdom of God is within us, (*Luke* 17:21) and we know from the Prophet that all the glory of the eternal King's daughter is within. (*Psalm* 44:14). Within us, in fact, is the clear understanding, the free will, the tenacious memory; and into us is infused the unction of the Holy Spirit, which perfecting these powers overcomes and annihilates all obstacles outside; within us, if we are good strivers, lives that Guest who said, "Have confidence, I have overcome the world." (*John* 16:33).

Trusting in this Guest, Catherine built for herself a cell not made with human hands, helped inwardly by Christ, and so was untroubled about losing a room with walls built by men. I remember—it has just come into my mind—that whenever I used to find myself pressed with too much business, or had to go on a journey, Catherine would say again and again, "Make yourself a cell in your own mind from which you need never come out." At that time I only understood what she meant superficially; but now, thinking back on her words, I am constrained to say with John the Evangelist, "These things his disciples did not know at the first: but when Jesus was glorified, then they remembered . . ." (*John* 12:16). It is remarkable how often it happens that I and the others who lived with her understand what she said and did better today than when she was amongst us.

Let us return to the story.

The Holy Spirit put into the virgin's mind another idea that enabled her to triumph over all the jeers and insults; this she revealed to me once when we were alone together, and I asked her how she had managed to retain her self-possession in the midst of all this ill-treatment. She told me that she had imagined her father as our Lord and Saviour Jesus Christ, her mother as his most glorious Mother, and her brothers and the other members of the family as the holy Apostles and disciples. With this in her mind, she had been able to serve them quite conscientiously and contentedly—much to their amazement. And also, while she was serving them, she could think about her Bridegroom and imagine she was serving Him too, and so when she was working in the kitchen she was all the time in the Holy of Holies and when she was waiting at table her soul could feed on the presence of the Saviour. O height of the riches of the eternal Counsel, in how many different and wonderful ways can you liberate those who trust in you from every kind of misery, guiding them through Scylla and Charybdis to the haven of eternal salvation!

So the matter remained: the holy virgin, with her eyes fixed unwaveringly on the reward promised her by the Holy Spirit, bore every offence with joyful patience, proceeding forward on the path marked out for her so that the joy of her soul might be complete. Unable now to have a room of her own and forced to be with the rest of the family all the time, with holy cunning she adopted her brother Stefano's room, as he had no wife or children, and during the day when he was out she could be alone there, and at night when he was asleep she could pray as much as she liked. Thus, ever seeking the face of the Bridegroom, she stood knocking untiringly at the door of the divine Tabernacle, praying continuously to the Lord that he would protect her virginity and singing with St. Cecilia the words of David, "Let my heart be undefiled in thy justifications." (*Psalm* 118:80). Thus wondrously fortified by silence and hope, the fiercer the persecutions became, the more she was sustained by graces and consolations, until her brothers, seeing her constancy, said to each other, "She has defeated us." But her father, a better person than the others, silently pondered his daughter's behaviour, and became more and more convinced every day that she was not being guided by any spirit of youthful caprice but by the Spirit of God.

What I have said in this chapter has been told me by Lapa, Catherine's mother, and Lisa, the wife of one of her brothers; and what I could not be told by the other people in the house I learned from the holy virgin herself.

CHAPTER FIVE

Catherine's Victory

———————•———————

W HILE the events narrated in the previous chapter were proceeding, the handmaid of Christ was one day praying fervently in her younger brother's room. The door was open, because she had been forbidden by her parents to shut herself up anywhere, and her father Giacomo came in looking for something, knowing his son was out. When he entered he looked round, and instead of seeing what he wanted he found his daughter there—though she seemed to be more God's than his, for she was kneeling in a corner praying, and above her head was a snow-white dove, which flew up as soon as he came in, and then, as it seemed to him, flew out through the window. Giacomo asked his daughter whose dove it was that had just flown away but Catherine said she had not seen any dove, or anything else. This amazed him, and he kept all these things in his heart, going over them in his mind again and again.

At this time, as has been said above, there was increasing in the mind of the holy virgin the desire which had first come to her as a child, and which she now wished to realize so as to safeguard her virginity, that is to say, to take the habit of the Order of Preaching Friars, whose founder and organizer and father had been the most blessed Dominic. Day and night she turned untiringly to the Lord, imploring Him to grant this wish of hers, developing too, as has been said above, a great devotion towards St. Dominic, who had always had such a splendid and most fruitful zeal for the salvation of souls. The Lord in His goodness, seeing the wisdom and fortitude with which His little disciple fought her battles and the fervour with which she was trying to make herself pleasing to Him, willed to grant her wish and, to give her a greater sense of security, comforted her with the following vision.

It was given, then, to the handmaid of Christ to see in a dream many holy fathers, and the founders of various Orders, including the most blessed Dominic. She recognized him at once because he was holding in his hands a most beautiful dazzling white lily, which, like Moses' bush, (*Ex.* 3:2) burned brightly without ever being consumed. All the people present advised her in turn to enter one of their Orders but she kept her eyes fixed on St. Dominic and gradually moved towards him. Suddenly he came forward to meet her, holding in his hand the habit of the Sisters of Penance of St. Dominic of whom there have always been a great number in the city of Siena. When he came up to her he comforted her saying, "Sweetest daughter, take courage and fear no obstacle, for you will undoubtedly put on this habit, as is your wish." These words filled her with great joy, and with tears of happiness she gave thanks to God and to Dominic, the famous athlete of the Lord, for giving her such perfect consolation. Then she was awakened by her tears and came back to her senses.

The virgin felt so encouraged and fortified by this vision that she was emboldened that same day to call her parents and brothers together and speak to them as follows: "For a long time you have been talking amongst yourselves and planning to marry me off to some mortal, corruptible man, as you have told me; and though I cordially detest the idea, as you must have been able to see from a number of signs I have given you, nevertheless I have kept quiet until now from the feeling of reverence that God commands us to show our parents. But now the time for keeping quiet is over, and I must tell you plainly what is in my heart and what my real intentions are. They did not come to me today; on the contrary, I have had them ever since I was a child, and they have only grown stronger with the passage of time. You must know then that when I was quite a little girl I made a vow of virginity to our Lord Jesus Christ, the Saviour of the world, and his most glorious Mother; and I did not do this childishly, but after long reflection and intentionally, and I promised Him that I would never marry anyone but Him through all eternity. Now that with the grace of God I have reached years of discretion and have more understanding you must know that there are some things so firmly established within me that it would be easier to soften a stone than to remove them from my heart. The more you go on about this the more you will be wasting your time; so I advise you to throw all thoughts of an engagement for me to the winds, because I have no intention whatsoever of obliging you in that respect: I must obey God rather than men. Further: if you want to keep me in this house as a servant I am quite prepared to stay and will willingly do my best to serve you; but if you prefer to cast me out you can rest assured that I shall not deviate from my intention by a hair's breadth. I have a rich and powerful Husband who will never let me die of hunger, and I am certain that He will never let me go without any of the things I need."

When the family heard this they burst into tears, and what with the sobs and the sighs no one was in a fit condition to say a word for some time. They had now fully realized the seriousness of the virgin's holy intention and did not dare oppose it, and they gazed dumbstruck at this girl who had hitherto always been so silent and shy but who had now revealed her thoughts so clearly and bravely and in such well-chosen words; and when they saw that she was prepared to leave home rather than break the vow she had made, which meant that there was no hope of her ever getting married, they were so moved that they found tears easier than words.

After a while they began to recover, and Catherine's father, who loved her tenderly, and who also feared God more than the others, remembered the dove he had seen and a number of other things he had noticed with amazement and said, "God forbid, darling daughter, that we should oppose the divine will from which it is clear your holy intention proceeds. We have realized this for some time as a matter of fact, but now we know for certain that you are not moved by youthful caprice but by an impulse of divine love. So keep your vow. Do exactly as you wish, and as the Holy Spirit teaches you. From now on we shall leave you in peace to your holy works, and put no more obstacles in the way of your holy exercises. Pray for us all a great deal, that we may be worthy of the promises of your Husband who in His grace singled you out from your earliest years." Then turning to his wife and sons he said, "From now on let no one upset this my dearest daughter or dare to interfere with her; let her serve her Husband freely and pray to Him for us unceasingly. We could never find a relative in any way comparable to this One, and we have no reason to lament if instead of a mortal man we are to have God and an Immortal Man in our family."

The matter ended in general lamentation, especially from Lapa, who loved her daughter very much in a worldly way, but the holy virgin, exulting in the Lord, gave thanks to her triumphant Bridegroom for leading her to victory. Then she humbly thanked her parents and prepared to make the utmost of the privileges that had been granted her.

Here I bring this chapter to an end.

You must know, reader, that I did not learn about the dove from the virgin's father, because he was already dead when I first met her; I was told about it by people who knew him well, and also by the maiden, who had often heard him tell the story. Indeed, they said that he had seen the dove several times and it had made him begin to feel a great veneration for his daughter and he had decided that she was to be left in peace. I have tried to write about this matter with as much moderation as I can, to avoid any suggestion of falsehood. With regard to the vision of St. Dominic, both I and my predecessor as her confessor learned about this from the holy virgin herself. And the speech she delivered to her parents and brothers too she described to me herself, relating everything in the greatest detail when I asked her how she had behaved during this time of persecution.

CHAPTER SIX

Catherine's Penances and Lapa's Persecutions

————•————

HAVING obtained her longed-for freedom to serve God, the virgin with admirable celerity began to direct her life towards serving Him. She was given a little room of her own in which she could pray and scourge herself as much as she liked just as though she were living in solitude, and with what penitential zeal she treated her body, and with what ardour she sought her Bridegroom, no tongue can tell.

This seems the right moment to speak of her unprecedented penances, so I shall break off my narrative at this point, dear reader, believing it appropriate to acquaint you with these matters forthwith. Before making a tour of the whole garden of her holy life, you must now taste some of its earlier fruits. But have no fear, for you will have the final fruits presented to you in all their beauty, God willing, when the narrative requires it; by proceeding in this way now you will be given a foretaste and be more ready to consider the fruits of her virtues later.

You must know, then, that in this little room were revived the ancient deeds of the holy Fathers of Egypt, which is all the more extraordinary considering the fact that they took place without Catherine's ever having been told about them or seen anything like them or given any thought to them before this time.

Consider, for instance, her abstinence from food and drink. As has been said above, the virgin had rarely eaten meat from early childhood, but from now on she would have nothing to do with it at all, and she became so used to doing without it that, as she confessed to me herself, the mere smell of it used to make her feel sick.

There is no need to marvel at this, dear reader. I must tell you that once, when I found her very ill and exhausted, I heard that she was not taking any of the food or drink that is usually given to invalids, and I managed to get some sugar put into the water she was drinking to try to build up her strength a little. When I told her about this she rounded on me and said, "It seems to me you want to take away the little bit of life I still have left!" I asked her what she meant, and learned that she had grown so accustomed to eating food without sugar and drinking pure water that sweet things were like poison to her. The same was true of meat.

At this time when she was living in her cell, she began to water down the wine she drank so much that it lost all its flavour and bouquet but kept a faint pinkish colour because Sienese wines are so red. When she was fifteen she gave up wine and drank nothing but well water.

She also gradually learned to do without any kind of cooked food except bread, and soon reached the point of living entirely on bread and raw herbs. When she was about twenty, I think, she gave up eating bread altogether, and lived entirely on raw herbs. In the end it was given her, not as a result of habit or natural disposition, but as I hope, God willing, to explain more fully later, through a divine miracle, to reach such a point that though her wasted body was plagued by complaints and subject to labours that others would never have been able to endure, nevertheless the vital juices were not consumed within her; and though her stomach would not digest anything her physical powers were not at all enfeebled by this lack of food and drink. It always seemed to me that her whole life was a miracle, for what was visible before our eyes was something that could not possibly have taken place as the result of a natural process, as I was told plainly by the doctors

I took to see her. But all these things, God willing, will be dealt with more fully later.

To end this part about her abstinence, you can rest assured, reader, that all the time I had the good fortune to be in Catherine's company she lived without eating or drinking, and endured unbearable pains and labours with an always joyful countenance without any help from nature. But it would be wrong to think that it was by any kind of effort or experience or habit of a natural kind that she reached this state or that anyone else could do such things. They were far too extraordinary for that, the result of fullness of spirit rather than any practice or habit of abstinence. As you know, fullness of spirit overflows into the body, because while the spirit is feeding the body finds it easier to endure the pangs of hunger. Can any Christian doubt this? Is it not a fact that the holy martyrs rejoiced in the torments of hunger in a quite unnatural way, as they did other bodily sufferings? How did they do this if not through fullness of spirit? I myself know from experience, and believe that anyone can prove it for himself, that while we are attending to God we find it easy to fast, but if we turn to other things we find it well-nigh impossible to go on with it. Why is this if not because in the former case the fullness of the spirit is sustaining the body with which it is hypostatically united? Such a thing may be above nature, but the body and the spirit naturally communicate both good things and bad to each other. I do not deny that some people find it easier to fast than others; but I do not see how a fast can go on as long as Catherine's did on any natural basis. Let this suffice for the moment for the matter of the virgin's abstinence.

But you must not imagine, reader, that she subdued her flesh in this way only. Attend to what follows. She joined a few boards together; and that was her bed. She sat on these boards to meditate, she remained prostrate on them to pray, and when it was time to go to bed she stretched herself out on them, dressed, to sleep.

Her clothes were made entirely of wool. For a time she wore a hair shirt, but being clean of soul she hated any kind of outward dirtiness too and for that reason she changed the hair shirt for a chain, an iron chain, which she wound so tightly round her waist that it sank into her flesh and almost chafed the skin away. I was told this by her spiritual daughters and companions, who often had to wipe her down after bouts of excessive sweating and change her clothes to bring her a little relief. Towards the end of her life, when her physical sufferings greatly increased, I ordered her under obedience to take this chain off, which she did, though extremely unwillingly.

In the beginning she used to stay awake at night until Matins, as, God willing, I shall relate at length later, but she gradually overcame her need for sleep until she needed no more than half an hour every other day, and only gave in to it when exhaustion forced her to. She once told me that she had found learning to do without sleep the most difficult thing of all.

When I knew her, if she had intelligent people to talk to she could have gone on talking to them about God for a hundred days and nights without stopping for any food and drink. She never got tired of talking about God; on the contrary, as time went on she seemed to grow ever more lively and enthusiastic. Again and again she has told me that she knew of no greater consolation in life than talking and arguing about God with people of understanding, and anyone who ever worked with her can vouch for this from personal experience; in fact it was quite obvious that when she could find time to talk about God and discuss things really close to her heart she took on a younger, healthier, happier air, even physically, but when she was not able to do this she went weak and seemed to have hardly a breath in her body.

I relate the following story in honour of the Lord Jesus Christ, Catherine's Eternal Bridegroom, and in praise of Catherine herself— and to my own confusion. When Catherine talked to me about God and entered into profound discussions of the highest mysteries, the conversation often went on for a very long time, and I, not possessing her spirit, and being weighed down by the weight of the flesh, would sometimes drop off to sleep. Catherine was always quite engrossed when she talked about God and she would go on talking away without noticing that I was nodding, but then after a while she would realize that I was asleep and she would wake me up by saying in a loud voice, "My dear man, do you really want to miss things useful to your soul, just for the sake of sleep? Am I supposed to be talking to you or the wall?"

Wishing to emulate Blessed Dominic who had appeared to her she disciplined herself with an iron chain three times a day—once for herself, once for the living, and once for the dead. In the story of St. Dominic's life it says that the famous Father usually did this, and for a long time she did the same. Later she had to give the practice up because she had begun to suffer from too many physical ailments. When I asked her privately how she did this penance she confessed with some embarrassment that she took an hour and a half over each application, and that the blood used to run down from her shoulders to her feet.

Just think, reader, what degree of perfection this soul must have reached if she was prepared to draw blood from herself three times a day to render to the Lord "blood for blood". Consider with how much virtue she had been enriched if within the walls of her own home she could do what she did without any instruction or guidance or example from human beings. Read the lives of the saints, the lives of the Egyptian Fathers, read the Holy Scriptures themselves, and tell me whether you can find anything comparable in them. You will discover no doubt that Paul, the first hermit, spent a long time alone in the desert, but he was brought half a loaf every day by a crow. You will find the celebrated Anthony practising extraordinary penances—but remember that he had visited a number of anchorites, from each of whom he had taken some example of virtue as others gather flowers. St. Jerome says that Hilary went to see Anthony when he was little more than a boy and then withdrew into the desert where after many fierce struggles he emerged victorious over himself. And the two Macariuses, and Arsenius, and all the others whom it would take too long to list in detail, had teachers, learned men who by their words and example guided them in the way of the Lord: this has always been the case, both in the desert and in any well-ordered and well-governed monastery. This true daughter of Abraham, however, lived not in a monastery or a desert but in her own home, without any help or example from any human being and in the face of hostility from everybody in the house, and yet she was able to reach a stage of perfection in the matter of abstinence which had never been attained by any of these saints. Faced with such facts, what can one say?

I beg you to listen to me for a little longer.

Holy Scripture relates that Moses twice (*Ex.* 34:28; 9:9) and Elias once (*3 Kings* 19:8) went for forty days without eating or drinking, and from the Gospels we know that the Saviour did the same; (*Matt.* 4:1–11; *Mark* 1:12–13; *Luke* 4:1–13) but no one has ever read that a fast went on for years. John the Baptist (*Matt.* 3:4; *Mark* 1:6) was inspired by God to go out into the wilderness, but according to what we read he lived on wild honey, locusts and the roots of herbs and never fasted absolutely. It is said, not in Holy Scripture but in the story of her life and the local traditions, that Mary Magdalene—and she alone—fasted for thirty-three years, hidden away in a rock—and I think personally that it was for this reason that the Lord and his glorious Mother gave the Magdalene to the virgin as her mother and teacher. What is one to say? It is clear that the holy virgin had an extraordinary grace direct from the Lord, a gift till now granted to no other, as, God willing, I shall explain later.

I should not like you to imagine, however, most loving reader, that I put the sanctity of this virgin in any way above that of the saints just mentioned, or intend to suggest any odious comparisons between the saints themselves. I am not quite as stupid as that, good reader; and since I have mentioned the Saviour as well as the saints, I must add that I know that any comparison between Him and the saints would be blasphemous. I have mentioned these saints not to compare them but to help you to appreciate God's bounty (for His generosity is so inexhaustible that never a day goes by without His finding new graces with which to adorn and perfect His saints) and this virgin's excellence.

In any case you know what the Church says so truly of every saint without detriment to any: "There was not found the like to him in glory." (*Ecclus.* 44:20). Everything comes from the power and infinite goodness of the Sanctifier, who can give each saint the glory of a special gift wherever He wills to do so.

I must not get too far away from the story I am supposed to be telling, but you should now be in a position to realize the state of exhaustion to which Catherine's body was reduced, tormented by such austerities and afflicted by such continual sufferings of spirit. Her mother, who is still alive, told me that before her daughter embarked upon these penances she was so strong and healthy that she could take an ass's or a mule's load upon her shoulders and carry it quite easily up two long flights of stairs from the front door to the attic. She said that at that age she was far bigger and fatter than she was when she was twenty-eight. It is not surprising that she wasted away as she did, in fact it is a wonder she didn't kill herself—the result of a miracle, I should say. During all the time I knew her anyone could see that her strength was very much reduced and insufficient—because, of course, growing in the spirit, it was natural that her body should waste away, the latter being, so to speak, subjugated by the former. Nevertheless she toiled bravely on, especially for the salvation of souls, even though she endured a continuous stream of sufferings. There seemed to be two Catherines in her, one that suffered in a state of exhaustion, and another that toiled in the spirit, and the latter, fat and healthy of heart, sustained and strengthened the weakened flesh.

Now I must return to the story and take up the thread of our discourse again, from which I seem to have wandered away.

The holy virgin, having obtained her cell, and permission to devote herself to the things of God, began to ascend towards her Bridegroom; but the old Serpent did not give up his attacks on her, despite the defeat he had suffered, and this time he again made use of a daughter of Eve, in this case her mother Lapa.

Lapa loved her daughter's body more than her soul, and was stung by the old Serpent in her maternal feelings to try to hinder her from doing penance. For instance, when she heard that her daughter was scourging herself with an iron chain she began to sob and to shriek. "Daughter, daughter," she cried, "I can see you dying before my very eyes! You'll kill yourself, of a truth you will. Oh, mercy me, who wants to take my daughter away? Who is bringing all these misfortunes upon me!" And the old woman went on and on, wailing and shrieking and acting like a mad thing, clawing at herself and pulling out her white hair as though she could already see her daughter lying dead. The whole neighbourhood was often roused by Lapa's cries, and there would be a rush to see what new misfortune had befallen her.

Then, when she found Catherine sleeping on bare boards, she dragged her into her own room and made her sleep in bed with her. But the virgin, illumined by the spirit of wisdom, would kneel down at her mother's feet and try to bring her back to reason, speaking gently and humbly to her, begging her to calm down, telling her that she would do as she wished and get into bed with her. So, for her mother's sake she would lie on the edge of the bed for a time meditating, and then when her mother had fallen asleep would get up as silently as a mouse and return to her holy exercises.

The Enemy of man hated Catherine's virtues so much that even this could not remain hidden from Lapa for long, so to avoid upsetting her mother further, the virgin adopted a subterfuge: when she was obliged to sleep with her she would take a plank or a few pieces of wood and quietly put them under the sheets so that when she lay down she could feel the usual hardness; in this way she did not have to give up her holy custom. After a few days, however, her mother found out what she was doing, but this time she said, "As far as I can see, I am wasting my time. You are getting more and more obstinate about these principles of yours, so I might just as well close my eyes to them and let you sleep how and where you please." And thereafter, acknowledging her daughter's strength of will, she allowed her to live as the Almighty inspired her to.

Here the chapter ends.

The information I have given about Catherine's fasts and penances and the way she went about them I obtained from the holy virgin herself. The rest I was told by her mother Lapa and by a number of women who often used to go into their house—though some things I saw or discovered for myself, especially, for instance, about the unparalleled gift of abstinence.

CHAPTER SEVEN

Catherine Takes the Habit of St. Dominic

———————•———————

H AVING achieved this further victory the holy virgin returned to her daily exercises and began to live the life of the spirit with renewed ardour, for she could feel herself being assaulted ever more closely and incessantly by the infernal Enemy. Every day brought sobs and tears as she begged the Lord to make her worthy to receive the longed-for habit He had promised her through the bountiful Blessed Dominic, for she felt that the vow of virginity she had made would never be safe from her own people until she had donned it, and that once she had received it there would be an end to all this stupid insistence on marriage, and she would be allowed to serve her true Bridegroom as she wished.

And so she gently pleaded with her parents, and implored the Sisters of Penance of St. Dominic—generally known in Siena as the *Mantellate*—to receive her into their sisterhood and grant her the habit. Lapa did not greatly favour the idea, though she did not openly oppose it, but she was still thinking of ways to take Catherine's mind off her austere life. She decided to visit the hot baths and to take Catherine with her, hoping that the pleasures of the world would make her forget her harsh penances. This she did, I believe, through the cunning of man's old Enemy, the Serpent, who, determined to snatch the ardent bride from the arms of the Eternal Bridegroom, insidiously suggested these malicious ideas to the simple-minded Lapa.

But no scheme made against the will of the Lord can avail, and the bride of Christ, surrounded to right and to left by victorious armies, turned the wiles of the Enemy to his discomfiture and her own advantage and in the midst of delights found the means to treat her body harshly. Pretending to be in search of better waters, she went off to the channels that carry the sulphureous streams along and received the boiling water on her tender flesh, afflicting her body more than she had ever done, even by beating it with an iron chain.

I remember Lapa telling me about this incident once when her daughter was there. Catherine calmly told me what I have written above and added that she had suggested taking her bath when everybody else was away, for she knew that if her mother was there she would never have been able to do it. I asked her how she had been able to endure the great heat without being afraid it would kill her, and with her dovelike simplicity she replied, "All the time I was in the water I kept thinking of the pains of Hell and Purgatory and begged the Creator I had offended so much to accept the pains I was voluntarily suffering at that moment in payment of the pains I knew myself to have deserved. As I had utter faith in His mercy all that I suffered became a pleasure and I did not get scalded despite the pain I felt."

When the period of treatment was over the pair returned home and the holy virgin immediately resumed her penances. At this her mother gave up all hope of getting her to change her manner of life, but she still kept bursting out in lamentations against her austerities. This did not, however, prevent Catherine, with her holy intention always in her mind, from worrying her to go and see the St. Dominic Sisters of Penance and get them to agree to her taking the much wished-for habit, and finally, anguished by her repeated requests, Lapa went off to see them. The sisters replied that it was not their custom to invest maids, either old ones or young ones, with the habit, and that only respectable widows of mature age who wanted to dedicate themselves to the service of God were eligible, because as they lived no kind of enclosed life but simply went on living in their own homes it was essential that they should be people of the utmost respectability.

The reason for this reply will be seen more clearly in the next chapter. For the moment let us get on with the story.

Lapa returned home with this answer, satisfactory from her own point of view but not so pleasing to her daughter. The virgin of Christ was not in the least put out, however, for she knew that God's promises can never come to nought but must always be fulfilled, so despite this rebuff she went on trying to persuade her mother to persist in asking the sisters to grant her the habit until, vanquished yet again by her daughter's entreaties, she did so, only to return with the same answer.

Meanwhile the virgin of Christ had been taken ill with a complaint that often attacks young adolescents. It may have been a result of the excessive heat she had had to endure from the boiling waters, but I rather think that it came about by divine intent and that there was some sort of mystery in it. Her whole body came out in blisters; and besides making her almost unrecognizable this gave her a very high fever. Lapa, who loved all her children dearly but had a special love for Catherine because she had brought her up on her own milk, was terribly upset about this, but this time she could not blame her daughter's abstinences because the trouble seemed to be a result of too much energy rather than too little, and in any case it was a common complaint amongst boys and girls of her age.

Poor Lapa remained at the bedside, applying what remedies she could and doing her best to cheer her daughter up, but though Catherine was weak in body she was stronger than ever in intention and seeing that this might be a good moment to get her mother to do what she wanted she said rather slyly, "Mother, if you want me to be well and strong again, satisfy my one wish, which is to receive the habit of the Sisters of Penance of St. Dominic; if you don't, I'm afraid that God and St. Dominic between them will see to it that you don't have me with you in any kind of habit."

Her mother, having had this sort of thing said to her again and again, finally took fright and went off at top speed to the sisters and spoke with such urgency that, overcome by her entreaties, this time they gave her a different reply. "If your daughter is not too pretty or attractive," they said, "we will accept her, out of consideration for her great enthusiasm, and yours: but, as we have already said, if she is very pretty we should be afraid of some scandal, people being what they are today, and in that case we cannot possibly give our consent." To this the mother replied, "Come and see, and judge for yourselves."

They then sent a few of their most sensible and practical-minded women off with Lapa to see the sick girl, to find out how pretty she was and whether she really meant what she said. When they arrived they failed to notice any of the holy virgin's charm, either because she was indeed not beautiful or because her illness had affected her so considerably that they could hardly tell what she really looked like, but when they heard the way she expressed herself and explained the seriousness of her intention they welcomed her sound sense and wisdom, first with amazement and then with increasing delight, realizing that though young in years she had an old head on her shoulders and excelled many older women in the sight of God. And so they went away edified and reassured, and described all they had seen and heard to their colleagues with considerable enthusiasm.

After this the sisters obtained permission from the Friars to hold a meeting at which they agreed unanimously that Catherine should be accepted as one of themselves; then they informed Lapa that as soon as her daughter was better she should take her to the Dominican church to receive the habit she so much desired, in the usual way, in the presence of all the Sisters and the Friars in charge of them.

When her mother told her this Catherine cried with joy and immediately gave thanks to her Bridegroom and to bountiful Father Dominic for thus promptly keeping his promise to her. Then she began to pray for a quick recovery, not for the sake of her body but so as to achieve her ambition without delay. To begin with, she had gloried in her infirmity and endured it gladly for the love of her Bridegroom, but now it began to weigh upon her, and she prayed earnestly to be freed from it because it was preventing her from fulfilling her wish. And her prayers were answered, for within a few days she was cured, He to whose will she conformed so assiduously being unable to refuse her anything. For everything that Catherine wanted and asked for was from One she loved with all her being, to whom she was devoted in utter self-subjection.

When she recovered her mother seemed to want to put the matter off again, but she was subjected to continual entreaties from her daughter, and finally she gave in. And so came the day and the hour ordained by Divine Providence when to the accompaniment of heartfelt joy Catherine was to receive the longed-for habit. Lapa and Catherine made their way to the church, and in the presence of all the delighted Sisters the Friar in charge of them clothed the holy virgin in the garments that our Fathers chose as symbols of innocence and humility, that is to say, white for innocence and black for humility.

In my view no religious habit could have been more suitable than this one as a symbol of the inward habit practised by this holy virgin. For she had adopted every means to mortify her body, extinguishing the life of the old man outwardly and all the deadly germs of pride—all this being signified by the black—and then, as has been said, she had chosen to adopt a virgin innocence of both body and soul and implored the Eternal Bridegroom, the true light, to make her all light too—this being signified no less aptly by the white. If the habit had been all black or all white it could only have symbolized one of these things, whilst if it had been any kind of grey it would have symbolized mortification but not clarity and purity of mind.

In my view, if those sisters had not been so hasty they would never have given her mother that first negative reply about granting her the habit, for the simple reason that Catherine was better suited to it and more worthy of it than they were themselves, for they could not boast of being virgins. The holy virgin should never have been denied that habit chosen by our holy Fathers to signify innocence for she had virginal innocence, which they had not, and virginal innocence is undoubtedly a higher thing than widowed chastity. I say quite boldly therefore that that habit did not acquire its highest honour in the city of Siena until this holy virgin put it on and wore it, for she was the first famous virgin to wear it there, and since then many other virgins have followed her example, so that we can say with David, "After her shall virgins be brought to the king." (*Psalm* 44:15). How this came about will be explained at length later.

Here I bring this chapter to an end, and shall now go on to describe the original foundations of the religious state in which Divine Providence had established this holy virgin, so that the idea of her sanctity may be more fully appreciated.

All that is contained in the present chapter I heard from the virgin herself and from Lapa her mother. The things concerning the adoption of the habit are known to all who knew her and have no need of further corroboration.

CHAPTER EIGHT

The Sisters of Penance of St. Dominic

———————•———————

I MUST tell all who read this chapter that I have read about everything contained in it or else heard about it in different parts of Italy from people worthy of credit and have also read about it in the life story of our holy Father Dominic.

This glorious defender of the Catholic Faith and "athlete of Christ" had a holy zeal for the health of the Church Militant. By his own labours, aided by his fellow Friars, he succeeded in ridding Toulouse and Lombardy of heresy, to such an extent that at his canonization process it was shown in the presence of the Supreme Pontiff that his words and miracles had converted over a hundred thousand people in Lombardy alone. In spite of this the poisonous doctrine held by these heretics had so perverted men's minds there that nearly all the rights of the Church were still held by laymen, who handed down her property as though it was theirs by hereditary right—a thing which unfortunately still goes on in Italy even today. As a result of this the Pontiffs were obliged to beg, not having the power to put down the error or the wherewithal to support the clergy and the poor as they were obliged to do by their office.

Seeing this, St. Dominic, unable to bear the thought of others enduring the extraordinary poverty that he had chosen for himself and his followers, began to fight zealously for the recovery of the Church's goods. He gathered together a number of God-fearing men personally known to him and suggested that they should form a kind of holy militia to recover and protect the rights of the Church and to oppose the wickedness of the heretics. They agreed to this, and volunteers came along who swore to do whatever was asked of them, even to giving up their goods and even their lives for the cause.

So that this holy work should not be thwarted, St. Dominic got the wives of these men to swear that they would not hinder their husbands but do all they could to help them. Promising eternal life to any married couple who kept their vow, he named them "The Brothers of the Militia of Jesus Christ", and to mark them out from others, and to make sure that they did a little bit more than usual, he bestowed upon them the colours of his own habit, so that both the men and the women always wore black and white clothes as the outward signs of innocence and humility. Lastly he ordered them to recite a certain number of Our Fathers and Hail Marys each day according to the canonical hours, so that they should take part in the Divine Office.

When this holy Father put off the burden of the flesh and ascended into heaven (multiplying thereafter the number of his miracles), the Apostolic Chair enrolled him in the Catalogue of the Saints and offered him to universal veneration. The men and women of the Militia of Jesus Christ, wishing to honour their now glorious Founder, decided to change their name, and called themselves "The Brothers of Penance of St. Dominic", being further induced to do this by the fact that the plague of heresy had by now almost abated—thanks to the merits and miracles of their Founder and the doctrine expounded by his Friars—and the purpose for which they had been founded no longer existed. The only thing that remained for them to do was to vanquish the Devil by means of penance, and so they chose the name "Brothers of Penance".

The band of loyal Preaching Friars grew daily—including one who shone like a morning star, Peter the Virgin and Martyr, who defeated more enemies after his death than when he was alive—and the pack of little foxes who had been eager to destroy the vineyard of the Lord of Hosts was almost completely wiped out; so, as I have said, with the Church of God restored by God to peace, the reason for the militia's existence and consequently its purpose came to an end. But as the Brothers of Penance died the women they left behind retained the influence of the religious lives they had led jointly with their husbands and showed no desire to re-marry, preserving their widowhood until their death.

Other widows not belonging to the Penance who had also decided to remain widows began to want to follow their observances to expiate their sins. The number of them grew in various parts of Italy and they began to ask the Preaching Friars of their own locality to instruct them in the way of life instituted by St. Dominic, but as there were no written rules a certain priest of holy memory, Fr. Munio, a Spaniard, the General of the Order, put their way of life down in writing, and it is now known as the rule, though it cannot strictly be called a rule since a rule can only refer to a state including the three main vows required by all the religious Orders.

These Sisters increased in merit and in number in various parts of Italy, and Pope Honorius IV of happy memory, hearing of their good name, published a Bull giving them the privilege to hear Mass in Dominican churches during an interdict. And when Pope John XXII promulgated his *Clementina* against the *Beghine* and the *Begardi* he stated in another Bull that the decree did not apply to the Sisters of Penance of St. Dominic in Italy and that the value of their state was in no way lessened by it.

This, reader, explains how it has come about that this way of life is only followed by women today, and why the sisters' first reply to Catherine's mother was that only acknowledged widows—not virgins—could be included amongst them.

Most of what I have said in this chapter I have found written down in various parts of Italy; the rest, very little as a matter of of fact, I have been told in answer to my enquiries by trustworthy old people of both sexes, by the Preaching Friars, and by the Sisters of Penance of St. Dominic.

And so I end the chapter and return to our main theme.

CHAPTER NINE

Wonderful Progress in the Way of God

———————•———————

W HEN the holy virgin took the habit she was not required to make the three main vows of the religious state for, as has been said, her position did not in itself require it, but she made a private resolve to observe them scrupulously nevertheless.

As regards her chastity, that went without saying, since she had already made a vow of virginity. With regard to obedience, she had resolved to be obedient not only to the Brother Director who was in charge of the nuns and to the Prioress but also to her confessor, and this she was until her death, so that when she was passing out of this world she could say to the Friar who was with her, "I cannot remember ever having been disobedient." It is true that some slanderers of the virgin's sanctity, liars prompted by envy and malice, dared to assert the contrary during her lifetime, but that the lie may be thrust down their throats I will have you know, dearest reader, that if this virgin had had no other afflictions during her life than those brought about by tactless spiritual directors she would have been a martyr of patience for that reason alone. These people did not understand her at all, nor did they believe in the magnitude of the gifts that heaven had bestowed upon her; they simply tried to guide her blindly along conventional ways. They quite failed to realize that the Divine Majesty was present within her, leading her forward in a marvellous manner, even though they could see obvious superficial proofs of this. They were like the Pharisees who saw signs and marvels but resented the cures performed on the Sabbath, saying, "This man is not of God, who keepeth not the sabbath." (*John* 9:16). Catherine, placed by the will of God amidst these vexations, did her best to obey these people, whilst at the same time she did not wish to abandon the way being taught her by the Lord, and was tormented by so many tribulations that no pen or tongue can easily describe them. Lord God, how many times was it said of her that she "casteth out devils by Beelzebub, the prince of devils," (*Luke* 11:15) *i.e.* that her visions were not from God but from the Devil. And yet it was plain to all eyes that leaving aside the actual physical miracles her whole life was a miracle!

At the right time we shall go into this question in more detail; for the moment I shall say no more about it.

As for the vow of poverty, Catherine observed this so strictly that when she was in her own home, where there was plenty or everything, she took nothing for herself but only for distributing to the poor, which she did with her father's full consent. She was such a lover of poverty that she told me in confession that she could never feel happy about her own home so long as the family was comfortably situated and used to pray constantly to the Almighty to put an end to their prosperity and reduce them all to a state of poverty. "Lord," she would say, "can this be the good I desire for my parents and brothers, or must I not rather desire for them eternal good? These goods bring many evils and dangers, and I do not want my own family to get involved in them." The Lord heard her prayers, for by a strange chain of events the family was reduced to a state of extreme poverty—through no fault of their own, according to the people who knew them.

Such are the original foundations on which the virgin based her spiritual life, and she merely broadened and deepened them after she had received the habit, as I must now go on to explain.

St. Dominic's promise having come true, this most faithful daughter began to gather honey from all directions, like a skilful bee, withdrawing ever more deeply into herself and enfolding her Bridegroom in an ever closer embrace. "Here you are, then," she would often say to herself, "in the religious life, and it is now no longer lawful for you to live as you have lived so far. Your secular life is over, the new religious life has begun and you must start living according to its rules. You must clothe yourself in purity, surrounding yourself with it in the way symbolized by the white tunic, then you must die to the world, as taught by the black mantle. So watch carefully how you behave, for you have to pass through a narrow way that few people choose to follow."

To observe the vow of purity better she decided to preserve an utter silence and never speak except at confession. My predecessor as her confessor has written that for three years she never spoke a word to anyone except him, and then only when she was making her confession.

She lived continually enclosed in her little cell, only emerging from it to go to church. She had no need to leave it for meals, for all she needed to eat she could eat there—her only cooked food was bread. She also decided always to eat her bread with tears: by making God an offering of tears before each meal she would first irrigate her soul and then take the food to sustain her body. She established a desert within the walls of her own home, and solitude in the midst of people.

Who could describe her vigils, her prayers, her meditations? Who shall number her tears? She made it a rule to stay awake every night whilst the Preaching Friars, whom she called her brothers, slept, until on the second bell of Matins, and not before, she would say to her Bridegroom, "Behold, Lord, my brothers your servants have slept until now, and I have kept watch for them so that you would preserve them from all evil and from the wiles of the Enemy. Now that they have risen to praise you, you watch over them and I will rest a while." And she would lie down on her planks with a piece of wood as her pillow.

Her most loving Bridegroom, who helped her in all she did, seemed to be as though drawn by her ardour, and not wishing to leave so noble a sheep without a shepherd or guide or such an apt and diligent disciple without a master, gave her as teacher not a man or an angel but

Himself. For, as she herself revealed to me, she would no sooner be enclosed in her cell than He would deign to appear to her and reveal things useful to her soul. While she was telling me about this in confession she said these actual words: "Father, you can take it as certain that I have never learned anything about the way of salvation from men or women but only from the Lord and Master Himself, the sweet precious Bridegroom of my soul the Lord Jesus Christ, either in the form of inspiration, or through His speaking to me as I am speaking to you now, before your very eyes." And she went on to tell me that when these visions first began to appear to her they generally came into her imagination but that sometimes she could also perceive them with her physical senses, so that she actually heard our Lord's voice. She said that in the early days she was afraid that this was a trick of the Devil, who often transforms himself into an angel of light, and this fear was not displeasing to the Lord, indeed He approves of it, saying, "The pilgrim must always go in fear, for it is written, 'Blessed is the man that is always fearful'." (*Proverbs* 28:14). And He went on, "Would you like me to teach you how to distinguish between my visions and those of the Enemy?" And when she said delightedly that she would He answered, "It would be easy to enlighten your soul by an inspiration to enable you to distinguish between one kind of vision and another, but to help you and others I would have you know that what the Doctors who have been taught by me say is true. When my visions begin they inspire fear, but as they develop they fortify; they begin with a kind of grief but they grow sweeter and sweeter. Whereas the opposite happens in the case of visions sent by the Enemy: at first they seem to give a kind of pleasure, contentment, sweetness, but as they go on pain and nausea begin to develop in the soul of the beholder. This is the truth, for my ways are utterly different from his ways. Undoubtedly the way of penance required by my commandments seems harsh and difficult to begin with, but the more it goes on the easier and sweeter it becomes, whereas the way of vice is pleasurable enough to begin with, but it becomes more and more bitter and painful as time goes on.

"But I will give you a sure and certain sign about this. Know for a certainty that since I am the Truth my visions must always bear fruit in a greater knowledge of truth in the soul. The soul needs knowledge of the truth, of me and itself, so it must know me and itself; knowing me and itself, it must necessarily despise itself and honour me—which is the true function of humility. Thus as a result of my visions the soul necessarily becomes more humble, and, recognizing its own nothingness, despises itself. The opposite happens in the case of the visions sent by the Enemy. As he is the father of lies and the king of all the sons of pride and is only able to give what he himself possesses, his visions always insinuate a kind of self-esteem and presumptuousness, in fact pride, into the soul, so that it gets swollen and full of wind. So if you keep a close eye on yourself you can discover where the vision comes from—the truth or the source of all lies; for truth makes the soul humble but lies make it proud."

The virgin, no careless disciple, treasured this salutary doctrine and later communicated it to me and many others, as with the grace of God will shortly be explained.

From this time onward the heavenly visions, revelations and visits from the Lord began to increase to such an extent that, as I have often said, it would be difficult to find two human beings who have so continually enjoyed each other's company as this holy virgin did that of her Bridegroom, the Saviour of all men, the Lord Jesus Christ. No matter whether she was praying, meditating, reading, watching or sleeping, she was comforted in one way or another by visions of Jesus; at times, even when she was talking to other people, this holy vision would remain with her and her mind would be conversing with the Lord while her tongue was talking to human beings. But this would not last long, for her soul would be so strongly drawn to her Bridegroom that she would soon lose the use of her senses and fall into an ecstasy.

From this proceeded all manner of wonderful things—her abstinence, which was far beyond anyone else's powers, her marvellous teaching, and the celebrated miracles that Almighty God allowed us to see personally while she was alive. And as it was the foundation, root and origin of all her holy deeds and the tangible evidence of her admirable inner life, and as, dear reader, I want you to be quite clear about this, I find myself obliged to reveal things about her which fill me with no small confusion. So that no incredulous person may say, "She was the only person who knew anything about these things—there were no witnesses—she is simply giving her own account—perhaps her account is not true—she could have been mistaken, or be telling lies," I must tell you what follows, something that I would never have divulged except out of concern for the honour of this holy virgin. But I prefer to be confused myself than rather see her denigrated and would rather blush before men than conceal my shame behind insults to her.

You must know then, dear reader, that I had heard Catherine's praises sung some time before I began to know her better, and God permitted for the sake of a greater good that I too should be tempted not to believe many of the things she said. I did all I could to discover whether her way of life came from God or not, whether it was based on fact or fiction, reflecting that this was the age of the third beast—the leopard (*Daniel* 7:6, 74) (which symbolizes hypocrites)—and that I had already come across quite a few of these animals, especially amongst women, who are proud to lose their heads and succumb to the wiles of the Enemy like the first mother of us all. These considerations would surge up in my mind and make me dubious and uncertain about Catherine and I was at a crossroads, a standstill, so to speak, not knowing which way to turn. In this state of indecision I made a petition to be guided by Him who can neither deceive nor be deceived.

It occurred to me that if I could be certain that Catherine's prayers had brought me a great and unaccustomed contrition for my sins it would be perfect proof that all her actions were guided by the Holy Spirit, for no one can feel contrition except through the Holy Spirit, and though we can never know whether we are in God's grace and worthy of His hatred or His love, nevertheless when contrition for sin rises up in our hearts this is always a great sign of the grace of God.

With these thoughts in my mind I went to her and begged her to pray for me and to ask God especially to forgive me my sins. In her great charity she said that she would be delighted to do this, whereupon I added that I should not feel easy in my mind unless I was given a Bull to prove this, like the ones given by the Roman Curia. With a smile she asked me what kind of a "Bull" I would like, and I said that what I really wanted was to feel a great and extraordinary contrition for my sins. She answered that she would certainly see to this. Realizing that she had divined my thoughts, I went off—at, if I remember aright, the next to the last hour of the day.

The following morning, finding myself suffering from one of my usual attacks, I was obliged to keep to my bed, being looked after by a friend of mine in our Order, a man from Pisa called Niccolo, a most devout man greatly beloved of God. The virgin heard about this, and as we were then housed in a Dominican convent not far from her home, she got up, ill though she was at the time, and said to her companion, "We must go and see Fra Raimondo; he is ill." Her companion said there was no need to go and pointed out that she was in a worse condition than I was, but she hurried off to see me all the same—a thing she did not usually do—and as soon as she arrived asked me what was the matter with me. I was so weak that I could hardly say a word to Niccolo, but forcing myself to answer her I said, "Why ever have you come, lady? You are in a worse state than I am!" But she at once started talking as usual about God and about the way we offend Him by not realizing how much we owe Him, and, feeling stronger, I got up for propriety's sake and went and sat on a little nearby couch so as to be more comfortable. I had forgotten all about the promise she had given me the previous evening.

She went on talking, and as she did so there came before my mind an unusual vision of my sins. I saw myself naked before the judgement seat of God, like a man facing sentence by the judges of this world. I saw myself sentenced to death. At the same time I realized the goodness and mercy of the Judge for, knowing that I should rightly die for my sins, He not only delivered me from death but dressed me in His own clothes, gave me food and shelter in His home, and, picking me out to serve Him, in His infinite goodness turned death into life, fear into hope, sorrow into joy and shame into a source of pride.

Under the effect of these reflections, or rather utterly clear visions, the cataracts of my flinty heart were loosed and fountains of water overflowed to lay bare the depth of my sins: I burst out into tears, so violently that (I say it with shame) I almost felt my heart would break. Catherine in her wisdom, having come for this very purpose, no sooner saw the state I was in than she stopped talking and let me go on crying and sobbing.

After a while, still crying, I began to wonder about this strange event, and then I remembered what I had asked her for the previous evening and the promise she had made. "Is this the 'Bull' I asked for yesterday?" I said. "It is," she replied, and getting up, and, if I remember rightly, tapping me on the shoulder, she said, "Never forget the graces of God!" And she went off, leaving me, edified and comforted, alone with my companion.

This I say in the presence of God, knowing I do not lie.

On another occasion I had further proof of this virgin's perfection, this time without going in search of it, and I wish to reveal it to her honour now, though I know I am only adding to my own shame.

Catherine was ill in bed in the above-mentioned convent, and wishing to speak to me about some revelations she had had she asked to see me privately. I went to the convent and, as she lay in bed, as usual she began to talk to me about God, and especially about what had been revealed to her that day. What I heard was so extraordinary—nothing of a like kind ever happens to anyone else—that I ungratefully forgot about the first grace I had received through her and felt doubtful as to whether what she said was true. While I was thinking these thoughts I turned and looked at her as she was speaking, and her face turned into the face of a strange man who, fixing grave eyes upon me, inspired me with a great fear. It was an oval, middle-aged face with a short beard the colour of corn, and it looked so majestic that it seemed to be that of the Lord. Moreover, at that moment it was the only face I could see.

Awed and terrified by this sight, I raised my hands and cried out, "Who are you, looking at me?" The virgin replied, "He who is." With these words the face disappeared and I could see the virgin's face quite clearly again, though I had been unable to make it out a few moments before.

I vow this is true as God is my witness, for this same God, the Father of our Lord Jesus Christ, knows that I am not lying. And I will add that I realize, as indeed is quite evident, that this miracle was performed by the Lord.

This vision (I say it with shame) gave me a great and unusual mental illumination concerning the train of argument which the virgin was pursuing at the moment, which I shall not reveal, and I felt I was experiencing what the disciples must have experienced when the Lord promised them the Holy Spirit saying, "And the things that are to come he shall shew you." (*John* 16:13).

There! I was made to look a fool, I don't deny it: the incredulous have forced me to confess it. But I prefer to be thought a fool by men, than to hide these proofs of the holy virgin's sanctity. And who knows whether the Lord may not have willed to manifest these things to me in my incredulity, so that I might in His good time reveal them as proofs of Catherine's sanctity and confute those who refuse to believe in it.

What do you say, you who are still incredulous, what do you say to that? If you will not believe Mary Magdalene and the disciples and still think them simple-minded, believe at least Thomas Didymus, who touched the Lord's wounds. If you refuse to act like believers, you cannot refuse to associate with unbelievers. Look! I stand before you as an unbeliever—more than an unbeliever—because after being given a proof that I myself had asked for I still persisted in my unbelief. And the Lord came and showed me His face, so that I could see Him, giving me ocular proof that He was speaking in Catherine: He gave Himself to be seen by the unbeliever Raimondo, as one day He had allowed

Thomas called Didymus to touch Him. Thomas after touching Him exclaimed, "My Lord, and My God!" (*John* 20:28)—does it surprise you then that after two such visions this unbeliever exclaimed, "True bride and true disciple of my Lord and my God"?

I have described these incidents, dear reader, so that when you come to hear about Catherine's visions and revelations, for which we have only her own word, you will not be tempted to doubt or despise them, but will rather concentrate on the holy example and sacred doctrine which the Lord, who accomplished all this, presented in a vessel naturally fragile and worthless but by Him made marvellously strong and precious.

Here I bring to an end this chapter, whose contents except for what happened to me personally I learned from the holy virgin herself.

CHAPTER TEN

Catherine's Wisdom

────────────────●────────────────

T HE foundation of belief having thus been laid, with the grace of
the Lord and the assistance of Him who is the chief cornerstone,
let us now pass on to the spiritual edifice itself. And as the souls of the
faithful are quickened and fed by the word of God, let us begin with
the extraordinary doctrine that was imparted to this holy virgin by her
Master, the Creator of all things.

The holy virgin told her confessors, of whom, though unworthy,
I was one, that at the beginning of her visions, that is to say when the
Lord Jesus Christ first began to appear to her, he once came to her while
she was praying and said, "Do you know, daughter, who you are, and
who I am? If you know these two things, you will be blessed. You are
she who is not; whereas I am He who is. Have this knowledge in your
soul and the Enemy will never deceive you and you will escape all his
wiles; you will never disobey my commandments and will acquire all
grace, truth and light."

Small words, yet great in value. A succinct doctrine, yet in its way
endless! Oh, immeasurable wisdom, wrapped in a few brief syllables,
however shall I understand you, who will help me to break your seals?
How shall I fathom the depths of your profundity? Perhaps this is that
length and breadth, that height and depth, that the Apostle Paul longed

to comprehend with all the saints of Ephesus? (*Eph.* 3:18). Or perhaps it is one with the Charity of Christ, transcending all human wisdom?

Dear reader, we must pause here, we must not pass by this pearl beyond price. We must resolutely dig the ground, for the signs given us promise wealth without end.

Infallible Truth said, "If you know these two things, you will be saved", and, "Have this knowledge in your soul, and the Enemy will never deceive you", and the other things related above. It is good, I think, to be here: let us make here three tabernacles, the first in honour of Jesus the teacher for giving our minds His words, the second to Catherine's piety in receiving these teachings and loving and revering them, the third for our own sakes, for we shall find life in these words if we keep them in our minds. Then we shall be able to dig and make these spiritual riches our own and not be mere shameful beggars.

"You," said the Lord, "are she who is not." And is this not so, indeed? All creatures are made from nothing, for "to create" means to make something from nothing. When creatures are left to themselves they tend to return to nothing, and if the Creator ceased for one moment to preserve them in existence, they would rapidly be reduced to nothing again. And when a creature commits sin, which is a nothingness, he approaches towards nothingness, and according to the Apostle no man can do or think anything by himself. (*2 Cor.* 3:5). None of this is surprising, for of himself no man has existence, nor can he preserve himself in existence. Whence the same Apostle says, "For if any man think himself to be something, whereas he is nothing, he deceiveth himself." (*Gal.* 6:3).

Thus, reader, it is apparent that all creatures are engulfed in nothingness—made from nothingness, tending towards nothingness, and by sin, as Augustine says, reducing themselves to nothingness—unable to do anything of themselves, as Incarnate Truth himself affirms, saying, "for without me you can do nothing" (*John* 15:5)—and unable to think anything of themselves, as has already been said. Whence we may conclude that the creature is not. For who will be rash enough to assert that a thing is, when it is nothing? True deductions from this, capable of removing all vices, have been made by holy men of God who were led by the Holy Spirit and filled with wisdom. For what wound of pride can enter into a soul that knows itself to be nothing? Who can glory in anything he does, when he knows that he himself has not done it, or imagine himself to be superior to others if in his heart of hearts he knows himself not to be? How can a man despise or envy others who despises himself as a nothingness, how glory in worldly wealth when he despises his own glory? Incarnate Wisdom said, "If I glorify myself, my glory is nothing." (*John* 8:54). Further, how will he dare to call things of the world his own when he knows that he himself is not his own property but belongs to Him who made him? This being so, what soul will take delight in the pleasures of the senses when it knows that it is daily fettering itself to non-being thereby? And lastly, who will be indolent when he knows that his being is not his own but something to be begged from Another? From these considerations, thus briefly stated, you will realize, reader, that all vices are driven out by those three words, "You are not".

I could certainly go on in this strain at great length if I was not holding up the life-story I am trying to write. Nevertheless, I must not omit the second part of this excellent doctrine.

This same Truth, then, said, "I am who am." (*Exodus* 3:14). Is this a new doctrine, do you think? It is both old and new. He who is speaking said it to Moses out of the burning bush. All the commentators on the Sacred Scriptures have discussed it at length, teaching that only He is, whose being is His essence, in whom there is no difference between His being and to be, who has His being from no one but Himself, from whom all other being originates and proceeds. He alone, therefore, can properly say this of Himself. In the words of the Apostle there is not in Him, as there is in creatures, "It is" and "It is not" but only "It is." (*2 Cor.* 1:18). Indeed He Himself commanded Moses to say, "He who is, hath sent me to you." (*Exodus* 3:14). Nor is this surprising, for if the definition of "creation" is carefully scrutinized it leads inevitably to this doctrine. For if "to create" means precisely to make something from nothing, it is clear that all beings proceed from the same Creator and cannot originate in any other way since Fie alone is the origin of being. This being so, it follows that creatures possess nothing of themselves but receive everything from the Creator, and this same Creator possesses all infinite perfection of being in Himself. If He did not possess in Himself this infinite power of being, He would not be able to make anything from nothing.

This is what the supreme King and Master willed to teach His bride when He said to her, "Know in your heart of hearts that I am truly your Creator, and you will be blessed." The Lord said the same words to another Catherine when, accompanied by a choir of saints and angels, he went to visit her in prison. He said to her, "Know, O daughter, your Creator." From this knowledge, beyond all shadow of doubt, proceeds all perfection of virtue and all proper order in the created mind.

Who but unreasoning and foolish men will not be glad to submit themselves to One they realize is the source of all they have? Who will not love with all his heart and mind so dear and rich a benefactor who freely gives everything that is good? Who will not burn with ever greater love for so lovable a Lover, who, without merit on the part of others, moved only by His eternal goodness, loves His creatures even before He creates them? And who will not always go in fear and trembling of offending or losing this great and tremendous Creator, this powerful, marvellous Giver, this ardent, gracious Lover? Who will not be ready to bear any ill for love of Him from whom he has received and still receives every good, and hopes to go on doing so? Who will grow weary of labours, or complain of sickness, if they please such a lovable Majesty? Who will not welcome with reverence, hear with attention, keep in the treasury of his memory, the words through which He speaks so worthily to His creatures? Who will not obey His salutary commandments to the utmost of his abilities and with a joyful heart?

These things all issue from that Perfect Knowledge which said, "Know that you are she who is not and I am He who is." Or, in other words, "Know, O daughter, your Creator." And when you consider, reader, the real value of this foundation, laid by the Lord in the beginning as an earnest to His bride of what was to follow, does it not seem to you to have been designed to support an edifice composed of all spiritual perfections, a construction never to be brought down or even shaken by any winds or storms?

I have already explained the foundation of the belief as well as the Lord has allowed me to; now you can see clearly what foundation the Supreme Architect had laid in Catherine's soul. Thus, reassured by this double foundation, you cannot remain any longer in uncertainty. You can be established in a firm and stable faith, not incredulous but believing.

To the above excellent doctrine the Lord added a further one worthy of note, one which, if I am not mistaken, is a consequence of the first. He appeared to her again later and said to her, "Daughter, think of me; if you do I will immediately think of you." Now bring to mind, reader, the words the Psalmist says to all the just, "Cast thy care upon the Lord, and he shall sustain thee; he shall not suffer the just to waver for ever." (*Psalm* 54:23). We shall now see how the holy virgin interpreted these words.

Discussing them with me in private, she said that the Lord had commanded her to shut all other thoughts out of her mind and to retain only the thought of Him. And to prevent any anxiety about herself or her spiritual condition from distracting her from the peace of the thought of Him, He added, "I will think of you", meaning, Do not fret about the salvation of your body and soul, for I who know and can do all things will think of it and look after it most carefully. Just try to think of me and understand me, for your perfection and final good are to be found in this.

O you who are the uncreated Goodness, what could be added to you if this your virgin bride or any other creature were to think or meditate about you? Can we give you anything? Why should you want us to think and meditate about you, except that you are goodness itself and long to come to us in order to draw us to you?

The virgin of the Lord used to conclude from this that since we give ourselves to God in holy baptism and in the life of the priesthood and the monastery, we should have no further anxiety about ourselves but simply try to please the Lord to whom we have given ourselves. And we should do this not with a view to the reward but for the sake of union, for the more firmly we are united to Him by love the more we please Him—the reward should not be desired except to the extent that it unites us with Him who is our infinitely perfect origin. Thus whenever I or any other of the friars was afraid of any danger Catherine would say, "What have you to do with yourselves? Leave it to Divine Providence. However much afraid you are, Providence still has its eyes on you and is always aiming at your salvation."

She developed such faith in her Bridegroom after she had heard Him say, "I will think of you", and had such a deep understanding of Divine Providence that she talked about it continually, and in the book[1] she wrote she discussed it at great length for many chapters, as anyone can verify by turning to it.

I remember that once there were a number of us on board ship with Catherine, and towards the middle of the night the wind which had been favourable died down, and the pilot had misgivings because he said we were in a dangerous position and if a beam wind came up we might get blown off our course and be stranded on an island. I mentioned this to Catherine and said mournfully, "Mother"—we all called her that—"don't you see what danger we're in?" "What have you to worry about?" she retorted sharply, and not only silenced me but banished my fear. But after a while a contrary wind sprang up and the pilot warned us that he would have to turn back. I told Catherine about this and she said, "Turn the wheel in the name of the Lord and see what wind He sends." The pilot changed direction and we began to go back in the direction we had been coming from, but Catherine lowered her head and prayed, and we had not gone more than the distance of a cross-bow shot when the

---

1. The Dialogue of Divine Providence.

original favourable wind sprang up again and the Lord took our ship in hand and at dawn we were delighted to find ourselves at our destination. Whereupon we sang aloud *Te Deum laudamus.*

I have introduced this story here not because it fits in chronologically but because of its relevance to the subject under discussion.

Anyone of any intelligence will realize that, as I said before, this second doctrine derives from the first, for if the soul knows that of itself it is nothing and that it owes everything to the Lord, it follows that it will not trust in its own operations but only in God's. In doing so the soul puts all its care on Him, and this to my way of thinking is what the Psalmist means by "casting one's care upon the Lord". But the soul does not give up doing what it can, for as it derives its confidence from love and love necessarily gives rise to a desire for the thing loved (which desire cannot be there unless the soul does the work possible to it), it works as hard as it loves. This means that it trusts in its own operations not as its own but as things done by the Lord, in perfect knowledge of its own nothingness and the perfection of the Creator.

Amongst all the marvellous things connected with this life-giving maiden I think one of the most considerable was her wisdom, and therefore I cannot refrain from mentioning here her other teachings, which all derive from the doctrine already expounded.

The holy virgin often used to talk to me about the condition of the soul that loves its Creator, and said that such a soul neither sees nor loves itself or anyone else but inwardly forgets itself and every other creature. I asked her to be more explicit, whereupon she said, "The soul that sees its own nothingness and knows that its whole good is to be found in the Creator forsakes itself and all its powers and all other creatures and immerses itself wholly in Him, directing all its operations towards Him and never alienating itself from Him, for it realizes that in Him it can find all goodness and perfect happiness. Through this vision of love, increasing from day to day, the soul is so transformed into God that it cannot think or understand or love or remember anything but God and the things of God. Itself and other creatures it sees only in

God, itself and others it remembers only in God. Thus it is like a man who dives into the sea and swims under water: all he can see and touch is water and the things in the water, while, as for anything outside the water, he can neither see it nor touch it nor feel it. If the things outside the water are reflected in it, then he can see them, but only in the water and as they look in the water, and not in any other way. This [she would say] is the true and proper way of delighting in oneself and all other creatures, and it can never lead to error, because, being necessarily always governed by God's ordinance, it cannot lead to any desire for anything outside God, because all the activity takes place within God and remains within Him."

I do not know whether I have succeeded in presenting her thought properly, because she had learned certain things from experience, like the Dorothea spoken of by Dionysus, and I—I am sorry to say—am so little expert in these matters that I do not possess the qualities to reproduce them properly. So you must meditate on them yourself, reader, and accept them according to the grace that God has given you. I do know, however, that the more you are united to God the more you will understand this prodigious doctrine.

From the above facts this mistress of the divine science went on to deduce another that she never tired of repeating to anyone she wished to direct in the way of God.

When a soul is joined to God in the way described, the more love it has for God the more holy hatred it feels against its own "sensitive part", or, as we call it, sensuality. Love of God naturally leads to hatred of sin committed against God, and so the soul, seeing that the incitement to all sin reigns in the sensitive part and has its roots there, is moved by a great but holy hatred of the sensitive part and does all it can not to destroy the senses but to annihilate the incitement that is rooted in them, and this cannot be done without great distress on the part of the senses. And because it is difficult for some root of sin, however small, not to remain in them—according to the words of St. John, "If we say that we have no sin, we deceive ourselves and the truth is not in us" (*1 John* 1:8)—the soul begins to feel a certain dislike for itself, from which arise holy hatred and contempt of self, a hatred and contempt that defend it against the wiles of men and the Devil. There is nothing that keeps the soul so safe and strong as this holy hatred, to which the Apostle referred when he said, "For when I am weak, then am I powerful." (*2 Cor.* 12:10).

"O eternal goodness of God," Catherine would say, "what have you not done! Out of sin you bring virtue, out of weakness strength, insult has brought mercy and sorrow happiness. Always, O sons, have within yourselves this proper hatred to make you humble, and you will always know yourselves to be humble. It will make you patient in adversity, moderate in prosperity, fixed in all the right ways, pleasing and acceptable to God and men." And she would add, "Beware, O beware, of anyone who does not have this holy hatred, for where it is missing love of self must necessarily reign, and that is the stagnant pool from which come all sins, the root cause of every evil lust." This was the sort of thing she would say to her followers every day, to foster in them this holy hatred and to incite them to fight against self-love.

When she discovered any fault or failing in anyone she would be moved by pity and say, "This comes from the love of self, which leads to pride and all the other vices." My God, many and many a time she said to my miserable self, "Do everything you can to uproot self-love from your heart and to plant this holy hatred there instead: for that is the one sure way to get rid of your defects." But, alas, I must confess that neither then nor since have I really understood the depth and value of her words or sought to put them into practice.

Dear reader, if you bring to mind the two cities described by Augustine in his book *The City of God*, one being built on self-love and rising to contempt of God, and the other being built on the love of God and leading to contempt of self, you will get some idea of this teaching, and if you understand what the Apostle meant when he said, "For power is made perfect in infirmity," (*2 Cor.* 12:9) words he heard from heaven while he was praying to be delivered from temptation, ending with "Gladly therefore will I glory in my infirmities, that the power of Christ may dwell in me," you will realize that the foundations of this holy virgin's doctrine were laid on the solid rock of Truth, Christ, who is indeed called "the Rock". (*1 Cor.* 10:4).

What I have said will suffice now for her teaching, given her by the Truth and by her in these latter days transmitted to us.

So I bring this chapter to an end, and this time there is no reason to cite any witnesses, for all that is contained in it I heard myself from Catherine's own mouth. But I advise anyone who reads it to reflect on the great merit that this holy virgin must have had in the eyes of the Lord to be clothed in so much light of Truth, and that she may therefore deserve to be believed in other things.

CHAPTER ELEVEN

The Closeness of Catherine's Relationship with the Saviour

———————————•———————————

WHEN the King of Peace raised the tower of Lebanon to defend Jerusalem against Damascus, the haughty King of Babylon, the enemy of peace, was angry and moved his army against it, determined to beat it down to its foundations. But the King of Peace, foreseeing this, had surrounded the tower with impregnable defences, and the enemy's spears not only flew against them in vain but bounced back and killed and wounded the very people who had hurled them.

I say this because the old Serpent, seeing this maiden soaring to the highest peaks of perfection and fearing—as in fact happened—that this would result in her own salvation and the salvation of many others and that her teaching and merits would defend the holy city of the Catholic Church, began to adopt a thousand cunning and malicious ruses to lead her astray. The Lord in His mercy allowed all this to happen to increase His bride's crown, and He supplied her with such strong spiritual weapons that she made more progress through having to fight than she would have done if she had been left in peace. For she was inspired to ask Him for the virtue of fortitude, begging Him fervently for it for many days. Finally, He mercifully granted her wish and said, "Daughter, if you wish to acquire the virtue of fortitude you must imitate me. Though I have divine power and could have annihilated all the powers of evil in quite a different way if I had willed to do so, nevertheless, wishing my actions to be taken as a model, I willed to act by way of the cross, so that I could teach you by words based on actions. If you want to have the strength to overcome all the enemy's powers, take the cross as your refreshment as I did. For indeed I, as the Apostle says, ran to such a hard and shameful cross because I had been offered joy, so that you would patiently choose pains and afflictions and embrace them indeed as consolations. And indeed they are consolations, for the more you suffer such things for My sake the more you make yourself like Me. If you conform yourself to Me in suffering, truly, as My Apostle says, you will become like Me in grace and glory. Therefore, O daughter, for My sake regard sweet things as bitter and bitter things as sweet and then have no fear, for undoubtedly you will be strong in all things."

Catherine heeded these instructions and resolved to find pleasure in tribulations; indeed she once told me in confession that nothing in this life brought her as much comfort as tribulation and suffering. Without these, she said, she would have been impatient at remaining in the body, but she was comforted by the knowledge that by enduring them her heavenly crown was increasing in splendour.

After the King of earth and heaven had armed His tower with the defence of sound doctrine, He opened its gates to its enemies to see whether they could take it by storm. They arrived in detestable hordes and besieged it on all sides, hoping that when it was cut off from all help they could raze it to the ground.

They began with carnal temptations, tempting Catherine not only inwardly with thoughts and fancies and dreams but with actual visions, which they put before her eyes and ears in the greatest variety of ways, taking aerial bodies. The subsequent battles are dreadful to relate, but the final victory makes sweet reading to pure minds.

Catherine rose gaily up against herself, against her own flesh and blood, lacerating her body with an iron chain until the blood flowed and increasing her vigils to the almost total exclusion of sleep. The enemies would not desist on this account, however, and assuming, as

I have said, aerial forms and increasing the number of their phantasies and apparitions, they appeared before her in great crowds as sympathizers and counsellors, saying, "You poor soul, why go on punishing yourself like this to no purpose? What good can all this suffering do you? Do you think you can go on with it? Never, unless you want to kill yourself and be the murderer of your own body. Better to stop being so foolish before you break down altogether. There is still time for you to enjoy yourself in the world—you are still young, and your body will soon again be healthy. Be like other women, get yourself a husband and have children and increase the human race. If you want to please God, remember that even saints have married: think of Sara and Leah and Rachel. Why have you adopted this single life, which you cannot possibly keep up to the end?"

Catherine paid no heed to all this but simply went on praying; to the assaults of the Tempter she quietly set up her Bridegroom. And when she was tempted to doubt whether she would be able to endure she answered, "I trust in the Lord Jesus Christ, not in myself." But they could not get another word out of her and after that she remained absorbed in prayer.

When she talked to us about this, she always told us as a general rule never to descend to the level of argument with the Enemy in times of temptation. Getting people to discuss the matter was exactly what he wanted, she said, for he has great faith in the subtlety of his wicked sophisms. As a chaste woman should avoid adulterers and refuse to speak to them, so a soul chastely united to Christ should refuse to discuss the Enemy's temptations but turn to its Bridegroom in prayer, relying on Him with absolute trust and faithfulness. All temptations, she said, could be overcome by the virtue of faith.

Thus did the bride of the Lord pursue her battle against Sisara, hammering the nail of faithful prayer into the temples of the Enemy. Realizing this, the Devil gave up flattery and adopted another form of attack. He brought vile pictures of men and women behaving loosely before her mind, and foul figures before her eyes, and obscene words to her ears, shameless crowds dancing around her, howling and sniggering and inviting her to join them. O my God, what a torment it must have been for the holy virgin to be forced to see and hear such things, even when she closed her eyes and ears in utter abhorrence! And to these afflictions was added a further source of suffering, for her Bridegroom, who had been in the habit of visiting her and bringing her many consolations, now seemed to have forsaken her and left her without assistance. Great was the bitterness felt by her soul, but not for one minute did she stop praying and mortifying her flesh. Moreover, at a suggestion from the Lord she adopted a defensive measure which she later taught me and many others as a means of warding off the Enemy's wiles. She said that all who love God experience tepidity at times; the fervour of the spirit grows cold, and this is either God's will for us or the result of some sin or an astute machination by the Devil. Some people, the less wise ones, finding themselves more or less deprived of the joys they have been accustomed to, abandon prayer, meditation, spiritual reading, penance, at this stage, and so become weaker and weaker—much to the Enemy's delight, for his whole aim is to get the soldier of Christ to lay down his arms. So when the wise "athlete of Christ" feels himself growing inwardly tepid, he should go on with his usual spiritual exercises and if anything increase them.

The holy virgin learned this from the Lord and she put this teaching into practice, speaking with holy hatred to herself as follows, "O vilest of creatures, do you imagine that you deserve content? Have you forgotten your sins and who you are, a miserable sinner? Is it not enough to be saved from eternal damnation, even though this means enduring pain and darkness for the rest of your fife? Why let these things make you apathetic and depressed? If you escape eternal punishment you will find happiness with Christ for all eternity. Did you decide to serve God to be comforted here or to enjoy Him in eternity? Cheer up, do your exercises as usual—indeed to every act of praise that you make, now add something more!" Thus with the spears of humility did the holy virgin wound and repulse the King of Babylon's pride, fortifying herself with the words of wisdom.

She confessed to me that there were so many hordes of devils in her cell—she could almost see them with her own eyes—rousing so many vile thoughts in her mind, that for a time at least she was glad to get out of it and take refuge in church. She thus spent even more time there than usual, for though she was still pursued by these denizens of Hell she found them less troublesome when she was inside. She said she would have fled up hill and down dale like St. Jerome to escape from those abominable monsters and obscene visions. But when she returned to her little room they were still there, talking and acting in the most licentious manner and attacking her like a swarm of maddening flies. She would at once take to prayer; and she was so insistent in her pleading that these hellish visitations gradually died down.

This had been going on for several days when all of a sudden, on arriving back from church and prostrating herself in prayer, she had an illumination from the Holy Spirit, who reminded her how a few days before she had asked the Lord for the gift of fortitude and He Himself had told her how to obtain it. At once she understood the mystery of the temptations, and in the joy this brought her she determined to bear these molestations with a cheerful spirit for as long as her Bridegroom required. Then one of the bolder and more malignant of the demons assailed her with these words: "You wretched creature, do you intend to live in this deplorable condition for the rest of your life? If you do not give in to us we shall persecute you to death." Whereupon Catherine, strong in the knowledge of what she had been told, promptly replied, "With joy I have chosen the way of suffering and shall endure these and any other persecutions in the name of the Saviour for as long as it shall please Him to send them, in fact I shall enjoy them."

On hearing this the horde of devils retired in shame, and there came from on high a great light that lit up the whole room, and in the light was the Lord Jesus Christ, nailed to the cross and bleeding as when he entered the holy of holies through the shedding of His own blood. From the cross He called down to the holy virgin, "Catherine, my daughter, you see how much I suffered for you? Do not be sad, then, that you must suffer for me." Then His appearance changed and He came closer to her, and to comfort her He spoke sweetly of the victory she had gained. But like Anthony she said, "My Lord, where were you when my heart was disturbed by all those temptations?" "I was in your heart," said the Lord. "May your truth always be preserved, Lord, and all reverence to Your Majesty," said Catherine, "but how can I possibly believe that you were in my heart when it was full of ugly, filthy thoughts?" "Did these thoughts and temptations bring content or sorrow, delight or displeasure to your heart?" asked the Lord. "The greatest sorrow and displeasure!" answered Catherine. "Well, then," said the Lord, "who was it who made you feel this displeasure if not I, who was hidden at the centre of your heart? If I had not been there they would have entered your heart and you would have felt pleasure in them, but my presence there caused them to displease you and when you tried to drive them away because they were upsetting you and you failed to do so, this made you unhappy and you suffered. But I, who was defending your heart from the enemies, was hidden there all the time, and though I permitted you to be attacked I was still there. Then when I decided that the time for battle was over I sent down my light and the powers of darkness took flight and vanished, for they cannot exist where my light is. Now, what but my light had taught you that pains are useful to help you to acquire fortitude, and that you must bear with them gladly for as long as I please? Then you promised to endure them all your life if need be, but you were relieved of them as soon as I revealed myself to you. For what pleases me is not the pains but the will of the person who endures them with fortitude.

"To help you understand these things better I will give you an example. Whoever would have thought that when my body was suffering and dying on the cross and then lay there with all the life gone from it, it had the life inseparably united to it hidden in it all the time? Not only the uncomprehending and the evil-doers but my own Apostles too who had been with me for such a long time were unable to believe this: they all lost faith and hope. Nevertheless, although it is true that my body was not alive with the life it had received from the soul, it was still united to the unending life by which all living things live; and by virtue of this, at the time determined from all eternity, my own spirit was reunited with it in more fullness of life and virtue than it had had before, endowed with the gifts of immortality and impassibility and other gifts which had not been granted to it in the first place, Thus when I so willed it the life remained hidden, but the Divine Nature being united to my body, when I so willed it it revealed its power. Now, since I have created you in my image and likeness and by taking on your nature have become like you, I never give up trying to make you like me in so far as you are able to respond: I try to create within your soul too, in this life, what then took place in my body. So, my daughter, since you fought the good fight not by yourself but with me, you deserve greater grace from me, and from now on I shall appear to you oftener and closer."

Here the vision ended, but Catherine was left in such a state of delight that it would be ridiculous to think of trying to describe it. What remained especially imprinted on her mind was the infinite tenderness with which the Lord had called her his daughter when he had said, "Catherine, my daughter." In fact when she described this vision to her confessor she begged him to address her like that in future, so that the joy she had felt might always be renewed.

From now onwards her most holy Bridegroom conversed with her on such intimate terms that to anyone who did not know what had gone before it would have seemed incredible and almost ridiculous. But to a soul that knows how indescribably sweet and good the Lord is it seems not only possible and fitting but quite reasonable. The Lord appeared to her very frequently indeed, and had long conversations with her. Sometimes He brought His most glorious Mother with Him, or St. Dominic, or both together, or it might be Mary Magdalene, or John the Evangelist, or Paul the Apostle, or other saints, either all together or each one separately, according to His pleasure. Generally, however, He came alone, and talked to Catherine as one friend to another, so much so, as she shyly confessed to me, that they would say the Psalms together, walking up and down the little room like two religious brothers saying their office. Isn't this amazing? What a marvellous demonstration of intimacy in our own times! Nevertheless, reader, it will not seem incredible to you if you really consider what has been said, and what will be said, and meditate on the unfathomable nature of God's goodness.

Upon each of His saints the Lord confers some special gift that he alone can rejoice in, so that not only all the saints together, but each one in particular, will manifest some facet of the Lord's greatness. As the Prophet says, "According to thy highness, thou hast multiplied the children of men": (*Psalm* 11:9) the Lord multiplies the number of the sons of men according to his highness, for as everyone is clearly in some way different from everyone else so every saint is distinguished from every other saint by some particular grace, and something is found in each one of them that is not in any of the others.

Since reference has been made to reciting the Psalms, I must tell you, reader, that this holy virgin knew how to read without being taught by human beings. I say "read"; she could never speak Latin, but she could read the words and say them properly.

She told me that when she decided to learn to read so that she could say the Divine Praises and the Canonical Hours, a friend of hers wrote the alphabet out and tried to teach it her, but after spending many fruitless weeks over it she decided not to waste any more time over it and to turn to heavenly grace instead. One morning she knelt down and prayed to the Lord. "Lord," she said, "if you want me to learn to read so that I can say the Psalms and sing your praises in the Canonical Hours, deign to teach me what I am not clever enough to learn by myself. If not, thy will be done: I shall be quite content to remain in my ignorance and shall be able to spend more time in meditating on you in other ways."

Then a marvel happened—clear proof of God's power—for during this prayer she was so divinely instructed that when she got up she knew how to read any kind of writing quite easily and fluently, like the best reader in the world. When I realized this I was flabbergasted, especially when I discovered that though she could read so fast she could not read separate syllables; in fact, she could hardly spell the words. I believe that the Lord meant this to be a sign of the miracle that had taken place.

From then on Catherine began to hunt for books of the Divine Office and to read the Psalms and anthems and the other things fixed for the Canonical Hours. She was especially struck by the verse with which each Hour begins and remembered it to the end of her life, "O God, come to my assistance; O Lord, make haste to help me." (*Psalm* 69:2). She often used to repeat this in the vernacular.

But her soul grew so contemplative that her vocal prayers gradually ceased and so frequent were her raptures that she could hardly reach the end of an "Our Father" without going into ecstasy. I shall be saying a good deal more about this later.

Let me end this chapter here; the next will bring us to the end of this first part of her life. What I have written here has been pieced together from what she privately told her confessors and her letters, in which she would sometimes advise people by relating events from her own life as though they had happened to someone else.

CHAPTER TWELVE

The Mystical Marriage

---•---

F ROM now on Catherine's soul increased in grace daily. She flew rather than walked along the way of virtue, and a holy desire developed within her soul to attain to perfect faith, so that, utterly subject to her Bridegroom, she might be utterly pleasing to Him. She began to pray to the Lord as the disciples had done, to increase her faith and make it perfect and as solid as a rock. The Lord spoke to her and said, "I will espouse you to me in faith." Catherine went on praying and praying and the Lord kept giving her the same answer.

Near Lent (when the faithful abstain from meat and fats) in the days when men celebrate the vain feast of the stomach, the virgin was to be found alone in her little room seeking through prayer and fasting the face of her eternal Bridegroom, praying endlessly for the same thing. Then the Lord said to her, "Since for love of me you have forsaken vanities and despised the pleasure of the flesh and fastened all the delights of your heart on me, now, when the rest of the household are feasting and enjoying themselves, I have determined to celebrate the wedding feast of your soul and to espouse you to me in faith as I promised."

Before He had finished speaking His most glorious Virgin Mother appeared with the most blessed St. John the Evangelist, the glorious Apostle Paul, St. Dominic (the founder of the Order) and the prophet

David with his harp. While David played sweet strains on the harp the Mother of God took Catherine's hand in her own most holy hand and presenting her to her Son courteously asked Him to marry her to Himself in faith. The Son of God, graciously agreeing, held out a gold ring with four pearls set in a circle in it and a wonderful diamond in the middle and with His most holy right hand He slipped it on to the virgin's second finger, saying, "There! I marry you to me in faith, to me, your Creator and Saviour. Keep this faith unspotted until you come to me in heaven and celebrate the marriage that has no end. From this time forward, daughter, act firmly and decisively in everything that in my Providence I shall ask you to do. Armed as you are with the strength of faith, you will overcome all your enemies and be happy."

The vision disappeared, but the ring always remained on Catherine's finger and though no one else could see it it was always before her eyes. In fact she frequently confessed to me in all humility that she could always see it on her finger and that there was never a moment when it was out of her sight.

Reader, you may know of another Catherine, a martyr and queen, who, as we read, was similarly married to the Lord after she was baptized. Well, here you have a second, most happy Catherine being solemnly married to the same Lord after achieving great victories over the flesh and the Enemy.

If you consider the properties of the ring she was given you will see how it agrees with the thing it symbolized or signified. Our virgin asked for a strong faith. What is stronger than diamond? As diamond can resist, overcome, break anything, however hard, and can itself only be broken by being sprinkled with the blood of a goat, so has a faithful heart the power to overcome all adversities and is itself only softened and broken by the blood of Christ. Then the four pearls symbolize the four different kinds of purity that Catherine had—purity of intention, purity of thought, purity of word, and purity of deed, as can be seen from what has already been said and will be proved again by what follows.

I believe that this marriage was meant to confirm the divine grace, and that the sign of this confirmation was the ring which she alone could see, so that when she went on to her task of rescuing souls from the swamps of this world she would never be downcast but always trust in God's grace as she bore them to the firm ground of salvation.

According to the Holy Doctors, one of the main reasons why Almighty God lets some people know that they will always be in His grace is because He plans to send them out into this perverse world to battle for the honour of His name and to save souls. This happened to the Apostles at Pentecost, when they received a visible sign of the grace they had been given, and also to St. Paul, who heard the words: "My grace is sufficient for thee." (*2 Cor.* 12:9). Other signs of a like kind have been given for the sake of mankind. Now in defiance of all convention our virgin too was to take part in public life for the honour of God and the good of souls (as with God's help I hope to describe later), and so she had the grace in her confirmed by a visible sign, so that she might be bold and firm in doing the things heaven enjoined her to do. But in her case there was something special, for whereas the signs given to others had been fleeting ones, with her the sign was permanent and she could see it all the time. I believe the Lord willed this because of her sex and the novelty of what she did and the slack condition of our times, all of which seemed likely to raise obstacles to the mission entrusted her by heaven, so that she needed special and continuous assistance.

And with this we come to the end of Part One of Catherine's life, which was made up of silence and seclusion. Now we shall go on to Part Two, in which I shall describe what she did in public for the honour of God and the salvation of souls, in all her actions there reigning the Lord Jesus Christ, who with the Father and the Holy Spirit lives and reigns, world without end, Amen.

PART TWO

PART TWO

CHAPTER ONE

Catherine's Divine Mission

———•———

T HE Heavenly Bridegroom, speaking in Canticles (*Canticles* 5:2:3) to his dearly beloved spouse, says to her: "Open to me, my sister, my love, my dove, my undefiled: for my head is full of dew, and my locks of the drops of the night." And she replies, "I have put off my garment, how shall I put it on? I have washed my feet, how shall I defile them?"

I have begun the second part of this story of Catherine's life with these words from Canticles because so far we have been discussing the embraces of Jacob and Rachel, and the better part chosen by Mary, but it is now time to speak at length of the fruitfulness of Lia and the assiduous ministerings of Martha. Thus I shall bring this bride of Christ before the eyes of the faithful not only with respect to her spiritual insight but also as regards the fruitfulness of her spiritual progeny.

A soul that has tasted how sweet the Lord is finds it very difficult to detach itself from this perfect sweetness. If this has to happen, the soul cannot help grumbling a little, resenting the fact that it has been called by God to produce sons and supply them with all they need. That is why I have begun by quoting the words of the Bridegroom as He awakens His spouse from her sleep on the bed of contemplation, where she has been lying unmindful of temporal things and washed clean of all filthiness, and invites her to open the door—not, of course, her own "door", but the "door" of other souls. Her own "door" is open already; otherwise she would never have been able to repose in the Lord. Nor, strictly speaking, would she have been able to call herself a spouse.

Catherine, having heard from the lips of her Shepherd and Heavenly Bridegroom that she was to be called from rest to labour, from silence to noise, from the seclusion of her cell to public life, answered plaintively, "I have already divested myself of all worldly cares; now that I have cast them aside, must I return to them again? I have washed the feet of my affections clean of every stain of sin and vice, must I then befoul myself again with the dust of the earth?"

Now let us apply what we have said to our particular purpose.

After the Saviour of men, the Lord God Jesus Christ, had sated this His bride with delights; after He had trained her in spiritual warfare with so many combats, and endowed her with excellent gifts by imparting to her an extraordinary doctrine; then, not wishing such a light to remain hidden under a bushel, but desiring that she should be a city set on a hill, visible to all, making full use of the talents He had given her, He called to her and said, "Open to me . . ." etc.

By this He meant: Open, by ministering to them, the doors of souls, that I may enter into them. Clear the way for my sheep, that they may come and graze freely. Open, again, to me (that is to say, to my honour), your casket of heavenly treasure—containing both doctrines and graces—that it may be poured into the laps of the faithful. Open to me, you who are by conformity of nature my sister, by intimate charity my friend, by simplicity of mind my dove, by purity of body and soul my immaculate one.

To all these things the holy virgin responded with perfect fidelity.

She told me in confession that, when by the Lord's command she was obliged to leave her cell and go and talk to anyone, she felt such a sharp pain in her heart that it seemed as though it was about to break, and that no one except the Lord would have been able to make her do it.

Now let us return to our story.

After the Marriage, the Lord, in a calm and orderly fashion, gradually induced her to have dealings with other people, without, however, depriving her of his divine society; in fact, as regards the degree of perfection, He rather tended to increase this in her, as we shall see later.

Sometimes, during the visits that He paid to her to teach her about the Kingdom of God, having imparted to her his divine secrets and said the Psalms and Canonical Hours with her, He would say:

"Go; it is dinner time, and the rest of the family are about to sit down at table; go and be with them, and then come back to me." At this Catherine would cry bitterly and say, "Why, sweetest Bridegroom, are you sending me away? Woe is me! If I have offended your Majesty, here is this little body of mine: let it be punished at your feet before you: I myself will be perfectly happy to do this. But do not let me be obliged to endure the harsh punishment of being separated from you, my most loving Bridegroom, in any way or for any time. What do I care for food? I have a kind of food unknown to those you order me to go to. Does man live by bread alone? Is not the soul of every wayfarer made to live by the word that comes out of your mouth? I, as you know better than I do myself, have avoided all other company so that I might find you, my Lord and my God; now that by your mercy I have found you, and, though unworthy, by your condescension possess you with delight, I surely cannot be obliged to forgo such an incomple treasure and involve myself again in human affairs, so that once again my ignorance returns and I quietly slip back and become a reprobate in your eyes. No, Lord; it is far from the immense perfection of your goodness, to order me or anyone else to be in any way separated from that same goodness."

To these words, and many more of a like kind, which the virgin, lying prostrate at the feet of the Lord, had spoken more by way of tears than with her lips, He would reply: "Be quiet, sweetest daughter; it is necessary for you to fulfil your every duty, so that with my grace you may assist others as well as yourself. I have no intention of cutting you off from me; on the contrary, I wish to bind you more closely to myself, by means of love of the neighbour. You know that the precepts of love are two: love of me, and love of the neighbour; in these, as I have testified, consist the Law and the Prophets. I want you to fulfil these two commandments. You must walk, in fact, with both feet, not one, and with two wings fly to heaven!

"Do you not remember that the zeal for souls which I planted and watered in your soul in the days of your infancy grew to such an extent that you planned to disguise yourself as a man and enter the Order of Preachers and go off into foreign parts, and so be more useful to yourself and other souls? The habit that you sought with such constancy, because of the great love you bore my faithful servant Dominic, who founded his Order mainly out of love of souls, you now possess. What is there to be astonished at or to lament about if I lead you to do what in infancy you desired to do?" And Catherine, somewhat comforted by this reply, would say, as once Blessed Mary had said, "How shall this thing be?" And the Lord: "According as my goodness shall ordain." And Catherine, like a good disciple imitating her Master, would answer: "Let your will, not mine, be done in all things, Lord, for I am darkness and you are light; I am not, whereas you are He who is; I most ignorant, and you the wisdom of God the Father. But I beg you, O Lord—if it is not too presumptuous of me—how can what you have just said come about; that is to say, how can I, wretched and frail as I am, be of use to souls? My sex, as you know, is against it in many ways, both because it is not highly considered by men, and also because it is not good, for decency's sake, for a woman to mix with men."

To these words the Lord would reply, as once the Archangel Gabriel had replied, that nothing is impossible to God, for He said: "Am not I He who created the human race, and divided it into male and female? I spread abroad the grace of my spirit where I will. In my eyes there is neither male nor female, rich nor poor, but all are equal, for I can do all things with equal ease. It is as easy for me to create an Angel as an ant, and to create all the heavens is as easy for me as to create the merest worm. It is written of me that I made whatever I willed to make, for nothing is impossible to me. (*Psalm* 113).

"Do you still remain doubtful? Do you imagine that I am unable to find ways of achieving whatever I have determined and predetermined on? However, I realize that you do not speak thus from lack of faith but from humility. Therefore you must know that in these latter days there has been such an upsurge of pride, especially in the case of men who imagine themselves to be learned or wise, that my justice cannot endure them any longer, without delivering a just chastisement upon them that will bring them to confusion. But since my mercy transcends all else I do, I shall first give them a salutary lesson, to see whether they will come to their senses and humble themselves; as I did with the Jews and the Gentiles, when I sent amongst them idiots whom I had filled with divine wisdom. To confound their arrogance, I will raise up women ignorant and frail by nature but endowed with strength and divine wisdom. Then, if they will come to their senses and humble themselves, I will behave with the utmost mercy towards them, that is to say, towards those who, according to the grace given them, receive my doctrine, offered to them in fragile but specially chosen vessels, and follow it reverently. Those who will not accept this salutary lesson, I shall with perfect justice reduce to such confusion that the world will look upon them as objects of contempt and derision. For it is indeed only just that those who try to exalt themselves should be humbled. Therefore, be bravely obedient when in the future I send you out amongst people. Wherever you may find yourself I shall not forsake you, or fail to visit you, as is my custom, and direct you in all that you are to do."

Having heard these words, the holy virgin bowed reverently before the Lord, and like a true child of obedience hurriedly left the cell and went off to join the rest of the family at table, fulfilling the Lord's command.

But here, dearest reader, we must stop, as I have to carry out what in the beginning I promised before God.

I have already, you may remember, said that I would write nothing down that was untrue, imaginary or exaggerated, but would restrict myself to what I had actually heard from the virgin herself or from others. Many and many a time she argued with me about different things, but I cannot remember what precisely she said. This comes of my negligence and, I say it with shame, my laziness. Many things, too, have gone out of my mind as a result of the affairs I have been engaged in since I last saw her, never to see her again. Perhaps there is also, as I myself believe, the matter of growing old; and in this case the first thing to go, I agree with Seneca, is one's memory. When memories come back into my mind, I use the words which seem to me to be most likely to have been said by her; but to the honour of Almighty God and his bride Catherine, I am bound to confess that, thanks to her, many, many things come back before my eyes which I had previously never even thought about. In fact she seems at times to be with me, telling me what to write.

All this, reader, can be taken as a rule in the matter of words. As to the facts, you must know that whatever I relate I have made myself fully conversant with, either through witnesses, or through writings, or from my own experience. I can also remember the gist of many other things she said, in particular as regards her doctrine.

I have been obliged to add this aside, for fear of offending against the truth.

Let us go back to the story.

The virgin, then, stood with her body amongst people but her soul entirely with her Heavenly Bridegroom. Everything she saw and heard was a burden to her, except for the thought of Him she loved. Overflowing with love as she was, the hours she spent in the company of others seemed endless, more like months or years, and as soon as she could she would return to her cell and seek once again Him whom her soul loved; and as soon as she had found Him would sweetly embrace Him, eagerly hold Him, and adore Him with ineffable devotion.

From this there began to grow within her a desire, which increased as long as she lived in the body, for frequent reception of Holy Communion, so that not only her spirit might be united with the Eternal Spouse but also her body with His body. She knew, in fact, that though the adorable Sacrament of the Body of the Lord produces spiritual grace in the soul and unites it to its Saviour, this union being the end for which the Sacrament was instituted, nevertheless anyone who truly feeds on it is at once united with His Body, though not with a union of the entire body. Therefore, wishing to unite herself ever more closely with the most noble object of her love, she determined to receive Holy Communion as often as she possibly could.

But we shall return to this later, in a separate chapter.

And so the Lord encouraged and assisted Catherine daily in the art of being on easy terms with people, so that He might ultimately draw from her the results He desired to obtain. And so it came about that, in order not to appear lazy in the eyes of the rest of the family, the virgin of the Lord began to occupy herself now and again with domestic affairs; and this led to such a number of extraordinary things, and they need to be taken such note of, that I prefer to describe them in a new chapter.

What I have written in the present chapter could only be verified by the holy virgin, for it was from her lips alone that I learned it.

CHAPTER TWO

Beginning of Catherine's Public Life

———————————•———————————

W HEN the virgin consecrated to God was thoroughly convinced
that it was her Heavenly Bridegroom's will that she should
occasionally mix with others, she decided to act in such a way that these
encounters should not be fruitless but should, on the contrary, give an
example of good living to the people she conversed with. Thus, for their
edification she began by performing acts of humility and then gradually
proceeded to acts of charity, not, however, forgetting continual devout
prayer, with which an unplleled penance was inseparably united.

She began to apply herself with the utmost humility to the lowest
kinds of housework, sweeping, kitchen-work, anything—and what a
splendid sight it must have been! But she was busiest when the servant fell
ill. Then she redoubled her labours, looking after the invalid and doing
the housework in her stead. The wonderful thing is that, even though she
was so busy, she never for one moment lost the delights of being with
her Heavenly Bridegroom, for she seemed to be so naturally inclined to
unite herself in mind with Him at all times and places, that no matter
what kind of work she was doing she was never deprived of His chaste
embraces. As the flame cannot but rise upwards, so her spirit, inflamed
by the fire of divine love, tended as though of its own nature towards the
things that are above, where Christ sits at God's right hand.

The result was that she very frequently suffered the kind of excess that is known as ecstasy, as I and all the other Friars who were spiritually regenerated by her witnessed on a thousand occasions. No sooner did the thought of her Heavenly Bridegroom come into her holy mind than she lost the use of her bodily senses, and her extremities, that is to say her hands and feet, became quite plysed. Her clenched fingers would press so tightly into the palms of her hands that it was as though they were nailed there, and it would have been easier to break them than force them open. Her eyes, too, shut tight, and her neck became so stiff that any attempt to move it would have been really dangerous.

On one occasion, her mother Lapa, who was quite in the dark about such things as ecstasies, saw her daughter looking so rigid and deathlike with her neck bent that she tried to straighten it; she only stopped when she heard shouts coming from the virgin's companion. When Catherine came back to her senses her neck was as painful as though it had been given a number of severe blows. When this matter was later mentioned in her presence she said that if her mother had used a little more force to straighten her neck she would undoubtedly have broken it.

In these ecstasies, in which the holy virgin became rapt like another Mary Magdalene, her body was sometimes raised up off the ground along with her spirit, and it was quite evident that a great power was attracting her spirit. We shall go into this, with a wealth of detail, later.

Now let us go on to a description of the miracle that took place at the beginning of these ecstasies.

One day Catherine was busy with the most humble tasks in the house, and was in fact sitting by the fire engaged in turning the spit; but her soul was not, for all that, any the less inflamed by the fire of the Holy Spirit, and, thinking of her soul's Love, and mentally conversing with Him, she was taken up into an ecstasy. Whereupon her hand stopped rotating the spit. Lisa, her sister-in-law, who is still alive to confirm this, saw the whole thing and ran up to turn the spit herself, leaving Catherine to enjoy the embraces of her Heavenly Bridegroom.

After supper, as the virgin was still in ecstasy, Lisa did all the clearing away and washing up herself, leaving her sister-in-law to go on enjoying the divine consolations. Then she went into the other room to look after her husband and sons as usual, and decided that after she had put the boys to bed she would go back into the kitchen and watch over her sister-in-law to see the end of the ecstasy. It was some time before she left the room and went through to where she had left the holy virgin rapt in ecstasy, and when she did so she found that her body had fallen right over the burning embers. There were always a lot of live coals in the house because they needed them for boiling up the dyes. When she saw what had happened Lisa let out a shriek: "Mercy, Catherine is all burned!" and ran and dragged her out of the fire. But she saw at once that Catherine's clothes and body had not been affected in the slightest degree by the fire, nor was there any smell of burning. The extraordinary thing is that there was not the slightest trace of ash to be seen on the virgin's dress, though by all accounts she must have been lying on the fire for several hours.

Can you imagine, reader, what a powerful invisible fire must have been hidden in the holy virgin's soul, if it was able to nullify the natural power of the visible fire? Don't you rather think that in some ways the miracle of the three young men had been repeated? (*Daniel* 3).

But this kind of miracle often happened.

One day, in the church of the Friar Preachers in Siena, she rested her head on the foot of a column, on which a number of saints were depicted, and a candle that had been lighted in honour of one of the saints fell on her head as she knelt in prayer and stayed there alight until it had burned itself right away. It seems incredible, especially in these days! A candle falls on the veil covering the virgin's head, stays there alight until it burns itself out, and not only does no harm to head or veil but leaves not the slightest sign of burning on the veil! Not until the wax was consumed did the light go out—just as though it had fallen on a sheet of iron or stone!

This miracle was witnessed by many of her companions, who told me about it afterwards. They included Lisa, Alexia and Francesca. Lisa is still alive; the other two, their mistress being dead, have followed her. But this is not all.

In other parts of the world, especially when she, or rather the grace of God through her, was reaping an extraordinary harvest of souls, the old Serpent would hurl himself upon her in a sudden burst of fury and be allowed by the Lord to push her into the fire, in the presence of many of her sons and daughters in Christ. These, with tears and screams, would do their best to pull her out of harm's way, but she would get up all smiles, without showing the slightest mark on her clothes or body and say to them, "Don't be afraid of the old Pickpocket!" That is what she used to call the Devil, because he is the naughty fellow who tries to snatch souls. In Siena, you see, the word "pocket" means in common parlance a little bag.

I have been told about these things by one of her spiritual sons, Neri di Landoccio di Siena,[1] who was present along with many others on two of these occasions. He is now living a holy life as an anchorite and I have known him for too long to have any doubts about the truth of what he tells me.

The whole thing is also confirmed by Gabriele, of the Sienese family of the Piccolomini, who has assured me that he too was present. In fact he went on to tell me that once, when the holy virgin was in bed near a great earthenware jar full of burning coals, the old Enemy attacked her with such violence that she banged her head against the vessel and broke it into pieces. Neither her head-veil nor her head itself was affected by the fire or the violent blow, and getting up as though nothing had happened, she said to her malignant persecutor, with a scornful smile, "Pickpocket, Pickpocket!"

The same sort of thing happened to Euphrasia,[2] as can be read in the lives of the Holy Fathers. But it is hardly surprising if God, who

---

1. See Part III, Chap. 1
2. The historians refer to several Euphrasias, and we do not know to which of these Raymond is alluding. Niceforo Callisto, in the seventh book of his *History*, tells of a

97

permitted this same Evil One to bear His beloved son to the top of the temple and the high mountain, should allow similar things to happen to his daughters!

Realize, dearest reader, that I have jumped ahead from the earlier events to those that happened later, but I was led to do so by the subject matter. Now I shall not be obliged to repeat myself about the miracles that the Lord performed through Catherine in the element of fire.

Let us return to the story.

Under the pressure and guidance of the Supreme Master, the holy virgin was learning daily more and more about how, so to speak, to enjoy the embraces of her Heavenly Bridegroom in a flowery bed and how to descend into the valley of lilies to make herself more fruitful; and she did not stop doing anything, or leave anything half done for the sake of something else—this being a proof of love and the highest perfection in anyone who is advancing. The source and basis of all she did was love; and so charity towards her neighbour surpassed all her other actions. These works of charity were of two kinds, since the neighbour is a composite of two substances, one spiritual, the other corporal. But as in teaching it is in the nature of things for the movement to be from imperfect to perfect things, we shall speak first of her corporal works of charity, and then of what she did for the good of souls. I do not believe, however, that it will be possible to describe all the latter. Further, on account of the excellence of her deeds, it will be necessary to distinguish between the things she did for those who were ill, and the things she did to help those who were in need, for both are surprising, and each one has a wonderful miracle behind it.

Euphrasia who was a virgin martyr in Nicomedia, who preferred to be beheaded rather than to be forced into a brothel. Another Euphrasia, who was born in the middle of the fourth century and died in Egypt in 410, was the daughter of an important personage at the court of Theodosius II; hating worldly vanities, she retired as a girl from the luxury of the court and on the death of her father distributed her inheritance to the poor, withdrew into a convent in Egypt, and consecrated herself to the religious life.

In the next chapter, therefore, we shall discuss the marvellous things she did to assist those who were in need, and in the following chapter the wonderful charity she showed towards the bodies of the sick.

I bring this chapter to an end without bothering to repeat the witnesses to the things related, having already mentioned them by name.

CHAPTER THREE

Charity Towards the Poor

———————•———————

WHEN the virgin perceived that the more charitable she was towards her neighbour the more she would be acceptable to the Lord, she prepared and equipped herself as thoroughly as she could to succour the needy. But as she had nothing of her own—being a true religious who had determined to observe the three main vows—so, not wishing to make use of anyone else's property, she went to her father and asked him for permission to give alms to the poor according to her conscience out of what the Lord granted him and his family. Her father readily agreed, for he was delighted to see his daughter advancing in the way of the Lord. And this was not a private agreement, for he made it an order for the whole house, saying, "Let no one try to stop my dearest daughter from giving alms, for I give her a free hand to give away anything I have in the house." Having obtained this permission, the holy virgin began to give her father's goods away lavishly; but as she possessed the gift of discretion in an especially high degree she did not give things away indiscriminately but was most generous to those she knew to be truly in need, even if they had not asked for anything.

In the meantime, it had come to her ears that not far from her home there were a number of needy families who would not come and knock at the door of her house because they were ashamed to ask for alms, but who were nevertheless suffering great poverty. She did not turn a deaf ear to this and early one morning, bearing a load of grain, wine and oil and whatever else she could find, she went off to the house of these poor people alone and unobserved like St. Nicholas. Providentially she found the door open, and being thus able to deposit what she had brought with her inside the house, she closed the door and hurried away.

One day she fell ill, and her whole body swelled up; she was unable to get up or stand on her feet. Hearing that there was a poor widow living nearby with sons and daughters all dying of hunger, she was at once moved by compassion and, during the night, she prayed to her Heavenly Bridegroom to grant her sufficient health to allow her to help the poor woman.

She got up before dawn and went round the house. Managing to find a small sack, she filled it with grain; then she got a big bottle and filled it with wine, and a smaller bottle and filled it with oil; then she found all the eatables she could and carried the whole lot into her room. Though she could have carried them one by one, it seemed impossible that she could take them all at once all by herself, considering the distance to the widow's house; nevertheless, doing the best she could, that is to say, taking one thing in her right arm, another in her left, loading a third on to her shoulders, and fastening another to her girdle and hoping for divine aid, she tried to lift them all at once—and immediately, with the miraculous help of the Lord, she lifted the entire load up as easily as if it had lost all its weight. She confessed to me and her other confessors that she carried all this load as easily as though it had been a wisp of straw, whereas it must in fact have weighed about a hundredweight.

As soon as the early morning bell rang to allow people to walk about out of doors, the holy virgin, young as she was, and despite her swollen body, emerged from the house bearing her pious load and hurried off as fast as she could towards the widow's house as though she was perfectly well and had nothing to carry.

Gradually, as she got nearer her destination, the load grew heavier and heavier, making it almost impossible for her to go on. Regarding this as a joke being played on her by her Heavenly Bridegroom, she called confidently on the Lord, and to gain further merit lifted her burden with difficulty and reached the door of the needy woman's house. Providentially it was ajar; so she put one of her arms through the crack, pushed it wide open, and deposited her burden inside. But as she put it down it made such a noise that it woke the poor woman up. Whereupon Catherine tried to hurry away, but found herself unable to: the Lord would persist in having his little joke with her, and the strength which through her prayers had been granted her to enable her to get up out of bed had by now been taken away from her completely and she was obliged to lie there in a worse state than ever, so weak that she was quite unable to move.

Saddened, but at the same time amused, she said to her Heavenly Bridegroom, "Why, sweetheart,[1] have you deceived me like this? Do you think it is a nice thing to do, to mock me and upset me by making me lie here? Do you want to show me up before all the people in the house here, and all the people who will soon be passing along the street? Have you forgotten the mercies you deigned to show your most unworthy servant? I beg you, give me my strength back, so that I may return home." And she struggled to get up, saying to herself as she did so, "You'll move, even if I have to die for it!"

In this way, crawling rather than walking, she had managed to move a little distance away, though not far enough, when the poor widow, who had by now got up, recognized the habit her benefactress was wearing and guessed who she was. Then her Heavenly Bridegroom, seeing how deeply depressed his bride was, and being in a way unable to endure this any longer, gave her some of her original strength back, so that after much struggling the virgin managed to arrive home before it was fully daylight and, thoroughly worn out, get back into bed. For

---

1. Perhaps a better translation would be "my dearly beloved."—*Publisher*, 2003.

her illnesses were not governed by the ordinary rules of nature but by what the Most High allowed, as, by God's will, will become clear as we proceed.

Thus, reader, you have seen repeated, not once but several times and in spite of grave infirmity, the deeds of St. Nicholas; let us inquire further and see whether we can find anything that bears any likeness to the generosity of the glorious Martin.

Once, when the virgin was in the church of the Preaching Friars in Siena, she was accosted by a beggar, who asked her for the love of God to help him in his need. Not having anything to give him, as she never carried gold or silver with her, she told him to wait until she had got home and then she would gladly give him as much as she could from what she was able to find. But the beggar (who I believe was not the man he seemed to be) persisted: "If you have anything to give me, give it me now, because the truth is I'm desperate."

Not wishing to send him away disappointed, she wondered what she could give him, and then she remembered a little silver cross that hung in the usual way at the end of those beads commonly known as "Paternosters" because one Paternoster is said for each bead. The holy virgin was in fact holding one of these Paternosters, with its little silver cross, in her hand, and she quickly broke the thread and gave the beggar the cross. As soon as he had been given it he went off perfectly content without asking anyone else for anything, as though he had been there for the sole purpose of getting that little cross.

During the night, while the virgin of the Lord was as usual at prayer, the Saviour of the world appeared to her holding this cross, now adorned with precious stones, in his hand. "Daughter," he said, "do you recognize this cross?" "I certainly do," replied Catherine, "but when it was mine it was not so beautiful." "You gave it me yesterday," said the Lord, "on an impulse of charity, as is signified by these precious stones: and, that your joy may be perfect, I promise you that I will present it to you, just as it is now, in the presence of the Angels and men on the Judgement Day; on that day, when I exalt my Father's mercy and

103

justice, I shall not conceal this work of mercy that you did to me, or allow it to be concealed."

With these words He disappeared, leaving the virgin's soul wholly occupied in humbly giving thanks, and inspired in the highest degree to perform more acts of charity, as will be described in the next episode.

The most lovable Bridegroom of Souls, allured by his bride's works of charity and mercy, tempted and provoked her for our instruction to greater things.

The hour of Terce had already sounded in the church, and the congregation had come out; but Catherine, who was accustomed to go on praying, had stayed behind with a companion on this day too. When she finally came down from the nuns' chapel, which is raised above the nave, intending to return home, behold! the Lord appeared to her in the likeness of a young man of about thirty-two or thirty-three years of age, half-naked, poverty-stricken and homeless, who asked her for the love of God to give him some piece of clothing. Fired more than usual by the desire to perform a work of mercy, she said to him, "Wait here for me a little while, dearest, while I go back into that chapel, and then I will give you the clothing." Once inside the chapel, with the help of her companion she carefully and modestly pulled down the sleeveless tunic that she wore under her outer tunic to keep out the cold, and cheerfully gave it to the poor beggar-man. He no sooner accepted it than he made another request: "Lady, now that you have supplied me with a woollen garment, will you give me some linen clothes too?" Catherine readily agreed, and said, "Follow me and I will give you all you ask for." The bride walked on in front, and the Bridegroom followed after, incognito. Entering her home, she went into the room where the linen clothes belonging to her father and brothers were kept, took out a shirt and a pair of trousers and with a smile offered them to the beggar. But even these did not satisfy him, for he said, "Lady, what use is this tunic to me without sleeves? Give me something to cover my arms too, then I can go away completely clothed." Whereupon Catherine, not in the slightest degree put out by this, but on the contrary

more enthusiastic than ever, set off on a careful search of the house
to see whether she could find a pair of sleeves. Then she happened to
see the serving woman's new dress hanging from a pole waiting to be
cleaned; so she took it down, quickly unstitched the sleeves, and courteously gave them to the beggar.

Having accepted these too, He who once put Abraham to the test
then said, "Look, lady, you have given me a new set of clothing, and
the Lord bless you, for whom you have done this; but I have a friend
in the hospital here and he too is in great need of clothing. If you
would like to send him anything, I will gladly take it to him from you."
Catherine, in no way put out by this new request, began to wonder
where she could find a coat to send to the wretched fellow in the poor-
house. She remembered that everyone in the house except her father
had taken her continual alms-giving amiss and had locked their possessions up to prevent her from giving them to the poor. So, realizing
that in justice she had already taken enough of the servant's clothes and
could hardly appropriate anything further, since the servant was a poor
woman herself, she was in two minds as to what to do, whether to give
the poor fellow her one remaining piece of clothing or not. Charity
suggested she should, but maidenly modesty said no. In this dispute
charity struggled with charity—the charity that looks to the soul and
the charity that has compassion on the body.

She reasoned, then, that if she were to go out without any clothes on
she would scandalize the neighbours, and that it was necessary to love
the soul more than the body, and not to run the slightest risk of scandalizing souls for the sake of giving alms. And so she said to the beggar man,
"Of course, dearest, if it was lawful for me to go about without a tunic I
would give you this one gladly; but I am not allowed to do so, and as I
haven't any other I beg you not to take it amiss, because I should be very
pleased if I could give you all you ask for." The other, smiling, replied,
"I know you would be very pleased to give me all you could. Farewell."
And as he was going away she seemed to perceive by various signs that
the poor man was no other than the One who frequently appeared to her

105

and talked to her as with a friend. At this her heart grew ardent, but at the same time she was dubious, for she considered herself unworthy of such a visit. Then she returned to her accustomed exercises and spent the rest of the day performing them.

During the night, while she was praying, there appeared to her the Saviour of the world, our Lord Jesus Christ, in the likeness of this beggar man, holding in his hand the tunic that Catherine had given him, now decked out with pearls and brilliant gems; and He said to her, "Most beloved daughter, do you recognize this tunic?" When she answered that she did, but that she had not given it to Him in that rich state, the Lord went on, "Yesterday, you gave me the tunic so generously, and clothed me when I was naked so charitably, that you rid me of the pains of both cold and shame; now I will give you from my holy Body a piece of clothing that will certainly be invisible to the eyes of men but which you nevertheless will be able to perceive, and by means of it your soul and body will be protected against all danger of cold until the time comes for you to be clothed with glory and honour in the presence of the saints and angels." And immediately with His most holy hands He drew forth from the wound in His side a garment the colour of blood, that shot shining rays in all directions and was made to the exact size of the virgin's body, and putting it upon her with His own holy hands, He said, "I give you this garment with all its powers for the rest of your life on earth, as a sign and token of the garment of glory with which at the appropriate time you will be clothed in heaven." With this the vision vanished.

The grace of this gift was so effective upon the holy virgin's soul and body that from that time forward she never wore any more clothes in winter than she did in summer, finding it quite sufficient to wear a single tunic over a petticoat. Not even when it was as cold as ice did she feel any need to put on more clothes, for as she could always feel this garment clinging to her body she had no need of any other.

Consider, reader, how perfect this virgin must have been if, imitating St. Nicholas in her secret alms-giving and St. Martin in giving away her clothes, she was considered worthy to have her works approved by a vision of the Saviour and words from His own mouth, and likewise to receive from Him the promise of an eternal reward, and to feel continuously within herself, with a perceptible, perpetual sign, how acceptable her gifts were to Him, the Giver of all.

Does it not seem more than likely to you that, when the Lord told the holy virgin that on the Judgement Day He would show her that silver cross, and clothe her with glory in heaven, He wanted to give her a full revelation of her final salvation, high glory and eternal predestination? You will not find these things in the lives of the saints, for when these did their extraordinary feats of alms-giving it was not revealed to them what eternal reward was to be theirs. "Martin clothed me with this garment before he was baptized," said the Lord; but He did not say, "I will give him a garment of glory in heaven," though this may have happened; nor was he given a perceptible token of the garment he was to receive in heaven, as happened in the case of our holy virgin.

These signs and revelations are not to be despised, for if the certainty of final salvation fills the soul with a satisfaction that no tongue or pen can describe, what must the result be of knowing that one is to obtain great glory in heaven? From such certainty in the soul follows an increase in all the virtues; patience, fortitude, temperance, care and diligence in the holy works of faith, hope and charity; and a continual growth of all good inclinations. And so what was at first difficult becomes easy, and that soul can do and endure anything for the love of Him who has revealed to it its eternal election and strengthened it in a way beyond words. From this, reader, you may see that there was something extraordinary about this virgin; but I can tell you that in what follows you will see greater and more extraordinary things still.

And now let us go back to what we were saying.

On another occasion the virgin of the Lord, burning incessantly with the fire of compassion, heard that a certain poor man, who had voluntarily given up the good things of the world for the love of God, was suffering from hunger. To comfort Christ in him, she put a number of eggs into the pocket that she used to wear sewn in under her tunic and set off. On her way to the man's house she went into a church, and immediately her spirit, finding itself in a house of prayer, began by its prayer to ascend to Him with whom she was always united, and she went into an ecstasy of the kind described in the previous chapter.

During this ecstasy her body happened to fall over on the side where the pocket full of eggs was, and the weight was such that a brass thimble of the kind that tailors keep on their fingers when they are sewing, which was in the pocket with the eggs, broke into three pieces, whilst the eggs that had been put there out of charity remained unscathed, as though they weren't there at all. And the marvellous thing is that those eggs bore the weight of the virgin's body for several hours without cracking, and what could not be borne by a brass ring was borne by the fragile shells of a few eggs. And it must not be imagined that the whole weight of the virgin's body was pressing on the ring alone: you only have to compare the size of the ring with that of all those eggs, and then think of the weight of the body that was pressing down.

The charity infused into the heart of this holy maiden was such that not only was she almost continuously aiding her neighbour by works of charity, but she also gave honour to the Highest by miraculous works of His Divinity. To demonstrate this, I should like to describe an extraordinary incident that was witnessed by all the men and women who were in the house at the time—which is to say, from what I have heard from reliable sources, about a score of people.

I was told, then, by her mother Lapa, her sister-in-law Lisa, her first confessor Fra Tommaso, and many others who frequented the house at the time, that in those days, when Giacomo had granted his daughter the fullest liberty in giving alms to the poor, it once came about that the family was reduced to drinking wine from a cask that had gone bad. Now the virgin would have regarded it as an insult to the honour of God not to give the poor the best of everything if she possibly could, and when she realized that the wine was bad she began to take good wine from another cask that had never been tapped and give some to the poor each day. This cask of good wine, on a normal estimate, contained just about enough to last the whole family a fortnight, or, at a pinch, three weeks. Before the wine from this cask was given to the family to drink, the virgin of the Lord had been giving a generous helping of it to the poor daily for a number of days, for no one had the right to prevent her from giving away whatever was in the house.

In the end, after quite a number of days, the person who looked after the cellar began to give the good wine to the family, but in spite of this the virgin went on giving it away too, in fact she now gave more away than before, reasoning that now that the whole family was drinking it the servants would not notice what she was doing. A fortnight went by, three weeks, a month, with the whole family drinking the wine too, and the cask showed no signs of giving out. The virgin's brothers and all the other people in the house were amazed at this and told their father about it, delighted that the cask should go on providing so much wine for such a long time and yet still seem to have plenty for the future. It was a delightful miracle for all who drank the wine, for they could not remember ever having drunk anything more pleasing or satisfying. This wine, then, delighted the people in the house not only because of the extraordinary amount of it but because of its exquisite quality too.

Whilst they were unable to account for this, the holy virgin, knowing the source of all good from whom this miraculous event proceeded, began to give out the wine openly and unstintingly to all the poor people she knew; but even so the cask showed no signs of drying up or the wine of losing its flavour. So a second month went by, and a third came, and still there was as much wine as ever, until harvest time approached and it was necessary to get all the jars ready for putting the new wine in. Then the people who looked after the household affairs decided to empty the cask so that it could be filled with the new wine, which was already running from the presses. But the divine Beneficence had other ideas.

The other jars had been prepared and filled with the new wine; but the presses were still running, so the young man in charge of the cellar ordered the cask to be emptied and prepared too. He was told that the wine had been drawn off the evening before and that a big flask of it had been taken, as white and clear as ever, and that still it showed no signs of coming to an end. This annoyed him, and he said; "Draw off all the wine in it and put it into another jar, then open the cask and get it ready to be filled with the new wine—we can't wait any longer for another one." Then a marvellous thing happened, of a kind absolutely unheard of in our day: the cask from which the wine had been flowing abundantly the day before was opened up, and it was found to be as dry as if it had not contained a drop of wine for months. Everyone looked at it in utter stupefaction, obliged to admit that the wine should have come to an end ages before. And only then, seeing with their own eyes how dry it was, did they begin to get some inkling of the miracle that lay behind the quality and quantity of that wine that had gone on for so long.

This miracle was performed in Siena, and the witnesses to it were all the people in the house, some of whose names I have given above: they were the people who told me about it.

With this I bring the chapter to an end.

CHAPTER FOUR

Charity Towards the Infirm

———————————●———————————

C ATHERINE felt wonderfully compassionate towards the poor, and for those who were ill her pity was unbounded. As a result of this pity she performed unprecedented labours, which to the ignorant will perhaps appear incredible. Nevertheless, we must not keep quiet about them; on the contrary, we shall describe them in full, to the greater glory of Almighty God.

What I am about to relate I have discovered amongst the writings of Fra Tommaso, and have also been told by Fra Bartolommeo di Domenico da Siena,[1] now Master of Sacred Theology and Provincial of the Roman Province, and by Lapa and Lisa and a number of other women as well, all trustworthy people.

In Siena there was a poor sick woman called Tecca who was obliged to go into hospital because she was too poor to get the proper treatment

———————————

1. Fra Bartolommeo di Domenico was born in Siena in 1343. He was a highly learned man and was rewarded with many honours in the Order. St. Catherine chose him as her confessor and spiritual director and he went with her on many of her journeys, including the one to Avignon. He was present at her death in Rome and worked a good deal for her canonization. Some say that he was elected titular bishop of Corona in Morea. He died of the plague in Rimini on July 3rd, 1415.

for her illness at home, and she was taken to a hospital[2] which was so short of money that she hardly had the bare necessities. The complaint she was suffering from was leprosy, and it increased to such an extent that it spread over her whole body; this made her more and more miserable, because everyone was so afraid of catching the infection that they would not go near her; they were more inclined to send her right away from the city, as is usually done with people suffering from this disease.

News of this reached the ears of the virgin, who immediately hurried to the hospital, full of burning charity, saw the poor woman, embraced her, and offered to help her and look after her for as long as she liked. And she suited the action to the word, for every day, morning and evening, she would go to see her all by herself, preparing the things she needed to keep her alive, feeding her, looking after her with care and diligence—looking upon this leper woman, in fact, as her Heavenly Bridegroom.

Although all this proceeded from the holy virgin's great virtue, in the mind of the invalid there grew up pride and ingratitude. It often happens, indeed, that people who do not possess the virtue of humility turn proud when they have reason to humble themselves and insult those to whom they should give thanks. So it was in the case of this sick woman, who responded to the holy virgin's humility and charity by becoming arrogantly demanding.

Seeing the virgin continually engaged in serving her, she began to demand almost as by right what was done for her out of generous charity, and would reprimand her helper with wicked words, heaping further abuse on her when she failed to bring her what she wanted. Sometimes, for example, in the morning, the virgin of the Lord would stay behind in church praying longer than usual. Then the angry patient would hurl taunts and abuse at her: "So at last there comes my lady queen of Fontebranda!" (This was the name of the district in which the virgin's home stood—and still stands.) Then she would go on, "Oh, what a gracious

---

2. The leper hospital, known as San Lazzaro, outside the Romano gate.

queen she is, spending day after day in the Friars' church! Were you there all morning, my lady, with the Friars? It seems as though you can never have enough of those Friars!"

With these words and others of a like kind she would try to provoke the maiden of the Lord, but the latter would pretend not to understand, and would calm her down by speaking to her as though she was her own mother, saying, "I shall soon get on with what you want me to do for you." And she would quickly get the fire going, put the cooking pot on it, get her food and all the other things ready, and wait upon her with such extraordinary care and diligence that even the bad-tempered patient marvelled at it.

Things went on like this for a long time without the virgin getting tired or losing any of her enthusiasm for the job. Many people were amazed, but Lapa was annoyed, and would grumble at her daughter, saying, "You'll catch the leprosy too, daughter. I shall never be happy about you looking after that leper woman." But Catherine, having put all her trust in the Lord, would turn away her mother's wrath with soft answers, convincing her that she had no reason to fear for her health and insisting that it was impossible for her to give up a job that had been laid upon her by the Lord; and so, removing everything that stood in the way of her performing this act of charity, she was able to persist in it.

But the age-old Adversary adopted another ruse, and—the Lord allowing it for the sake of a more glorious triumph by His bride—tried to make the infection attack Catherine's hands. From daily contact with the leper woman's body, her hands did in fact begin to show signs of infection—and one look at them was enough to convince anyone that the infection was in fact leprosy. The virgin did not allow this to interfere with her holy intention, however; in fact she would rather have had her whole body covered with leprosy than turn back from the work once begun, for she despised her body as filth and never attempted to cure it of anything that afflicted it, so long as she could thereby render a service pleasing to her Eternal Bridegroom. The infection lasted quite a long time, but to the holy virgin, through the greatness of her heavenly love, it seemed no longer than a second. But He who chastises to heal, and humbles to exalt, and who arranges that all things work together for good for those who love Him, seeing with delight the fortitude of his bride, would not suffer the infection to last.

It was not long, in fact, before the sick woman's life approached its end, and finally, in the presence of the holy virgin, who effectively consoled her, she died. Then, despite the horrible appearance of the body, Catherine carefully washed it, clothed it, laid it decently in the coffin, and finally, the funeral rites having been performed, buried it with her own hands. As soon as the body had been buried, all trace of the leprosy disappeared from the virgin's hands, and they looked as though they had never been infected at all, in fact they were now more beautiful than any other part of her body, and seemed to have increased in beauty as a result of the infection.

Reader, do you see what a multitude of virtues were assembled together in this one work done by the holy virgin? Charity, the queen and exemplar of all the virtues, prompted her to embark upon this service and see it through; through humility she became subject in all things to an invalid who had earned general contempt; and patience enabled her to endure vituperation cheerfully and to accept that repulsive disease with resignation in her own body. Clearly, these virtues were assisted by a sure and shining faith, enabling her to look with the eyes of faith, not upon the leper woman, but upon the Bridegroom whom she desired to please; nor was there lacking fortitude in hope, by which she persevered to the end. It is clear that the miracle was a result of this holy multitude of virtues; for the malady that she had caught from the leper woman while she was alive was cured by Christ at once, as soon as the sick woman was dead and buried. Are not these things marvellous, to all who can see the truth? They are indeed, but those that follow will seem still more marvellous to you, dear reader, if you will follow me attentively.

In this same city of Siena, which we have already mentioned so often, in the days when the virgin of Christ had dedicated herself for the love of God to the service of the poor and sick, there lived a certain member of the Sisters of Penance of St. Dominic, by name Palmarina, who had dedicated herself and all she possessed, according to the custom of the city, to the house of the Misericordia.[3]

Although Palmarina was bound by a dual religious obligation, she was also caught up in one of the Devil's strange and horrible toils. From a secret source of pride and envy, she nursed a cordial hatred of the holy virgin, Christ's bride, to such an extent that she could never bear to see her or even hear her name mentioned. She spoke all the evil she could of her both in private and in public, and in complaining about her and maligning her she was never-ending. She showed all the signs, in fact, of a profound hatred. The virgin did all she could to placate her with acts of humility and kindness, but the woman had nothing but contempt for them. So, as usual, Catherine was obliged to turn to her Heavenly Bridegroom and plead with Him, saying special prayers on behalf of her enemy. By so doing, she, in the Apostle's words, (*Rom.* 12:20) heaped coals of fire upon Palmarina's head, and her prayers, like mounting flames, ascended to the Lord in search of mercy and justice. Not that the maiden of the Lord asked for anything but mercy for the murmurer; but as both mercy and justice are praised in Him whom she implored, it was not fitting that mercy should be shown without justice.

The Lord was indeed severe in His justice, but in judging He showed great mercy in consequence of his bride's prayers. He struck Palmarina in the body, that she might be cured in soul: the extent to which the latter had grown obdurate in its obstinacy, and the degree of the sweetness of the charity in which He had clothed His bride, the Lord made clear by the manner of His justice. Then He redoubled the

---

3. This house or Hospital of Mercy had been founded in about the middle of the thirteenth century by St. Andrea Gallerani and was situated in the road now known as the Via della Sapiema. In 1408 the building was ceded to the University, and in 1816, when the University moved to St. Vigilio, it passed into the hands of the Academy of Arts.

virgin's zeal for souls, by showing the inestimable beauty of Palmarina's soul, already condemned by its sins but miraculously saved by Catherine's merits and prayers.

Though Palmarina had been struck down by bodily illness, the sickness of her soul did not improve; on the contrary it seemed to grow worse, for she showed more unreasoning hatred of the holy virgin now that she was ill than when she had been well. When Catherine realized this, she endeavoured to placate her by acts full of humility and meekness. She frequently went to see her, appeared before her submissively, and with kind words and charming ways did all she could to comfort her, endeavouring to serve her as much as she could in every possible way. But the woman was as hard as flint and would yield neither to words nor to loving charity; she made no attempt to respond to Catherine's courteous behaviour, poured scorn on all she said and did, and angrily told her to leave her alone. The just Judge, seeing this, laid the hand of His justice so heavily upon this enemy of charity that she suddenly took a turn for the worse and found herself in danger of dying without the Sacraments.

News of this came to the virgin's ears, whereupon she at once shut herself up in her cell and began to pour forth ceaseless prayers to her Bridegroom that this soul should not be allowed to be lost on her account. In her mind, as she confessed to me, she said to him: "O Lord, can it be that a poor thing like me should come into the world so that souls created in your image should be cast into eternal fire? Can your will permit that I should be the cause of the eternal ruin of one of my sisters, when I should be a means to her eternal salvation? Far from the multitude of your mercies be this dreadful justice, and far from your eternal goodness be it to permit this! It would have been better for me not to have been born than to be the cause of damnation to souls redeemed by your blood. Woe is me! Are these the promises You so generously made me, when you predicted that I should help towards the salvation of my neighbour, as I desired? Can the fruits that you were to obtain through me come down to this, the damnation of one of my sisters? I have not the slightest doubt that my own sins lie behind all these things. Of course I could not expect anything different to result from anything I do, nevertheless I shall not stop pleading with your eternal mercy, or weary of imploring your infinite goodness, until the evils I have deserved are changed to good and my sister is freed from everlasting death."

While the holy virgin was speaking thus, more with her mind than with her lips, it was divinely revealed to her that this soul on the brink of death was falling into a desperate and pitiable state so that her compassion was increased. When the Heavenly Bridegroom told her that His justice could not let such an inveterate hatred, conceived in such malice, go unpunished, the virgin threw herself to the ground, saying, "O my Lord, if you will not grant me the mercy I have asked for for my sister, I shall not leave this spot alive. Punish me for all her sins, for I am the cause of her wickedness and I should be punished, not her." And she went on, "I beg you, O most merciful Lord, by all your goodness and mercy, not to allow my sister's soul to issue from her body until she has been given your grace and obtained your mercy."

Such was the efficacy of this prayer that that soul could not leave its body, though Palmarina lay in agony for three days and nights. Those who knew her and saw her agonizing for all this long time marvelled at it and spoke about it with grief; but the holy virgin went on praying until she so to speak had conquered the Unconquerable and captured the Almighty with humble tears. For the Lord, as though He could no longer resist her, in His mercy sent a light from on high to enlighten that agonizing soul, and allowed her to recognize her fault and be sorry for it, and to ask for salvation.

No sooner had the holy virgin realized all this, through a revelation from the Lord, than she went with all speed to see Palmarina, who manifested her pleasure and respect for her from whom she had formerly shrunk with what signs she could, and with words and gestures confessed her sin. And then, having received the Sacraments, with great contrition of heart she died.

117

After her death the Lord showed Catherine this soul that had been saved; it was so beautiful that, as she confessed to me herself, no words can describe it, though it was still not clothed in the glory of the Beatific Vision but only had the beauty of nature and baptismal grace. And the Lord said to her: "See, most loving daughter, for you I have retrieved this soul that was already lost." And He went on, "Do you not think it gracious and beautiful? Who would refuse any labour to win so lovely a creature? If I who am the Ultimate Beauty, from which all other beauty proceeds, was so carried away by the love of souls that I willed to descend upon earth and shed My blood to redeem them, how much more should you be prepared to do for one another, that such a creature should not be lost? That is why I have shown you this soul: that you may burn ever more ardently to procure the salvation of all souls, and induce others to do the same, according to the grace that is given to you."

Thanking the Heavenly Bridegroom for these words, Catherine lovingly implored Him to grant her a special grace, the ability to perceive the beauty of all the souls she came into contact with, so that she would be the more prompted to work for their salvation. The Lord consented to this, and said: "Since, despising the flesh, you have given yourself wholly and entirely to me, who am Supreme Spirit, and since, for the salvation of Palmarina's soul, you prayed with such anxiety and concern, see, I give your soul a special illumination which will enable you to see the beauty or ugliness of all the souls who come to you, so that your spiritual senses will henceforth perceive spiritual conditions, as the bodily senses perceive the qualities of bodies, and not only of the souls present before your eyes, but of all whose salvation you ardently long for and fervently pray for, even though you have never seen them." And the grace of this gift was so lasting and effective that from that time onwards Catherine knew more about the spiritual motions and qualities of the people she came across than she did about their bodies.

When in fact I told her privately that some people were grumbling because they had seen men and women on their knees before her and she

118

had done nothing to stop it, she replied, "The Lord knows I hardly ever notice anything of the physical movements of the people around me. I am so engrossed in reading their souls that I don't pay any attention to their bodies." So I said, "Do you mean to say that you can see into their souls?" And she answered: "Father, I reveal to you in confession that since the time when as a result of my insistent prayers my Saviour granted me such grace that He delivered a certain soul, destined by its own sins to the everlasting fire, from the abyss of eternal damnation, and then showed me the beauty of that soul, practically no one has ever come before me without my being able to see his state of soul intuitively." And she added, "Father, if you could see the beauty of a rational soul, you would not doubt for a minute that you would be prepared to give your life a hundred times over for the salvation of that soul, for there is nothing in this world that can compare with such beauty."

On hearing this, I made her tell me what had happened, and she revealed what I have written above. But when she had to mention the sin that Palmarina had committed against her, she was brief and mild in what she said, and I only heard the full gravity of this hateful sin later, from many trustworthy sisters who had known the two people.

I will give proofs of what I have said.

I remember that I acted as interpreter between the Supreme Pontiff Gregory XI of happy memory and our holy virgin, as she could not speak Latin and he could not speak Italian. In the course of their talk the holy virgin bewailed the fact that at the Roman Court, which should have been a paradise of heavenly virtues, there was a stench of all the vices of hell. The Pope, on hearing this, asked me how long she had been at the Court, and on being told that it was only a few days said to her, "How have you managed to get to know the state of the Roman Court in a few days?" Whereupon Catherine's attitude suddenly changed from one of subservience to one of majesty. I saw it with my own eyes: she stood up straight and broke out into these words: "To the honour of Almighty God I dare to say that I could smell the sins being committed in the Roman Court better when I was in Siena where

I was born than the people who committed them and are still committing them today." The Pope was speechless, and I in my bewilderment
puzzled over the matter, and above all wondered how such words came
to be spoken with such authority in front of such a high Pontiff.

It also happened during our journeys in various parts of the world,
where neither she nor I nor any other of her companions had ever been
before, that we came across persons previously unknown to us, decently
dressed and to all appearances respectable, but whose lives were in fact
obstinately rooted in evil. Catherine, immediately aware of the state of
sin they were in, could not exchange a word with them or look them
in the face while they were speaking to her. When they insisted on
speaking to us, she would say, raising her voice a little, "We should cure
ourselves of our sins and free ourselves from the Devil's shackles before
we speak of God!" With this she would hurry away, and we would learn
later that these people were in fact entangled in sins of evil living and
persisted in them impenitently.

Once, I am sorry to say, we came across a woman who was the mistress of a high prelate in the Church. While this woman and Catherine
were talking together, I was present too, and while the woman seemed
decent enough in her dress and behaviour, I noticed that she was never
able to look the virgin straight in the face. Wondering at this, I took
the trouble to find out who the woman was, and was told that she was
as described above. I mentioned this to the virgin, and she told me, privately, "If you had smelt the stink that I could smell while I was talking
to her you would have been sick."

These things, reader, I bring to your notice with the sole aim of
enabling you to realize what sublime gifts were granted to our virgin
by the Lord. So please do not imagine that by introducing them I have
allowed myself to wander too far away from my story: as you will see,
they are all part of it.

Meanwhile, the Enemy of the human race, seeing that the virgin
was acquiring a great store of merit through tending the sick, and was
reaping a rich spiritual harvest in the hearts of her fellow-men, thought

up another means to weary her. But his iniquity defeated its own ends, for, in attempting to kill the fruit of this tree planted by the side of the heavenly waters, he only—thanks be to God—succeeded in establishing it more firmly.

It happened that at this time another of the Sisters of Penance of St. Dominic, whose name was Andrea (it was the custom in Siena to give men's names to women), had fallen ill with what doctors call cancer of the breast, which had gone on eating away the flesh, spreading as cancers do until practically the whole breast was affected. This horrible sore gave out such a frightful stench that you had to hold your nose when you went near it, and the result was that no one would help the poor woman or even go and see her. When the virgin of the Lord got to know of this, she realized that heaven had reserved this unfortunate woman especially for herself, and she immediately went off to see her, comforting her with a kind and cheerful countenance and joyfully offering her her services for as long as the illness lasted. Andrea was all the more glad to accept because she had been so completely abandoned by everyone else.

And so the virgin began to look after this widow—youth serving age; the one languishing with love of her Saviour serving the one languishing with illness, and she did everything expected of her, even though the stench grew more and more unbearable. She was with the sick woman continuously, without stopping up her nose, unbandaging the sore, wiping it, washing and dressing it, showing no sign of repulsion, seemingly unwearied by the length of time it took her; and doing everything with such grace and cheerfulness that the sick woman herself was amazed to see such constancy of soul, such warmth of affection and charity.

But the Enemy of all men and virtue now had recourse to one of his usual tricks in an attempt to nullify this act of charity which was so hateful to him, and he began to assault Catherine.

One day, when she uncovered the ulcer and a more nauseating smell than usual came out of it, the Devil, being unable to affect her will, which was founded on the rock of Christ, assaulted her stomach, which under the effect of the horrible stench began to turn over and made her feel sick. Then the servant of Christ grappled with herself and said to her body, "Ah, you presume to abhor this sister, who has been redeemed by the blood of the Saviour, do you—you who could fall into the same sickness or an even worse one? As God lives you shall not remain unpunished!" And she immediately bent her face down over the sick woman's breast, put her mouth and nose to the horrible sore and remained there until the Spirit had conquered the rebellious feeling of nausea and tamed the flesh that was trying to oppose the spirit. When the sick woman saw this she cried out, "Stop, daughter! Stop it, dearest daughter! Don't infect yourself with this horrible filthy pus!" But the virgin of the Lord would not get up until she had defeated the Enemy; who after this went into hiding for a while.

Realizing that so far as the virgin was concerned there was nothing to be done, the Devil transferred his infernal attention to Andrea herself, whom he found less strong-minded and impregnable.

Being the sower of cockles, he began to plant within Andrea's mind a certain annoyance at finding herself being looked after by Catherine. And this annoyance slowly increased in wickedness until it finally became rank hatred; and though she knew that Catherine was the only person who would wait on her and help her, her hatred manifested itself in an inordinate jealousy.

It is a sign of hatred to tend to believe ill of the person hated: thus this old invalid, now even more sick in mind than she was in body, was led on by the age-old Adversary to such a degree that she began to suspect this purest of virgins of impure living. When Catherine was not with her, she imagined her committing all kinds of wickedness. Thus do the incautious fall!—first they are annoyed by their neighbour's good works, which they had begun by being delighted with; then they hate them; and thence they regard all their doings as evil—exactly as Isaias says of a blind mind: "Woe to you that call evil good and good evil." (*Isaias* 5:20). The holy virgin, however, remained as firm as a rock in the midst of these misfortunes, and with her eyes fixed steadfastly on her Heavenly Bride-groom went on looking after her with her accustomed joy, responding with firm patience to the age-long Adversary, from whom, as she could see, all these difficulties came. But the more cheerfully Catherine fulfilled her pious office, the more she angered him until he excited the blind mind of the sick old woman to such a pitch that she openly accused this most innocent of virgins of vicious living.

News of this spread amongst the nuns, and some of the older ones went to see the woman to find out if what they had heard was true, and she, thoroughly in the Devil's toils by now, insisted with utter shame-lessness and lies that all that she had said about the virgin was indeed true. This infuriated them, and they sent for Catherine and attacked her with insults and reproaches and all manner of coarse vile words, asking her how she had allowed herself to be deceived to the extent of losing her virginity. Catherine patiently and modestly replied: "I assure you, ladies and sisters in the faith, that by the grace of God I am a virgin." That was all she would say, however much they went on lying and insulting her, "Indeed I am a virgin. Indeed I am a virgin."

Despite all this, she went on with her work, and although it was very distressing for her to have to listen to such an infamous charge she went on looking after her calumniator as conscientiously as ever.

As soon as she was free she would run into her cell and set herself to prayer, saying, more with her heart than with her lips: "Almighty God and most beloved Bridegroom, you know how fragile a virgin's reputa-tion is, and how the purity of anyone wedded to you must be free from every stain. Thus you willed that your most glorious Mother should have a putative husband. You know too that all these things have been invented by the Father of Lies, to take me away from a service I entered upon for love of you. Therefore, O Lord my God, knowing that I am innocent help me, and do not allow the old Serpent who was con-quered by your Passion to have any power against me." And she prayed and wept. Then the Saviour of the World appeared to her, holding in his right hand a crown of gold studded with pearls and precious stones and in his left a diadem of thorns, and He said to her: "Dear daughter, you must know that it is necessary that at different times and different places you must be crowned with both these crowns. Choose then, which you prefer: to be crowned during your life on earth with the crown of thorns, and I will keep the other for you for the life without end; or to receive the precious one now and to have the crown of thorns reserved for you after your death." She answered: "O Lord, I have long renounced my own will and have chosen to follow yours; hence the choice is not mine. But since you wish me to reply, I will say at once that in this life I prefer to be always conformed to your most holy Passion and for love of you to embrace any pain as my refreshment."

With these words she took the diadem of thorns passionately with both hands from the hand of the Saviour, and pressed it down so hard that the thorns pricked her head, so that, as she told me herself, even after the vision was over her head felt sore from the pricks of those thorns. Then the Lord said to her:

"All things are in my power; and as it is I who have permitted this scandalous thing to happen, so too can I easily remove it. You, meanwhile, go on with this service you have embarked upon, and do not give way to the Devil, who wants you to give it up; then I will give you complete victory over him, and his schemes against you will all fall back on his own head, and all will be to your greater glory." So the handmaid of the Lord was left comforted and reassured.

While this had been going on, her mother Lapa had got to hear about the tales that the nuns were spreading about her daughter under Andrea's influence, and although she had no doubt whatever about her daughter's innocence, she was highly incensed against Andrea. She went off to her daughter, her heart overflowing, and began to shout at her: "Oh, didn't I keep telling you not to go and help that stinking old woman? Just see what it has brought you! She has accused you of vile living before all your sisters! If you go on seeing her and looking after her, I shall never call you daughter again." This, too, came about by the instigation of the old Enemy, to prevent Catherine going on with her holy labours. At these words of her mother's Catherine was quiet for a while; then she went up to her and threw herself at her feet, saying humbly, "Dearest mother, do you expect God to stop showing his daily mercies to sinners, because of human ingratitude? Did the Saviour refuse to accomplish the salvation of the world when He was on the Cross, because of the insults that were hurled at him? Know in your charity that if I was to abandon this sick woman there would be no one else to take my place, and she would die at once. Are we supposed to cause anyone's death? She has been practised upon by the Devil; now perhaps she will be enlightened by the Lord and will see the error of her ways." With these and other words she succeeded in gaining her mother's blessing, and went back to the sick woman and looked after her quite happily, as though she had never said a word against her.

Andrea was amazed at this, and seeing no signs of disturbance on Catherine's part could not deny that she had been outwitted in every respect. This brought a secret feeling of repentance, which the sight of the virgin's constancy strengthened every day.

Then the Lord had mercy on the old woman and in honour of his bride showed her a vision. One day it seemed to her that when the maiden of the Lord came into her room and approached her bed a light came from on high and shone round the bed so pleasingly and comfortingly that she quite forgot her own unhappy condition. Unable to understand the cause of this, she looked all round her and then she saw the virgin's face become transfigured and transformed until she no longer looked like Lapa's daughter Catherine but someone of angelic majesty. Then the light enveloped her like a mantle. When Andrea saw this she was greatly moved and realized how profoundly guilty she had been in letting her tongue run loose in scandalous stories about such an excellent virgin. The vision, which she witnessed with wide-open eyes, lasted for some time, and then vanished as it had come.

When the light had gone, the old woman remained comforted, but at the same time sad with the kind of sorrow which, as the Apostle says, leads to salvation. (*2 Cor.* 7:10). And, a little later, weeping bitterly, she asked the virgin's pardon, confessing that she had sinned gravely in slandering her so unjustly. It seemed in fact as though that visible light had brought with it an invisible light in which the invalid could see the tricks that Satan had played on her. Then the virgin of the Lord threw herself into the arms of her calumniator, did every-thing she could to comfort her and assured her that she would not leave her and did not feel in the slightest degree offended. "Dearest mother," she said to her, "I know that it was the Enemy of the human race who caused all these scandalous things to happen and took you in so completely; so it is him I have to be offended with, not you. In fact, I ought to thank you, because like the most loving friend you were concerned to defend my honour." Having comforted Andrea with these words, and finished looking after her in her usual careful way, she then went back to her cell, so as not to waste time on things of no account.

Andrea, now sincerely aware of how deeply she had sinned, con-fessed with sighs and tears to all who went to see her that she had made a great mistake and allowed herself to be taken in by the Devil's wiles. Acknowledging her guilt, she protested loudly that the virgin she had calumniated was not only pure but holy and full of the Holy Spirit, and asserted that she had proof of this. Some of the people present asked her privately how she could now say all this about the virgin, and she replied passionately that she had never felt or known what sweetness of mind and spiritual delight were until she had seen the virgin trans-formed and surrounded by that indescribable light. And when these people persisted in asking whether she had seen everything that had happened with her own eyes she said that she had, but that she had no words to describe the beauty of the light or the sweetness she had felt in her soul during those moments.

Thus the news of Catherine's sanctity began to spread abroad amongst men; and where the age-old Adversary had imagined that he would succeed in deceiving her, with the co-operation of the Holy Spirit he was forced in a way to exalt her.

After this experience, the holy virgin, who had shown that she could not be cast down in adversity, did not get puffed up when all was going well, and she went on with her works of charity without a pause, applying her whole soul to the knowledge of her own nothingness. "He who alone is" rewarded her; but the insatiable Enemy, who can be scotched but not killed, returned to his first method of attack, and tried to bring the Lord's triumphant fighter low by upsetting her stomach.

One day when the maiden of Christ had removed Andrea's bandages in order to wash and clean the sore, at once, thanks to the Devil rather than nature, she was assailed by a stench so unbearable that her inside turned over, and a great sensation of nausea convulsed her stomach. The virgin of the Lord did not like this at all, because in these days of repeated victories, obtained with the help of the Holy Spirit, she had reached new heights of virtue; so, rousing herself to holy anger against her own body, she said to it: "Long live the Highest, the sweet Bridegroom of my soul! This which you find so abhorrent, let it enter into your bowels!" And she collected up into a bowl the fetid stuff that had been used to wash the sore, along with all the pus, and, going away a little, gulped it all down. When she had done this, the temptation to feel repugnance passed away.

When, incidentally, I was told about this, Catherine was present, and I remember that secretly she whispered to me, "Never in my life have I tasted any food and drink sweeter or more exquisite." I found the same sort of thing among the papers left by Fra Tommaso, her first confessor, who notes how the virgin confessed to him that she had smelt a most sweet and pleasant smell when she had bent down and put her mouth to the sore in the way described above.

I do not know, reader, what credence you will give to what I have said, but when I have finished my account of this event I will add briefly what the Lord suggests to my mind about it.

These victories, then, having been graciously granted to his bride by the Heavenly Bridegroom, on the night following the last of them, while she was praying about them, the Lord and Saviour Jesus Christ appeared to her, bearing imprinted on his body the five most holy wounds which He had suffered for our salvation when He was crucified, and said to her: "Beloved, many battles you have fought for love of me, and so far, with my help, you have won them all. By this you have made yourself pleasing and acceptable to me, but yesterday you made yourself especially pleasing to me, for not only did you despise the attractions of the body, not only did you show indifference to what people said about you and overcome the Enemy's temptations, but, annihilating your bodily nature with the ardour of my charity, you cheerfully drank that abhorrent drink. I therefore say to you that since with that act you transcended your own nature I will give you a drink that transcends every human nature and expectation." And putting His right hand on her virginal neck and drawing her towards the wound in His own side, He whispered to her, "Drink, daughter, the liquid from my side, and it will fill your soul with such sweetness that its wonderful effects will be felt even by the body which for my sake you despised." And she, finding herself thus near to the source of the fountain of life, put the lips of her body, but much more those of the soul, over the most holy wound, and long and eagerly and abundantly drank that indescribable and unfathomable liquid. Finally, at a sign from the Lord, she detached herself from the fountain, sated and yet at the same time still longing for more; for the satiety did not breed disgust, nor the longing pain.

O Lord of ineffable mercy, how good you are to those who love you, and sweet to those who taste you! But how much more so, to those who abundantly drink you! For drink is swallowed most quickly and easily, and most easily changed into the substance of the person taking it. I do not think, Lord, that either I, or anyone else who has never experienced this, can have an adequate idea of it. There are things outside our range, like colours to a blind man and music to the deaf. But not being entirely ungrateful we ponder and admire in so far as we can the graces that you liberally grant your saints, and thank Your Majesty according to our ability.

I advise you, reader, to give your attention to the act of extraordinary virtue performed by our bountiful virgin. Consider the great charity that prompted her to undertake a form of service so abhorrent to the bodily senses. Then consider, I pray you, her zeal, whereby she persevered in that service despite the natural repugnance of the flesh. Observe, I implore you, the firm and incomple constancy that could not be shaken by the worst slander or disheartened by the hateful wagging of a wicked tongue. Consider, finally, the soul absolutely devoted to Christ, which did not grow puffed up when praised, and in a way above all the forces of the flesh and against nature forced her stomach to gulp down something that the eye cannot even bear to look at. I do not believe that such things have ever happened before—or if they have, there have been very few of them, especially in our day, for the sort of people who could do such things have become rarer than the phoenix.

Now let us admire the wonderful sequel. The holy virgin took that drink from the Saviour's side, and thereafter her soul was diffused with such an abundance of graces that her body felt the effect of them also. So that from that time forward she never wanted food or was able to take it, as we shall show in more detail later.

Here I end this chapter, which has turned out to be rather long. But its length does not lessen its importance.

I shall not repeat the names of the witnesses to what has been said, as I have already given them. However, for the sake of the future as well as the present, I must insist that all that I write was either confessed to me by Catherine herself or I found it amongst the writings of Fra Tommaso, her first confessor, or else I was told it by Friars of my own Order and reliable women whom I have already named, who were companions of Catherine's. When necessary I shall quote them again.

CHAPTER FIVE

How Catherine Lived

———————————•———————————

A FTER the incomple Bridegroom had proved his chosen one in the fire of many tribulations, and taught her how to beat the old Adversary in all her battles with him, the one thing that remained for Him to do was to give her the full reward for her triumph. As, however, the souls on earth who by the eternal decree and promise of this same Bridegroom were to be helped by her had not yet received the full benefit of her aid, it was necessary for her to remain for a little while longer among the living. But she was given a token of the eternal reward.

And so this Lord and Heavenly Bridegroom, willing that His bride and servant should begin to lead a heavenly life in this vale of tears, and at the same time continue to have dealings with those on earth, prepared and trained her with the following revelation.

One day, while the virgin was praying in her little room, the Lord and Saviour of the human race appeared to her and announced what was to happen in these words. "Know, sweetest daughter," He said, "that in the time to come your earthly pilgrimage will be distinguished by such marvellous new gifts from me that the hearts of ignorant carnal men will be amazed and incredulous. Many even of those who love you will have doubts, and believe that what you do is all a deception, whereas in fact it will be a result of a superabundance of love on my part. I shall infuse such a fullness of graces into your soul that they will overflow, and even your body will feel their effects and begin to live in an unprecedented way. Furthermore, your heart will burn so strongly for the salvation of your fellow-men that you will forget your sex and change your present way of life; you will not avoid the company of men and women as you do now, but for the salvation of their souls will take upon yourself every kind of labour. Many people will be scandalized by the things you do, and oppose you, so that the thoughts of their hearts may be revealed. But you must not be anxious or afraid, for I shall be always with you, and I shall free your soul from the evil tongues and the lips that utter lies. Carry out undauntedly whatever the Spirit prompts you to do, for through you I shall snatch many souls from the jaws of hell and by my grace transport them to the kingdom of heaven."

To these words, which, as she confessed to me herself, the Lord repeated several times, especially, "You must not be anxious or afraid," the holy virgin replied, "You are my Lord, and I am the least of your servants. May your will be done always, but remember me according to your great mercy, and do not forsake me."

The vision vanished, and the maiden of Christ remained lost in thought, wondering what this future change would mean.

From that moment the grace of Jesus Christ began to increase daily in Catherine's heart and the Spirit of the Lord to overflow within her; so that even she was astounded, and almost fainted from the wonder of it, singing with the Prophet, "For thee my flesh and my heart have fainted away: thou art the God of my heart, and the God that is my portion for ever." (*Psalm* 72:26). And, "I remembered God, and was delighted, and was exercised; and my spirit swooned away." (*Psalm* 76:4).

The virgin of Christ languished with love of her Lord, and the only relief she could find was in weeping of soul and body. Every day there were groans and tears. But not even incessant tears could bring alleviation of her pain. Then the Lord, as it seemed good to Him, inspired her to have frequent recourse to the altar of God, to receive our Lord Jesus Christ, the joy of her body and soul, in the sacrament from the hands of the priest as often as she could, so that during her earthly pilgrimage she might at least taste Him sacramentally, even if she could not as yet sate herself fully on Him, as she longed to, in heaven.

But this led to still greater love, and hence still greater languishing; but by the power of faith it helped to assuage the furnace of charity which the breath of the Holy Spirit fanned in her heart more brightly every day. She developed the habit of communicating almost daily, and was only prevented from doing so, as frequently happened, by illness or through her concern for the good of souls.

Her longing to receive the Lord was so strong that when she could not satisfy it her body suffered hardship and faintness, for as it shared in the abundance of her spirit so it was obliged to share in its afflictions. But of this, with the Lord's help, we shall speak at greater length elsewhere.

Now let us return to her admirable manner of life.

Thus, then, as she herself confessed to me in secret, and as I have also seen in the writings of the confessor who preceded me, after the vision described above there began to descend into her soul, especially when she received Holy Communion, such an abundance of graces and heavenly consolations that, overflowing and pouring out into her body, they affected the radical humour itself;[1] changing the nature of her stomach in such a way that not only did she have no need of food but she could not in fact take any without it causing her pain. If she forced herself to eat, her body suffered extremely, her digestion would not function, and the food had to come out with an effort by the way it had gone in. It is difficult to estimate the amount of suffering that this holy virgin experienced through swallowing food.

At the beginning such a way of life seemed incredible to everyone, even to the people in her own home and those most intimate with her; and what was in fact an extraordinary gift from God they called a temptation and a trick of the Devil.

---

1. In the Middle Ages the 'radical humour' was supposed to be a fluid that was the principle and basis of all life.

This mistake was also made by her confessor who has already been mentioned several times by name, for, out of zeal for goodness, certainly, but without a great deal of insight, he decided that the virgin had been led astray by the Enemy, disguised as an angel of light; and so he forced her to eat every day, and told her not to believe in her visions because they came from the Devil. Though Catherine told him that she knew from experience that she felt stronger and healthier when she refrained from eating, and tired and ill when she did eat, he remained unconvinced and went on insisting that she must eat. Being a true daughter of obedience she did her best to obey, but this so exhausted her that she seemed almost on the brink of death.

At this stage she went to see this confessor and said: "Father, if I went in for an excessive fast that was likely to bring me to death's door, it is true, isn't it, that you would forbid me to do it, so that I would avoid dying and being guilty of self-murder?"

"Certainly," he answered, "of course!"

So she said, "Isn't it worse to die from over-eating than from fasting?" and when he answered yes, she went on; "Well then, if, as you have seen again and again, and can see now, I am not at all well when I eat, why not forbid me to eat in the same way as you forbid me to fast?" To this reasoning he had not a word to reply; and as he could see quite clearly that Catherine showed all the signs of being on the point of death, he said, "Do as the Holy Spirit prompts you to do, for I can see that God is doing great things in you."

And this seems a good opportunity, reader, to beg you to consider how much Catherine suffered—beyond all description—from the people in her home, who simply would not understand that the Lord was granting her extraordinary gifts. The holy virgin herself revealed this to me in confession when I first began to enjoy the honour of knowing her, and she repeated the same thing again later when we had occasion to discuss the matter.

These people judged her words and actions, not by the standard set by the Lord Himself in shedding His graces so lavishly into His bride's soul, but by the usual standard, and often their own private one. Standing in the valley, they pretended to be able to measure the high tops of the mountains; ignorant of first principles, they nevertheless drew final conclusions, and blinded by the brilliance of so much light, they rashly criticized the colours. And so they foolishly complained about the rays that came from this star; tried to teach her, failing to realize that it was she who was teaching them; and, being themselves in the dark, took it upon themselves to argue with the light. They found fault with her amongst themselves, and behind a façade of righteousness did their best to dispge her to others. They even complained to her confessor, and got him against his will to agree to reprimand the virgin.

How much spiritual unhappiness Catherine had to endure from this behaviour of theirs cannot easily be described, though I could easily go into it all if I had the time.

Obedient as she was, and rooted in contempt of self, she was no expert in the art of finding excuses for herself, nor did she dare set herself up against anything her confessor said or did. The result was that, knowing quite clearly that the will of the Highest was in conflict with all their opinions, and yet from fear of the Lord not wanting to fail in obedience or give scandal to anyone, she found herself in a state of uncertainty. On all sides were causes of grief, and her only consolation was prayer. To the Lord she shed tears of sorrow and hope, praying Him with humble persistence to reveal His will to her opponents, and especially her confessor, whom she was most fearful of offending.

She was not able to follow the words of the Apostles when they said to the high priest, "We ought to obey God rather than men" (*Acts* 5:29) because it could immediately be pointed out to her that the Devil often transforms himself into an angel of light, and that she was therefore not obliged to believe every spirit, and least of all trust in her own prudence, but should follow the advice that had been given her. The Lord heard her prayers in this as in many other things, and often enlightened the mind of her confessor, who altered his advice to her; nevertheless, neither he not any of the others who murmured against the virgin, women or men, had much sense of discretion. If they had remembered how frequently Catherine had been taught by the Lord to know all the Devil's wiles; how used she was to fighting against him; how often she had triumphed over him; if, furthermore, they had considered the gift of intelligence that had been divinely granted her, as a result of which she could say proudly, with the Apostle, "We are not ignorant of his devices," (*2 Cor.* 2:11) they would certainly have kept quiet and, mere beginners that they were, they would not have presumed to put themselves above a perfect mistress of the art—adding their little trickles to an already swollen stream.

I said this forthrightly at the time, and I say it again now, not without reason considering some of the people whom I hope will hear it.

Good reader, let us get back to the story.

After the virgin had had the first vision she was so full of the Holy Spirit that she went without food or drink for the whole of Lent until the feast of Our Lord's Ascension; and yet despite this she was always bursting with life and happiness. No wonder, for as the Blessed Apostle says, "the fruit of the Spirit is charity, joy and peace." (*Gal.* 5:22). And the First Truth announced that "Not by bread alone doth man live but by every word that proceedeth from the mouth of God." (*Deut.* 8:3; *Matt.* 4:4). It is also written that "the just man liveth by faith." (*Rom.* 1:17).

In the end, as the Lord had predicted, and as she herself had told her confessor, she was able to eat on Ascension Day, when she had wheaten bread and oil and vegetables. For it was not possible for any rich food to enter her stomach, either by natural or by supernatural means. When that day was over, however, she resumed her habitual fasting. Then she gradually reached a state of total abstinence almost unheard of in our times. But if her body took nothing, her spirit fed most sumptuously in its stead. While these things were happening, in fact, the holy virgin was devoutly receiving Holy Communion very frequently indeed, and on each occasion she was given so much grace that, with her bodily senses and all their inclinations thoroughly mortified, her soul and body were both equally nourished by the power of the Spirit. From this anyone with any faith must conclude that her life was wholly miraculous.

I myself have often seen that poor body, sustained by no more than a few glasses of cold water, reduced to such a state of exhaustion that we were all worried, imagining that she was about to die at any moment. Instead, as soon as any opportunity arose to honour the Divine Name, or do good to some soul, there would be a sudden wonderful change, and without the help of any medicine Catherine would regain all her life and strength and be strong and cheerful. She would get up, walk about, and go about her work as easily as the people who were with her and who were in good health: she did not know the meaning of fatigue.

I ask you: where did all this come from, if not from the Spirit who delights in such works? What could not be done by nature, He did by miracle. Is it not perfectly clear that it was He who gave strength to her soul and body?

Further: when the virgin first began to live without eating, her confessor, Fra Tommaso, asked her if she ever felt any desire for food and she replied, "I feel so satisfied by the Lord when I receive His most adorable Sacrament that I could not possibly feel any desire for any other kind of food." Then, when he wanted to know whether she felt any pangs of hunger when she did not receive the Sacrament, she replied, "When I am unable to receive the Sacrament, I am quite satisfied if I can be near it and see it; in fact I get so much pleasure out of merely seeing a priest who has touched the Sacrament that I lose all desire for food even then."

Such, then, was the virgin of the Lord; satisfied, though fasting, empty without but full within, dry to look at but inwardly watered by rivers of living water and at all times full of life and happiness.

But the tortuous old Serpent could not see these great gifts of God without a feeling of furious hatred, and he incited everyone against Catherine, spiritual men and worldly men, religious and secular alike.

Do not be scandalized, reader, by these devout religious people. Believe me, if self-love is not rooted out of them envy reigns among them more dangerously than it does in any other class of people, especially when they see someone doing things that they find impossible. Read the lives of the famous Fathers of the Thebaid, and you will find one of the Macariuses going there dressed as a layman, staying with a group of monks under Pacomius,[2] and after many trials being accepted into their way of life by Pacomius himself. And when the monks saw what wonderfully austere penances he did, they rose up in rebellion against Pacomius and said, "Either you get rid of him, or we all leave this monastery today." And this was said by men who were supposed to be perfect! What can we expect today, then, from our own religious?

I do not wish to go on about this, otherwise there are a lot of things I could say that I know from my own experience. It is enough for our present purpose, however, for you to know that as regards the holy virgin's fasting, everyone had something to say against it.

Some said, no one can be above the Lord: if Jesus used to eat and drink, and his glorious Mother did the same, and the Apostles too, to whom the Lord said, "And in the same house remain, eating and drinking such things as they have," (*Luke* 10:7) who is there who can surpass them, or believe himself to be their equal? Others said that all the saints have taught by word and example that no one should do anything out of the ordinary but follow the general practice. There were those who whispered that any excess was dangerous, and always had been, and was to be avoided by anyone who truly feared God. Some, as has been said, trying to make out that at least the virgin's intentions were good, called it a trick of the Devil. Then worldly people and the professional scandalmongers said that it was all a pretence on Catherine's part to

2. St. Pacomius was one of the greatest of the Desert Fathers. He died in 348 on the island of Tabenna in the Thebaid. He was the monks' first legislator, and drew up a Rule in Coptic: the original has been lost, but a copy of it, translated from the Greek by St. Jerome, still exists.

make herself seem important, and that far from fasting she used to have excellent meals on the sly.

If I failed to speak out against these false and foolish ideas to the extent the Lord inspires me and grants me the talent to do so, I should feel that I was guilty in the eyes of the First Truth. Therefore, good reader, do me the goodness to note this: that if what the first set of murmurers said about the Saviour and his glorious Mother and the holy Apostles was true, it would follow that John the Baptist was greater than Jesus Christ himself. For our Lord said with his own mouth that John came neither eating nor drinking, whilst the Virgin's son did come eating and drinking. It would also follow that Antony, the two Macariuses, Hilary and Serapion and a host of others who observed a long and well-nigh continuous fast, far beyond what was customary amongst the Apostles, were greater than the Apostles too.

If these murmurers try to make out that John in the desert and the Fathers in Egypt did not preserve a strict fast, because they did occasionally have something to eat, what would they say about Mary Magdalene, who spent thirty-three years in a cave without eating anything, as is clearly stated in the story of her life and is evident from the place, now inaccessible, where she lived? Is it to be imagined that she was greater than the glorious Virgin, who did not live in a cave or observe any such fast? What will they say about all the various Holy Fathers who went without eating for days on end? Of some it is expressly stated that having received the Sacrament of the Lord they are nothing else.

Let these people learn, if they do not know it already, that the value of a person's sanctity is to be weighed and judged, not on the basis of any fasting but according to the degree of that person's charity. Let them learn too that people ought not to judge things they know nothing about. Let them hear what that same Incarnate Wisdom of God the Father says about them: "Whereunto then shall I liken the men of this generation? They are like to children sitting in the market place and speaking one to another, and saying: We have piped to you, and you have not danced: we have mourned, and you have not wept." (*Luke* 12:32). And He goes on, as we have said above: "For John the Baptist came neither eating bread nor drinking wine . . . and you say: Behold a man that is a glutton and a drinker of wine." (*Luke* 7:33–34). These words of the Saviour's should suffice to silence this first class of murmurers.

To the second set of detractors, that is to say, those who detested the holy virgin's unusual manner of life, it merely needs to be said that though we are not required to play at being original, nevertheless we must accept whatever God demands of us; otherwise we would despise God's special gifts. Scripture, it is true, tells us that the just man should not seek after what is above him, but it immediately goes on to add: "For many things are shewn to thee above the understanding of men." (*Ecclesiasticus* 3:25). In other words, you must not of yourself seek after anything that is above you, but if the Lord reveals anything to you that is above you, you must accept it with thanksgiving. In our particular case, what is involved is precisely one of God's special providential gifts; who then can adduce any charge of singularity?

Such was the virgin's own view, as she made clear when, in the cloak of true humility, she answered those who asked her why she did not act like everyone else. She said, "God for my sins has afflicted me with a special kind of illness that makes it impossible for me to eat; I should like to be able to eat, but I can't. Pray for me, that God will forgive me my sins, which make me have to suffer all these evils." As though to say, God is doing this, not me, and thus, that there might not be a shadow of suspicion of vainglory in it, laying all the blame on her own sins. And in saying this she did not belie her real thoughts on the matter, for she firmly believed that all this murmuring against her was permitted by God as a punishment for her sins. All the evil that happened to her she attributed to her sins, and all the good to God: this was her unchanging rule in all things.

This suffices, too, as a reply to the third group, who said that excesses are to be avoided. For excesses cannot be vicious when they come from God, and man must not attempt to avoid them. And we have surely made it quite clear that this was so in the case in question.

Perhaps the fourth lot, who said that the fasting was a trick of the Devil, will be kind enough to tell me whether it is in fact likely that the virgin would have allowed herself to be taken in in this way. Has it not already been made sufficiently plain by actual examples that she always triumphed over the Devil's wiles and temptations? Let us assume that she was deceived: who was it then who kept her body in such a robust condition? The Devil? Who then maintained her soul in such a state of peace and joy, deprived as it was of all material satisfactions? This is a fruit of the Holy Spirit, not the Devil! For it is written that the fruit of the Spirit is charity, joy and peace. (*Gal.* 5:22).

I do not believe that any of this could in truth be ascribed to the Devil; but if these people want to deny the truth come what may, what guarantee have we that they themselves were not deceived by the old Serpent? If in their view the Devil could deceive and lead astray a virgin who triumphed over him time and time again, whose body lived and grew far above the scope of every natural power and virtue, and whose soul remained constantly in a state of spiritual and not sensual enjoyment, how much more could he deceive people to whom, as we know, these things did not happen? It is more likely that they are in the hands of the Devil when they say such things, than that she was, when no one else has ever suggested that she was misled.

Lastly, to the professional scandalmongers, whose tongues have grown accustomed to telling lies, the best answer is silence, not words. No person of any sense or decency will take any notice of them or consider them worth replying to. What decent person is safe from their tongues? If they and their like call Beelzebub Lord and Father, is it surprising that they tell similar lies about one of his household? So they will have to be satisfied with silence.

This, then, as the Lord has granted me, is my reply to those who criticized this holy virgin's special way of life.

Catherine meanwhile, full of the spirit of discretion and the desire to imitate her Heavenly Bridegroom in all things, remembered how that same Lord and Master had exercised restraint when Peter was asked to pay the didrachmas for Him, although He could not be obliged to pay. After showing Peter that there was no reason why He should pay the tribute, He nevertheless added, "But that we may not scandalize them, go to the sea and cast in a hook, and that fish which shall first come up, take: and when thou hast opened its mouth, thou shalt find a stater: take that and give it to them for me and thee." (*Matt.* 17:26).

Having pondered on this, the holy virgin, to silence the faultfinders and prevent people from being scandalized by her fasting, decided to sit down with the family once a day at table and find out whether she could make herself eat like everyone else. The food she forced herself to take did not include meat or wine or fish or eggs or cheese or even bread; nevertheless, this eating, or rather attempt at eating, produced such pains in her body that anyone who had seen her would have felt sorry for her, no matter how hard-hearted he was.

As we have shown above, her stomach could not digest anything, the heat did not consume the vital humours, with the result that what she had taken in had to come out by the same way as it had gone in, otherwise it caused her acute pains and swellings over most of her body. The holy virgin did not swallow any of the vegetables or other things that she masticated, for she spat out all the large bits; but because it was impossible for some little bits of food or juice not to go down into her stomach, and because she liked to drink fresh water to refresh her throat and jaws, she was obliged to throw up everything she had swallowed every day. To do this she often had to introduce a small branch of fennel or some other shrub into her stomach, despite the great pain it caused her, as this was generally the only way in which she could get rid of what she had swallowed. She did this throughout the rest of her life because of the grumblers, particularly those who were scandalized by her fasting.

Seeing the pain she endured in getting rid of the food she had eaten in this way, I once out of compassion tried to persuade her to leave the critics to their criticizing and not go on putting up with such a martyrdom simply on their account. With a contented smile she said:

"Father, don't you think it is better for me to have my sins punished in this world rather than to have to face a punishment without end? Their criticisms are highly useful to me, because they help me to pay my Creator back in a finite way, whereas I owe Him something infinite. Should I try to escape from divine justice? Of course not! I am receiving a great grace, because justice is being done to me in this life." What could I answer? I preferred to say nothing, for if I had spoken I should not have been able to find anything suitable or worth saying.

With such considerations in mind, she called this painful behaviour "doing justice", saying to her companions, "Let us go and do justice to this miserable sinner." Thus she drew some particular kind of profit from everything that happened to her, whether it was the Devil's wiles or being persecuted by humans; and every day, too, she taught us to do the same.

One day, discussing the gifts of God with me, she said, "If everyone knew how to use the grace God gave them they would benefit from everything that happens to them." And she added, "This is what I would like you to do whenever something new happens to you, whether you like it or not: think to yourself and say, I intend to get some benefit from this. If you really did this you would be rich in no time."

Unhappy man that I am, I failed to treasure up these and all her other precious words! Don't you, reader, be as lazy as I was, but remember the words, "Blessed is the man who learns from the misfortunes of others." And I pray the Author of all Piety to enlighten you, and to goad me into imitating this virgin as hard as I can all my life.

With this I end this chapter; the bulk of its contents are guaranteed by the virgin herself, and by her words and open acts, and by my predecessor as her confessor.

CHAPTER SIX

Ecstasies and Revelations

———————•———————

A T THIS time, when the Lord had granted His bride a particular way of living as regards the body, he likewise comforted her soul with great and extraordinary revelations, and the supernatural vigour of her body certainly resulted from this abundance of spiritual graces. And now that we have described in the utmost detail Catherine's bodily life, it is requisite to go on to recount the vigour of her spirit.

Know then, reader, that from the time when this virgin drank the water of life from the Lord's side, she abounded in such fullness of graces that she was almost always in a state of contemplation, and her spirit was so absorbed in the Creator that she spent most of her time in a region beyond sense. This, as I have shown in Part One, I experienced personally time and time again, and so did others, who saw and touched, as I did, her arms and hands, which remained so numb while she was in a state of contemplation that it would have been easier to break them than to get them to move. Her eyes remained tightly shut, her ears could not hear the loudest noise, and none of her bodily senses performed its accustomed functions. You will not find this astonishing if you follow carefully all that follows.

The Lord began to appear to His bride not only privately, as He had done at first, but in public too, in fact before everyone's eyes and quite familiarly, both when she was walking about and when she was standing still, and He set such a fire blazing within her heart that she herself told her confessor that she could not find words to express the divine experiences she had.

Once, when she was praying to the Lord with the utmost fervour, saying to Him as the Prophet had done, "Create a clean heart within me, O God, and renew a right spirit within my bowels," (*Psalm* 50:12) and asking Him again and again to take her own heart and will from her, He comforted her with this vision. It appeared to her that her Heavenly Bridegroom came to her as usual, opened her left side, took out her heart, and then went away. This vision was so effective and agreed so well with what she felt inside herself that in confession she told her confessor that she no longer had a heart in her breast. He shook his head a little at this way of putting it, and in a joking way reproved her; but she repeated it and insisted that she meant what she said. "Truly, Father," she said, "in so far as I feel anything at all, it seems to me that my heart has been taken away altogether. The Lord did indeed appear to me, opened my left side, took my heart out and went away." Her confessor than pointed out that it is impossible to live without a heart, but the virgin replied that nothing is impossible to God, and that she was convinced that she no longer had a heart. And for some time she went on repeating this, that she was living without a heart.

One day she was in the church of the Preaching Friars, which the Sisters of Penance of St. Dominic in Siena used to attend. The others had gone out, but she went on praying. Finally she came out of her ecstasy and got up to go home. All at once a light from heaven encircled her, and in the light appeared the Lord, holding in His holy hands a human heart, bright red and shining. At the appearance of the Author of Light she had fallen to the ground, trembling all over, but He came up to her, opened her left side once again and put the heart He was holding in His hands inside her, saying, "Dearest daughter, as I took your heart away from you the other day, now, you see, I am giving you mine, so that you can go on living with it for ever." With these words

He closed the opening He had made in her side, and as a sign of the miracle a scar remained on that part of her flesh, as I and others were told by her companions who saw it. When I determined to get to the truth, she herself was obliged to confess to me that this was so, and she added that never afterwards had she been able to say, "Lord, I give you my heart."

After the reception of this heart, then, in such a gracious and marvellous way, from the abundance of its graces poured forth Catherine's great works and her most marvellous revelations. In point of fact she never approached the sacred altar without being shown many things beyond the range of the senses, especially when she received Holy Communion. She often saw a baby hidden in the hands of the priest; sometimes it was a slightly older boy; or again, she might see a burning fiery furnace, into which the priest seemed to enter at the moment when he consumed the sacred Species. When she herself received the most adorable Sacrament, she would often smell such a strong sweet smell that she almost fainted. Seeing or receiving the Sacrament of the Altar always generated fresh and indescribable bliss in her soul, so that her heart would very often throb with joy within her breast, making such a loud noise that it could be heard even by her companions. At last, having noticed this so often, they told her confessor Fra Tommaso about it. He made a close inquiry into the matter and on finding it was true left the fact in writing as an imperishable record.

This noise bore no resemblance to the gurgling that goes on naturally in the human stomach; there was nothing natural about the noise at all. There is nothing surprising in the fact that a heart given in a supernatural way should act in a supernatural way too, for, as the Prophet says, "My heart and my flesh have rejoiced in the Living God," that is to say, "They have jumped out, into the Living God."

The Prophet says, "the *living* God", to signify that this special beating or heart action, being caused by the true Life, does not bring death to the person to whom it happens as it would in the ordinary course of nature, but Life.

After the miraculous exchange of hearts the virgin felt a different person, and she said to her confessor Fra Tommaso, "Can't you see, Father, that I am not the person I was, but am changed into someone else?" And she went on, "If only you could understand how I feel, Father! I don't believe that anyone who really knew how I feel inside could be obstinate enough not to be softened or be proud enough not to humble himself, for all that I reveal is nothing compared to what I feel." She described what she was experiencing, saying, "My mind is so full of joy and happiness that I am amazed my soul stays in my body." And she also said, "There is so much heat in my soul that this material fire seems cool by comparison, rather than to be giving out heat; it seems to have gone out, rather than to be still burning." And again, "This heat has generated in my mind a renewal of purity and humility, so that I seem to have gone back to the age of four or five. And at the same time so much love of my fellow-men has blazed up in me that I could face death for them cheerfully and with great joy in my heart." All this she told her confessor alone, in secret; but from others she hid as much as she could.

Words and happenings like this give some idea of the abundance the Lord had infused into the holy virgin's soul at this time, in a way far beyond the ordinary. But if I tried to describe everything in detail it would mean writing several books; so I have decided to collect together only a few things that nevertheless provide extraordinary evidence of Catherine's sanctity.

You must now know then, dearest reader, that while this abundance of graces was being poured from on high into Catherine's soul, many remarkable visions were being revealed to her from heaven, and it would be a sin to pass them all over in silence.

First of all the King of Kings appeared to her with the Queen of heaven, His Mother, and Mary Magdalene, to comfort and strengthen her in her holy intentions. The Lord said to her, "What do you want?" And she, weeping, said to Him, as Peter had done, "Lord, you know what I want; you know, because I have no will but yours and no heart but yours." At that moment she remembered how Mary Magdalene had given herself wholly to Christ when she had wept at His feet; and she began to feel something of the delightful sweetness and love that the Magdalene must have experienced at that time; and so she turned her eyes towards her. The Lord, as though to satisfy Catherine's desire, said to her, "Sweetest daughter, for your greater comfort I give you Mary Magdalene for your mother. Turn to her in absolute confidence; I entrust her with a special care of you." The virgin gratefully accepted this offer, commended herself with great humility and veneration to the Magdalene, and begged her earnestly and passionately to take care of her now that she had been entrusted to her by the Lord. From that moment the virgin felt entirely at one with the Magdalene and always referred to her as her mother.

In my view this had a very serious significance. As Mary Magdalene spent thirty-three years—a period of time which equals the Saviour's own age—in her cave in continual contemplation without taking any food, so, from the time of this vision until the time she was thirty-three, when she died, Catherine devoted herself with such fervour to the contemplation of the Most High that, feeling no need of food, she found nourishment for her mind with the abundance of graces she received. And as Mary Magdalene was taken up into the air by the angels seven times a day so that she could listen to the mysteries of God, so Catherine was for most of the time taken out of the world of the senses by the power of the Spirit, to contemplate heavenly things and praise the Lord with the Angels. The result was that her body was frequently lifted into the air, as many people, both men and women, claim to have seen. But we shall discuss this in more detail later.

During these raptures, while she was contemplating the marvels of God, she would be all the while muttering wonderful phrases and the most profound sayings, some of which were written down, as we shall explain when the time comes.

I myself once saw her rapt and heard her muttering in this way, and when I went up to her I distinctly heard the words *Vidi arcana Dei.*

She kept on repeating, in Latin, *Vidi arcana Dei*; that was all. After a long time she came back to her senses but she went on saying the same words, *Vidi arcana Dei*.[1]

I then thought I would like to know why she kept on repeating this phrase, and I said, "Mother, why do you keep repeating the same words? Why don't you explain the meaning of them to us as usual, but simply go on saying these words and nothing else?" She answered, "It is impossible for me to say anything else, or to say it in any other way." So I said, "What is the reason for this new kind of behaviour? Up till now, even without my asking you, you have always let me know what the Lord has let you see; why won't you answer my questions this time, the same as usual?" She replied, "I should feel such remorse if I tried to explain in our inadequate words what I have seen that I should feel as if I was in a way insulting or blaspheming against the Lord. The distance between what is heard by a mind rapt in God, and enlightened and assisted by Him, and what can be expressed in words, is so great that the two things seem to be at opposite poles. That is why I cannot possibly make any attempt to explain what I have seen, for they are things that cannot be said."

It was therefore highly fitting that Almighty God should in His providence have given the virgin to Mary Magdalene as her daughter, and Mary Magdalene to the virgin as her mother; for it was proper for penitent to be united with penitent, lover with lover, contemplative with contemplative.

The virgin herself, when she was describing these things, could only say that a sinner had been given as daughter to another who had also once been a sinner, so that the mother, mindful of human frailty, and of the generous compassion shown towards her by the Son of God, might have compassion on the daughter's frailty and obtain generous compassion for her too.

Her first confessor, Fra Tommaso, amongst whose writings I found a description of this vision of the Magdalene, relates that the virgin told

---

1. "I saw the hidden things of God."—*Publisher*, 2003.

him in confession that after these happenings it seemed to her that her heart entered into the Lord's side and became one heart with His. Then her soul seemed to melt in the vehemence of the Divine Love, whereupon she kept saying to herself, "Lord, you have wounded my heart! Lord, you have wounded my heart!" This happened, says Fra Tommaso, in the year of Our Lord 1370, on the feast day of St. Margaret, virgin and martyr.

In the same year, on the day after the feast of St. Lawrence,[2] Catherine wept so loudly during Mass that this same priest was afraid that she would disturb the priests who were saying the Mass and told her to try to stifle her sobs when she went up to the altar. Being a true daughter of obedience, Catherine went far away from the altar, and begged the Lord to grant her confessor a special illumination that would enable him to realize that there are some movements of the Spirit of God that cannot be repressed. Fra Tommaso records that what the virgin asked for was revealed to him so clearly that from that time onwards he never again had the courage to tell her anything.

He describes this episode very briefly, as though to avoid praising himself; but I rather think that he had finally learned from experience that such spiritual favours cannot be inwardly restrained.

Let us get back to Catherine. While she remained there, a long way from the altar, thirsting for the adorable Sacrament, saying in a low voice, but loud in spirit: "I want the Body of Our Lord Jesus Christ," lo, as so often happened, the Lord Himself appeared to her, determined to satisfy her, and, drawing her mouth towards the wound in His side, made a sign to her to sate herself to her heart's content on His body and blood. She did not need to be invited twice, and drank long from the rivers of life at their source in the holy side; and such sweetness ascended into her soul that she thought she must die of love. When her confessor asked her how she felt and what she felt at the time, she answered that she did not know how to describe it.

---

2. August 11th.

A similar thing had happened to her in the same year on the feast of St. Alexis.[3] The night before, while she was praying, feeling an increasing desire for Holy Communion, it was revealed to her that she would certainly receive Holy Communion the following morning: this was said because she was often wilfully denied Communion by the unperceptive monks and nuns who were in charge of the community at the time. Having had the revelation, she at once begged the Lord fervently to purify her soul and dispose it to receive such an adorable Sacrament worthily.

While she was praying and pleading with the greatest fervour, she felt as it were a river of heavy rain falling on to her soul, but it was not water or any other ordinary liquid, it was blood mixed with fire. This so purified her soul that her body experienced the same sensation too and felt purified not merely of its foulnesses but of the corruption at the very roots of desire.

The next morning she found that the physical ailments with which she was afflicted in those days had increased so much that it seemed obvious that she could not possibly move a single step. But Catherine was so sure that the promise would turn out to be true, and so trusted in the Lord, that she got up and to the amazement of everyone was soon going off to church. She did in fact get there, and installed herself in a chapel near the altar. And then she remembered that her superiors had forbidden her to receive Communion from whichever of them happened to be there, and so she began to hope that her confessor would come and celebrate at that altar. Immediately it was revealed to her from heaven that this would happen, and so she waited in perfect confidence.

Her confessor, who describes all this in his writings, says that he did not feel prepared or inclined to say Mass that morning, and knew nothing about Catherine being in church. But all at once the Lord touched his heart, and he began to feel an ardent desire to celebrate,

---

3. July 17th.

and so, guided by the Lord, he betook himself to an altar he was not in the habit of visiting—and it was precisely the one near where the holy virgin was waiting for God's promise to her to be fulfilled.

Catherine's presence, and her request to him for Holy Communion, convinced him that God's providence had ordained that he should celebrate Mass, which he had not thought of doing, at an altar which he hardly ever visited. So he did so, and at the end offered the holy virgin her Communion. She went up to the altar with her face bathed in tears and sweat, but shining and as though on fire, and received the Sacrament with such devotion that he marvelled at it and was greatly edified. Having communicated, she remained so absorbed in God and engulfed in the deepest mysteries of the Godhead that for the rest of that day she could not say a word to a soul, even after she returned to her senses.

The next day her confessor, who had seen her with such a burning face while he was giving her the Sacrament, asked her what had happened to her, and she said, "Father, I don't know what colour I was but when I received that ineffable Sacrament from your hands I could not see any shapes or colours, but what I saw took such absolute hold of me that all other things seemed no better than revolting dung—not only temporal riches and the pleasures of the body, but any kind of comfort or delight even of a spiritual kind. And so I begged and prayed that even those spiritual pleasures might be taken away from me, as long as I might please God and finally possess Him. So I prayed that He would take my will away completely and give me His own instead. And this He did, for He answered me and said, 'Behold, O sweetest daughter, I give you my will, which will make you so steadfast that nothing whatsoever that happens to you will move you or change you in the slightest'." And so it was, for, as we who were with her know, from that time onwards she was entirely contented, and never upset herself no matter what happened to her.

Later, when talking to her confessor, the virgin said again, "Father, do you know what the Lord did to my soul that day? He behaved like a mother with her favourite child. She will show it the breast, but hold it away from it until it cries; as soon as it begins to cry, she will laugh for a while and clasp it to her and, covering it with kisses, delightedly give it her full breast. So the Lord behaved with me. That day, He showed me His most sacred side from afar, and I cried from the intensity of my longing to put my lips to the sacred wound. After He had laughed for a little while at my tears—at least that is what He seemed to do—He came up to me, clasped my soul in His arms, and put my mouth to where His most sacred wound was, that is to say, to the wound in His side. Then with its great longing my soul entered right into that wound, and found such sweetness and such knowledge of the Divinity there that if you could ever appreciate it you would marvel that my heart did not break, and wonder how ever I managed to go on living in such an excess of ardour and love."

These things happened, it is said, on the feast day of St. Alexis.

In the same year, the Lord's power was manifested once again over her on the eighteenth of August, when she was receiving Holy Communion in the morning.

The priest had taken the Sacrament in his hand and had no sooner told the virgin to repeat, "Lord, I am not worthy that Thou shouldst enter under my roof," and she had received the Communion, than it seemed to her as though her soul entered into the Lord and the Lord into her, as the fish enters into the water and the water surrounds it; and she felt so absorbed in God that she could hardly get to her cell, where she immediately fell down on her self-made plank bed and remained there for a long time like one dead.

Later, her body rose into the air and remained there without anything supporting it, as three witnesses I shall name claim to have seen. Finally she came down again on to the bed and then in a very hushed voice she began to utter words of life that were sweeter than honey, and so full of wisdom that they made all the people there cry. Then she began to pray for the whole world and for some people in particular, above all her confessor.

At the time her confessor was in the Friars' Church, not thinking about anything that might have led him towards recollection; in fact, as he says himself, prayer was the last thing he was feeling in the mood for. But during the time when the virgin was praying for him, all at once he found his mind turning towards holy things, and he felt a wonderful sense of devotion that he had never felt before; within his heart there was a new and quite indescribable sensation. In his amazement he wondered where such a grace could be coming from at that hour, and he was still thinking about this when one of the holy virgin's companions happened to come to him. "Father," she said to him, "I must tell you that at such and such a time Catherine was praying very hard for you." By the time she mentioned he suddenly realized the origin of the unexpected illumination he had had, and he went on to ask her more about it. He learned that while the virgin had been praying for him and the others, asking the Lord to give them eternal life, she had stretched her right hand out, saying, "Promise that you will do it." While the hand was stretched out she seemed to feel a great pain, whereupon with a deep sigh she said, "The Lord Christ be praised," which she was accustomed to say during the struggles that took place during her illnesses.

Her confessor then went to see her and asked her what had happened in the vision, and, being under obedience, she told him what I have just described and then went on: "I kept on begging for eternal life for you and the others I was praying for and the Lord was promising it to me, when, not through unbelief, but so that I could have definite proof of it, I said to Him, 'What sign will you give me, Lord, that you will do what you say?', and He said, 'Put out your hand.' I stretched it out to Him, and He took out a nail, put the point of it in the middle of my palm and pressed my hand so hard against it that it felt as though it had gone right through, and I felt as much pain as though the nail had been struck by a hammer. And so, through the grace of my Lord Jesus Christ, I now have the wound in my right hand, and though it is invisible to others I can feel it, and there is a continual pain from it."

As we are talking about Catherine's experiences at Holy

Communion, and her stigmata, I feel obliged, good reader, to tell you what happened in Pisa much later, when I was there myself.

Arriving in Pisa with a number of other people, of whom I was one, Catherine was put up by a citizen who had a house near the Santa Cristina chapel.

On the Sunday, at the virgin's request I said Mass in this church, and, to use the official expression, I "communicated" her. When she had received Communion she went as usual into ecstasy, her spirit, thirsting for its Creator—that is to say, the supreme Spirit—absenting itself as far as it could from the senses. We were waiting for her to come back to herself, so as to receive some kind of spiritual encouragement from her, as we often did on these occasions, when to our surprise we saw her little body, which had been lying prostrate, gradually rise up until it was upright on its knees, her arms and hands stretched themselves out, and light beamed from her face; she remained in this position for a long time, perfectly stiff, with her eyes closed, and then we saw her suddenly fall, as though mortally wounded. A little later, her soul recovered its senses.

Then the virgin sent for me and said quietly, "You must know, Father, that by the mercy of the Lord Jesus I now bear in my body His stigmata." I replied that while I had been watching the movements of her body when she was in ecstasy I had suspected something of the sort; I asked her how the Lord had done all this. She said, "I saw the Lord fixed to the cross coming towards me in a great light, and such was the impulse of my soul to go and meet its Creator that it forced the body to rise up. Then from the scars of His most sacred wounds I saw five rays of blood coming down towards me, to my hands, my feet and my heart. Realizing what was to happen, I exclaimed, 'O Lord God, I beg you—do not let these scars show on the outside of my body!' As I said this, before the rays reached me their colour changed from blood red to the colour of light, and in the form of pure light they arrived at the five points of my body, hands, feet and heart." "So then," I said, "no ray reached your right side?" "No," she replied, "it came straight to my left side, over my heart; because that line of light from Jesus's right side struck me directly, not aslant." "Do you feel any pain at these points now?" I asked. She heaved a great sigh, and answered, "I feel such pain at those five points, especially in my heart, that if the Lord does not perform another miracle I do not see how I can possibly go on, and within a few days I shall be dead."

While she was saying these things, and I was rather sadly pondering upon them, I was trying to see if I could discover any signs of this great pain. She finished telling me what she wanted me to know and then we came out of the chapel and went back to the house where we were being put up. When we got there, the virgin had no sooner stepped into the room she had been given than her heart gave out and she fell senseless. We were all called, and gathered round her, and as the occurrence seemed more serious than usual we all started weeping, afraid that we were going to lose her whom we loved in the Lord. It is true that we had often seen her rapt out of her senses, and also at times had found her considerably weakened by the abundance of her spirit; but until this moment we had never seen her stunned in quite the same way.

After a short time she returned to herself, and when we had all had our meal she spoke to me again, telling me she felt that if the Lord did not cure her she would soon be dead. I did not remain deaf to these words, and summoning her spiritual sons and daughters I begged and implored them with tears in my eyes to join together in a joint prayer to the Lord that He would deign to leave us our mother and teacher for a little while longer, so that, weak and sickly as we were, not yet strengthened by heaven in the holy virtues, we might not be left orphans amongst the dangers of the world. All, men and women, promised with one heart and voice to do this, and so went to her and said, weeping, "Of course we understand, Mother, that you long for Christ your Heavenly Bridegroom, but your reward is already secure; have compassion on us whom you will leave behind, still too weak to weather life's storms. We know that nothing will separate you from your sweetest Bridegroom, whom you love with the most burning love; and therefore we implore you to pray to Him to let you stay amongst us, for if you go away now we shall have been your followers in vain. Our prayers are as fervent as we can make them; nevertheless we are afraid that through our own fault they will not be heard, since we are so unworthy; so may you, who truly desire our salvation, gain for us what our own merit cannot obtain."

To these words, which we addressed to her with tears, Catherine replied, "For some time now I have renounced my own will, and neither in this matter nor in any other do I want anything but what the Lord wants. I long for your salvation with all my heart, but He who is my salvation and yours knows how to procure it better than we do, and so in all things may His will be done. Nevertheless I will gladly pray for what is best to happen." This reply left us all miserable and perplexed.

But the Highest did not despise our tears, for on the following Saturday Catherine called for me and said, "It seems to me that the Lord wills to satisfy you, and I hope that you will soon have your wish." And it happened as she said.

The following Sunday she received Holy Communion from my unworthy hands, and whereas on the preceding Sunday her body had been as though blighted while she was in ecstasy, on this day the ecstasy she fell into seemed to give it more life than ever. To her companions, who stood there marvelling that in this rapture she gave no sign of suffering the usual pains, but seemed rather to be enjoying a sort of peaceful refreshing sleep, I said, "I hope to God that the tears with which we asked for her life to be preserved for us have indeed been acceptable to the Lord, as she said they would, and that despite her eagerness to go to her Heavenly Bridegroom she will return to us and alleviate our misery." Such were my words, and in a short time we had proof that they were justified, for when she revived she seemed so full of vigour that we no longer doubted that our prayers had been granted. O Father of infinite mercy, what will you do for truly faithful servants and beloved sons, if you consent so readily to the pleadings of sinners like us?

Bearing in mind what I had seen, for greater reassurance I asked the virgin, "Mother, can you still feel the pain of those wounds that were inflicted upon your body?" She answered, "The Lord, to my great displeasure, has granted your prayers, and those wounds no longer give my body any pain; instead they have made it stronger and healthier and I can feel quite clearly that the strength comes from the places where the agonies came from before."

The events that I have described will show you, reader, with what extraordinary graces this virgin's soul was enriched, and they will teach you that when even sinners pray for the salvation of their souls they are heard by Him who wills all men to be saved.

One thing is certain, and that is that if I wanted to describe all this virgin's ecstasies I should lack for time, not for material. For the moment I hasten to describe one that in my view is about the most remarkable that I could relate, and then, with God's help, I shall bring this chapter to an end.

I found four full written records left by the saint's confessor, Fra Tommaso, packed with information about the marvellous visions and unheard-of revelations she had. At one time the Saviour Himself introduces her soul into His own side, and there reveals to her no less a mystery than that of the Trinity; at another, the glorious Mother of God herself fills her with ineffable sweetness with milk from her most holy breast; again, Mary Magdalene frequently has intimate conversations with her, in which she tells her of the ecstasies she had in the desert seven times a day; then all three come and walk about with her and talk to her quite casually, bringing her soul delight beyond description. Nor do other saints fail to appear and comfort her, especially Paul the Apostle, whom she never mentioned without delight, John the Evangelist, sometimes St. Dominic, often St. Thomas Aquinas, and, most frequently of all, the virgin of Montepulciano, Agnes, whose life I wrote twenty-five years ago.[4]

---

4. The Life or *Leggenda* of St. Agnes was written by Bl. Raymond when he was about thirty-five and was living in Montepulciano as confessor to the nuns there.

As regards St. Agnes, it was revealed to Catherine that she was to be her companion in heaven. But more of that later.

I cannot in conscience end this chapter without first presenting for the benefit of my readers a few interesting particulars about what happened to Catherine with respect to her visions of Paul the Apostle.

On the feast day of the Apostle's conversion our virgin was rapt in ecstasy and her spirit ascended so high that for three days and nights she gave not the slightest sign of life. Those present believed her dead, or on the point of death. A few, however, who understood what was happening, considered that she had been taken up by the Apostle into the third heaven. Time passed, and the ecstasy came to an end; but her spirit, drunk with the heavenly things it had seen, seemed so reluctant to return to the things of earth that she remained in a sort of daze, like a drunkard who is stupefied but not asleep.

Just at this time her confessor, Fra Tommaso, and a certain Friar Donato of Florence, who were on their way to see an important person in the Order of Hermits living as a hermit, called upon the virgin and, finding her full of this holy stupor, drunk, so to speak, with the spirit of God, said to her in an effort to wake her, "We are on our way to see such and such a person, who is in the hermitage; do you want to come with us?" Now Catherine was a great lover of holy places and servants of God, so she said, still half-asleep, yes, but having said this she was immediately afflicted by great remorse of conscience, because she had told a lie; and this so distressed her that she at once came back to her senses and for as many days and nights as she had been in ecstasy she wept and wept and wept, saying to herself, "O most perverse and iniquitous of women, are these the things that the Most High, in His infinite goodness, has revealed to you? Are these the truths you have learned in heaven? Is this the doctrine that the Holy Spirit has deigned to reveal to you—that, returning to earth, you should lie? You knew quite well that you did not want to go with those Friars, and yet you went and said yes, lying to your confessors and fathers of your soul. O wickedness, worst of iniquities!" And she refused to eat or drink anything for the space of three days and nights, as had happened during the ecstasy.

Consider, reader, the marvellous ways and laudable methods of Divine Providence. So that the greatness of her latest revelations should not rouse the virgin to pride, God permitted her to fall into this kind of lie—if it can be called a lie, seeing that there was no intention to deceive in it; moreover, the people who actually heard her answer knew that it was said in sleep. And so, through this humiliation, which was like a lid on a special vase, Catherine was able to preserve what the Lord had given her, and her body, which had almost passed away through the elevation of her spirit, returned in this way fortified. In point of fact, although the joy of the spirit overflows on to the body by virtue of the union between them, nevertheless the excessive elevation of spirit which takes place as a result of a vision of the third heaven, that is to say, an intellectual vision, deprives the body of its quickening powers to such an extent that if God does not restore it with another miracle it is bound to die. It is a known fact that an act of understanding does not require any object of sense for its instrument except as a means to the representation of the intelligible object; now, if Almighty God by a special grace presents such an object to the intellect in a supernatural way, the intellect, finding its own perfection in Christ, immediately leaves the body behind and endeavours to unite itself with it. But God, in His excellent wisdom, first by a revelation of His light draws up the intellect that He has created, and then permits some affliction to plunge it down into the depths, so that, drawn thereby into the middle of the knowledge both of the divine perfection and of its own defects, it may soar in safety, passing freely over the sea of this world, to arrive safe and sound at the gates of eternal life.

This, I believe, is what the Apostle meant when he wrote to the Corinthians: "And lest the greatness of the revelation should exalt me, there was given me a sting of my flesh," etc. (*2 Cor.* 12:7) and, further on, "For power is made perfect in infirmity," etc. (*2 Cor.* 12:9).

But let us return to our subject.

You must know, reader, that what Catherine saw at that time she did not, as she usually did, describe to her confessor, because, as she told me much later, she was unable to find words to describe these things, which, as the same Apostle says, cannot be described in human words. Her fervour of heart, her assiduity in prayer and the effectiveness of her admonishments made it quite clear that the virgin had seen divine mysteries only to be understood by those who see them directly.

Again, at another time, as she told her confessor, who put it down in writing, the same blessed Apostle appeared to her and advised her to devote herself to deep and continual prayer. Catherine did not remain deaf to this advice, and during the vigil of the feast of St. Dominic, while she was praying in church, she had many visions of St. Dominic and other saints of the Order. These revelations or visions remained so impressed on her mind that even when she was describing them to her confessor she could still see them in front of her. I believe that this was heaven's way of letting her know that she should reveal these things to her confessor, or confessors, in order to help others.

On this day, then, shortly before vespers, Catherine was absorbed in these revelations when a certain Friar happened to come into the church, Bartolommeo di Domenico da Siena, now a Master of Sacred Theology and at that time a companion of the virgin's confessor, Fra Tommaso. Catherine had perfect confidence in this Friar, and when Fra Tommaso was away he would act as her confessor instead. As soon as she realized, more with the eyes of her mind than those of her body, that Fra Bartolommeo was coming towards her, she got up and went to meet him, saying that she needed to speak to him about something private; so they sat down and she began to describe what the Lord was revealing to her about St. Dominic at that moment. "I can see St. Dominic," she said, "better and more clearly than I can see you, and he is nearer to me than you." And she began to talk about his glories, as will shortly be described.

In the meantime one of the holy virgin's brothers, Bartolommeo, went by. Distracted by his shadow, or the sound of his footsteps,

Catherine turned her head slightly to look towards him, saw that it was her brother, and then at once turned back. Whereupon she immediately burst into tears, and was quite unable to speak.

The Friar waited for her to stop crying. A long time went by, and finally he asked her to go on with what she had been describing, but she was still sobbing and he could not get any answer out of her. When at last she was able to speak, she said, amidst sobs, "Unhappy me! Woe is me! Who will avenge my iniquities? Who will punish such a terrible sin?" Friar Bartolommeo asked her what sin she meant, and when she had committed it, and she replied, "Didn't you see a miserable woman turn and look at someone going by while the Lord was revealing his wonders to her?"

"But," said the Friar, "you only turned your eyes away for a moment, a split second: I didn't even see you do it." Catherine said, "If you knew how the Holy Virgin had scolded me for it, you too would weep for my sin." She wouldn't say another word about the vision but went on crying until she had made her confession.

When she got back to her own room at home she was still crying, and then, as she told her confessor later, St. Paul appeared to her and gave her a severe scolding for having lost that little time in turning her head. She assured her confessor that she would rather face the shame of the whole world than have to suffer again the blushes she felt while the Apostle was reprimanding her.

Paul may have appeared to Catherine on some other date to judge by what I have recently seen in other writings, but the actual date of the occurrence is unimportant; what is certain is that his severe reprimand was occasioned more by her allowing her attention to be distracted than the loss of time, and that it was his reprimand that upset Catherine so much. Later she said to her confessor, "Just think what Christ's reprimand will be like at the Last Judgement, if that of one of his Apostles could make me so afraid!" And she added that if it had not been for the vision of a very gentle shining Lamb that had been there before her eyes while the Apostle was speaking to her she would have been heartbroken with shame. From this time onwards she was more careful and recollected; she husbanded God's great gifts to her perfectly and directed her desires with ever more zeal and fervour towards greater things.

Reader, I wanted to relate these two experiences in this chapter because I believe them to be highly useful in helping to teach humility to both the perfect and the imperfect.

As I myself have been miraculously called by St. Dominic to be a member of his Order, I should consider myself lacking in gratitude if I were to pass over his glory in silence, as it was revealed to this virgin. I therefore thought this a suitable place to describe in detail the vision mentioned above.

I was told then, by the said Fra Bartolommeo, who is still with me, that on that day when the virgin was talking to him, he was assured by her that she could see the Eternal Father in a vision, generating from His mouth, as it seemed to her, the Son co-eternal with Himself, who then Himself appeared to her after assuming our human nature. Utterly absorbed as she was in what was happening, she also saw the most blessed patriarch Dominic emerging from the breast of the same Father, surrounded by brilliant light, and heard a voice coming from that same mouth, saying, "Sweetest daughter, I generated these two sons, one according to nature, the other by adoption in love and gentleness." As Catherine marvelled greatly at hearing St. Dominic honoured by such a flattering comparison, the Eternal Father himself explained the words that He had uttered. "Just as this Son of mine, generated by nature from all eternity, assumed a human nature and was obedient to me unto death, so my adopted son Dominic, in all he did from infancy to the end of his life, was ruled by obedience to my commandments. Never once did he transgress against a single one of my laws, because he preserved perfect virginity of mind and body and the grace of baptism in which he had been spiritually reborn. Just as this natural Son, the eternal Word of my mouth, preached to the world the things I commanded Him to preach and gave testimony to the truth, as He said to Pilate, so my adopted son Dominic preached the Truth of my words to the world, to both Catholics and heretics, and not only by himself, but also through others; not only while he was alive, but also through his successors, by means of whom he went on preaching and still goes on preaching today. As my natural Son sent out His disciples, so this adopted son sent out his Friars, therefore, as my natural Son is my Word, so this adopted son is the bearer and announcer of my Word. For this purpose, by an extraordinary gift from me, he and his Friars have been enabled to understand the truth of my words and never to forsake this truth. Further, as my natural Son devoted all His life and actions to the salvation of souls, so my adopted son Dominic directed all his efforts and powers to the task of freeing souls from the snares of vice and error. This was the main reason why he founded and developed his Order: zeal for souls. I tell you that in almost all his works he resembled my natural Son; and so, as you can now see, the image of his body bore a great resemblance to the image of the body of my most sacred only Son."

While the virgin was relating these things to the said Friar Bartolommeo, there took place the event we have already amply described.

Now let us come to the last vision.

You must know, beloved reader, that by this time Catherine's soul had received such an abundance of graces, revelations and visions, that the power of love they generated in her soul began to make her languish and grow weak, and indeed her weakness increased to such an extent that she was unable to get up out of bed. Her only suffering was love for her Heavenly Bridegroom, whom she called upon unceasingly as if out of her mind, "O sweetest and most beloved Son of God!" sometimes adding, "and of the Virgin Mary!" Utterly absorbed in these thoughts and feelings of Paradise she lived without sleep or food.

The Bridegroom, who had kindled this holy fire within her so that she would grow ever more inflamed, appeared to her continually, and she, all on fire, would say to Him: "Why, O most beloved Lord, do you allow this contemptible body of mine to keep me away from your embraces? In this wretched life I find nothing that attracts me. I seek no other but you, I love nothing but you, for if I love anything it is for your sake that I love it. Why, then, by a worthless body must I be prevented from enjoying you? O, my most merciful Lord, release my soul from this prison and free me from this mortal body!"

To these entreaties, addressed to Him with tears and sighs, the Lord replied: "Dearest daughter, when I was on earth I did not do my own will but the will of my Father; and though, as I told my disciples, I had a great longing to eat the last Pasch with them, nevertheless I waited patiently until the proper time came, which had been determined by the Father. So you too, despite your great longing to be united with me, must wait patiently until the time determined by me." And Catherine said, "As it is not your pleasure now, your will be done. But I pray you to be good enough to listen to one little request from me: that during the time you want me to remain in the body you will allow me to share in all the sufferings you endured, including your final Passion, so that, as I am not able for the moment to be united with you in heaven, I may be united with you through your Passion on earth."

The Lord answered her in the affirmative, and kept His promise. In fact, as Catherine confessed to me, she now began to feel the Saviour's sufferings, of which she had already had some experience, more strongly than ever in her soul and body. But so that all this may be better understood, I shall give her own account of it.

The virgin often talked to me about the Saviour's Passion, and assured me that from the time He was conceived Jesus had always carried the cross in His soul, because of the immense desire He had for the salvation of mankind. "It is certain," she would say, "that Jesus Christ, the mediator between God and man, was from the moment of His conception full of grace, wisdom and charity, and there was no need for Him to make any further progress in these things because He was perfect from the beginning. But, loving God and the neighbour in the most perfect way, and seeing God deprived of His honour and the neighbour of his true end, He was greatly afflicted until He had restored the honour of obedience to God and salvation to the neighbour. And the desire

He felt was no slight affliction, as is known to all who have had any experience of it, but the biggest of crosses. That was why He said to His disciples at the last Supper, 'With desire I have desired . . .' etc.; (*Luke* 22:15) and He said this because at that supper He gave them a pledge of the salvation He was to effect before eating with them again."

The virgin connected these words up with others that the Saviour had said when He was praying, and she commented on them in a way that I have never read or heard of except from her. She said that the words, "My Father, if it be possible, let this chalice pass from me . . ." etc., (*Matt.* 26:39) were not to be understood by the strong and perfect in the same way as by the weak who are afraid of death. The Saviour was not in fact asking for the hour of His Passion to be cancelled or postponed. As, from the moment of His conception, He had undertaken to drink the chalice of the desire for the salvation of mankind, so now, as that time drew near and He drank it with greater desire, He asked for that to be fulfilled which He had for so long and with such great anxiety desired: that is to say, that the chalice which He had been drinking throughout His life should at last be completely emptied. He was not, therefore, asking for a respite but for a quick fulfilment. The Lord Himself made this clear when He said to Judas, "That which thou dost, do quickly." (*John* 13:27). And although this chalice of desire was a most grievous thing for Him to drink, yet, as a son obedient in all things, He added, "Nevertheless not as I will, but as thou wilt," (*Matt.* 26:39) thus showing Himself prepared for a delay in the fulfilment of His desire, if the Father so willed. So that when He said, "Let this chalice pass from me," He was not, according to Catherine, referring to the chalice of His future Passion, but to that of the present and past.

When I mentioned that the Doctors who have interpreted these words agree in saying that the Saviour was speaking as a real man, whose senses were naturally afraid of death, and as the head of the elect, the weak as well as the strong, so that the weak would not despair if they felt any fear of death, she replied, "If the works of the Lord are studied attentively, they will be found to be so full of meat that everyone will find the part of the meat that suits him and fits in with his salvation. If the weak find comfort for their weakness in this prayer of the Lord's, it seems necessary that the strong and perfect too should be able to find an increase of their strength in it; which would not be the case if this kind of interpretation could not be made. It is better, therefore, for it to be interpreted in several ways so that everyone can have his share in it. If it was interpreted in one way only, it would only suit one kind of person." When I heard this I was silent in admiration of her grace and wisdom.

I have come across another interpretation of these words amongst the writings of the virgin's confessor, Fra Tommaso, which include a collection of her sayings and deeds.[5]

He relates that during an ecstasy Catherine learned how the Lord suffered His Agony and the sweat of blood, and that He directed this prayer to the Father for those who, He foresaw, would not enjoy the fruits of His Passion; but because He loved justice He added the reservation, "Nevertheless, not as I will but as thou wilt." Catherine also said that if He had not added this reservation the whole world would have been saved, it being impossible for a prayer by the Son of God not to achieve its effect. This agrees with the Apostle's words to the Hebrews about Him: "Who . . . was heard for his reverence," (*Hebrews* 5:7) which are generally thought by the Doctors to refer to the prayer in the Garden.

In addition to what I have already said, she told me other things, and taught me that the suffering that Jesus endured for our salvation could not have been borne by anyone else without his dying of it many times over, if that were possible. As in fact the love He had and has for us is of inestimable worth, so was the Passion He endured at the behest and impulse of love of inestimable worth too. His sufferings far surpassed the actual nature of things or the most quintessential evil of those who persecuted Him. Who would ever have believed, for instance, that the thorns

---

5. This collection, made by Fra Tommaso della Fonte, which Raymond made great use of, has been lost.

would have penetrated His skull right to the brain? Or that the bones of a living man would have come apart as a result of being pulled? It is written, "They have numbered all my bones." (*Psalm* 21:18). But because the love by which He endured all these sufferings was so great, He accepted the greatest pains invented so that He might reveal Himself to us most perfectly. Undoubtedly that was one of the main reasons for His Passion, to show us His utterly perfect love for us; and it could not have not been revealed to us in a more fitting way. It was not the nails that held Him to the cross, but love, not human strength that overcame him, but his own love. If this were not so, how could His enemies have triumphed over Him, when it would have been enough for Him to say one word to have annihilated them completely?

These things, so profound and to the point, I was told about the Lord's Passion by this most wise of virgins, and she also told me that she had experienced something of each of His sufferings in her own body. Something: for she considered it impossible for anyone to be able to endure the whole Passion of Jesus Christ. She also said that the greatest pain suffered at the Crucifixion was in the breast, because of the rending apart of the bones, and to prove this she mentioned the pains in her own breast: all others had passed, but that pain, no. Although she suffered continual pains in her sides and head, the pains in her chest, she said, were the most violent; because of the proximity of the heart this seems to me not unlikely, either in her case or in the case of the Saviour himself. The bones in the chest, in fact, being arranged by nature to protect the heart and lungs, cannot be sundered without strong repercussions on the heart, and perhaps only a miracle could have saved anyone else from dying from such a thing.

However that may be—to return to our subject—after the holy virgin's body had endured the Passion, which lasted several days, of course her physical powers were greatly weakened, but the love in her heart was increased. In undergoing that most bitter Passion, she had in fact a tangible experience of how much the Lord had loved her and the whole human race, for there was kindled in her heart such a violence of charity and love that it was not possible for her heart to remain whole and not break in two. The same thing happens when a pot is filled with fermenting liquor; the repressed force, finding itself hemmed in, cracks the pot and the liquid rushes out because there was not a proper balance between the contents and the container.

But why am I wasting time on comparisons? The force of this love was such that the virgin's heart broke in two down the middle, and so, with the vital veins broken, solely through the vehemence of the divine love, and through that alone, she expired. Do you find this impossible to believe, reader? You must realize that many people were present at her death, and some of them are still alive. It was they who first told me about it; I shall give their names later.

I went off to see her in a state of the utmost concern, and did all I could to find out what she was thinking, imploring her to tell me the truth. Instead of answering me, she burst into tears. After a while she said, "Father, would you feel sorry for a soul that had been freed from a dark prison, seen a light that made her blissfully happy, and then was once again locked up in darkness? That unhappy person is me! And it all happened to me because of my own fault, God's providence having so decreed." These words increased my curiosity to know how anything so portentous had happened to her, and I said, "Mother, was your soul really separated from your body?" She replied, "The fire of Divine Love and the longing to be united with Him I love had burned up so high that even if my heart had been made of stone or steel it would have been split apart in just the same way.

"I am convinced that no created thing could have made my heart proof against the violence of that love. So you can take it as certain that my heart broke from top to bottom and split apart, solely as a result of the violence of that love, and I still seem able to feel the wound that splitting apart made. This will give you some idea whether my soul was separated from my body. And I saw divine mysteries that no living soul can utter because memory has no hold over them and there are no words capable of describing things so sublime: any words that were used would be like mud compared with gold. One thing I do retain from the experience, however, is this; that whenever I hear people talking about what happened to me I get very upset, because it reminds me of what a worthless state I have been reduced to after rising to such heights of nobility; and the only way my disappointment can express itself is in tears."

On hearing this, desirous as I was to learn the most minute details of what had happened to her, I said, "Mother, you never keep any secrets from me; well, then, I beg you, describe this miraculous event to me down to the last detail." She said: "In those days, after many ecstasies and visions and after receiving many spiritual favours from the Lord, I fell ill, entirely overcome by love of Him, and had to go to bed, where I prayed to him continuously to take me from the body of this death, that I might be more closely united with Him. I did not obtain this, but I did finally manage to get Him to communicate the pains that He had felt to me, in so far as I was able to bear them."

Then she told me what I have related above about the Lord's Passion. She went on: "From these teachings about His Passion I got a much clearer idea of how much my Creator had loved me, and this so increased my love that I languished to the point of wanting only one thing, that my soul should depart from my body. Each day He Himself increased the fire that He had lit within my heart until it could bear it no longer, and the love became as strong as death: then the heart broke in two, as I said, and my soul was set free from this flesh of mine. But unfortunately for all too short a time!"

"How long," I asked, "did your soul remain outside the body?" "Those who saw my death," she answered, "say that four hours elapsed between the time I expired and the time I came back to life. Quite a lot of people in the neighbourhood went and told my mother and family the sad news. But my soul, which believed it had entered eternity, lost all account of time."

"And during those hours, Mother, what did you see?" I asked. "How did your soul come back into the body? Tell me all about it: don't hide anything from me."

"Father," Catherine said, "my soul saw and understood everything in the other world that to us is invisible: that is to say, the glory of the Saints and the pains of sinners. I have already told you: the memory cannot keep anything of it and words are not adequate to describe it; but as far as I can I will try to tell you about it. You can be certain, then, that my soul contemplated the Divine Essence; that is why I am now always so discontented with being in the prison of the body. If I was not sustained by love of Him and love of my fellow-men, for whom He sent me back into the world, I should die of misery. Nevertheless, it is infinite comfort to me to know that I suffer what I do suffer: it is through suffering that I shall enjoy a more sublime vision of God. For this reason alone, my tribulations do not weigh on me; in fact they bring comfort to my soul, as you and the others who are with me can witness daily.

"I also saw the torments of the damned and the souls in Purgatory, but there are no words that can adequately describe these. If poor mortals had a glimpse of the least of those torments they would undoubtedly prefer to die ten times over rather than have to bear such a thing for one day. I was specially struck by the punishment meted out to those who sin in the married state, who do not respect their vows as they should and seek to satisfy their lust." I then asked her why this sin, which is no more serious than any other, should be punished so severely. She replied, "Because the people concerned don't regard it as important and consequently are not sorry for it as they are for the others, and so they succumb to it more readily and frequently." And she added, "This fault is all too dangerous, however trivial it may seem, because no one who commits it bothers to get remission of it through repentance."

Having come to the end of this aside, she returned to her main theme. "While my soul was seeing all these things, the Heavenly Bridegroom, whom I believed myself to be possessing fully, said to my soul, 'Do you see how much glory is lost by those who offend against me, and what torments they are punished with? Then return to life and make them understand their errors, the danger and the harm they do.' And as my soul showed itself highly reluctant to do this, the Lord went on, 'The salvation of many souls makes it necessary for you to go back! You must change your present way of life; your cell must not be a home to you any longer; instead, for the good of souls you will have to leave even your own city. I shall be with you always, in your goings out and in your comings in, and you will carry my doctrine and the honour of my name to high and low, to lay folk, clerics and religious. I shall put a kind of wisdom in your mouth that none will be able to resist. I will lead you before Popes, before the Heads of the Christian Church and its people; and through the weak, as is my custom, I shall humble the pride of the powerful.' While God was speaking thus to my soul in a spiritual or intellectual way, it suddenly, in a way I cannot understand or describe, found itself back in the body, and as soon as it realized this, it was assailed by unbearable misery, and for three days and three nights I could do nothing but weep; and even now when I think back on that experience I still feel I must cry.

"Don't be surprised at that, Father! The surprising thing is rather that my heart is not broken anew with misery every day, considering the sublime degree of glory I possessed, which now alas has forsaken me. The purpose behind all that experience was the salvation of my fellow-men; so no one must be scandalized if I love with a love without equal those whom the Lord has made it my task to correct and lead from the false way to the true after buying them at the highest of all prices. For their sake I have been separated from the Lord, and His glory has been withdrawn from me for who knows how long? Hence, as St. Paul said, they are my glory, crown and joy! I say this to you," she concluded, "so as to remove the thorn from your heart that others have in their hearts too, who grumble because I am everyone's friend."

When I had heard all this, and comprehended it as far as the grace granted me allowed me to, I decided that it would not be a good thing to spread this news abroad, especially in view of the thoughtlessness of our day and the unbelief of people who love no one but themselves. I therefore forbade the monks and nuns entrusted to my care to say a word about it so long as she was alive.

I had also noticed that some people began by listening to the virgin's advice, but as soon as they heard it they forsook her because they could not receive the word. But when Catherine's frail life had run its course and she ascended into Paradise, not to return until the General Resurrection, I decided (and still believe) that I was obliged to reveal all about this event, so that such a gift from the Divine Mercy and such a great and evident miracle should not remain hidden through any negligence on my part.

So that you may see, reader, how clearly Divine Virtue revealed the event, you must know that when the time for her first departure from this life was drawing near, her confessor, Fra Tommaso delle Fonte, was summoned by her companions and daughters in God to attend to her in the usual way, and commend her soul to the Lord. He took Fra Tommaso di Antonio with him and hurried along to attend to her needs, saying the prayers with sorrow in his soul. Another Friar, Bartolommeo di Montuccio, heard about this and went along after him, taking with him Friar Giovanni da Siena, a lay brother, who now lives in Rome. These four Friars, all still living, were the unhappy witnesses of this holy virgin's passing.

She had no sooner breathed her last than Giovanni, the lay brother, was overcome by grief, and wept and sobbed so much that he burst a vein in his chest; in fact, being shaken by a fit of coughing, a common enough thing in these cases, he began to spit clots of blood, which threatened sudden death or an incurable ailment. To those present a second sorrow was thus added to the first, for while they were still shedding tears over the virgin's death they found themselves obliged to weep for the Friar's, which they saw fast approaching.

Faced with this crisis, the virgin's confessor, Fra Tommaso, said with great faith to Fra Giovanni, "I know for certain that this virgin has great merits in the eyes of God; so put the hand of her holy body on the spot where you feel these atrocious pains and you are sure to be cured." This Giovanni did in the presence of all the assembled company and he was cured at once. Friar Giovanni will tell this to anyone who cares to ask him about it, and, if it is considered necessary, he will even confirm it on oath.

For the rest, in addition to the Friars named above there was also present at her demise one of her companions and daughters in the Lord, Alessia, who is now, I imagine, in heaven with Catherine, for she only lived a little while after the virgin's death.

The virgin was also seen dead by most of the people in the neighbourhood, particularly those men and women who were acquainted with her, for as is usual on such occasions they hurried to her home to see her, and there was not one who did not believe that she was really dead.

Lastly, with regard to the rising in the air and remaining there, as mentioned at the beginning of this chapter, this was witnessed by a number of the Sisters of Penance of St. Dominic, including a certain Catherine, the daughter of Ghetto da Siena, who was for a long while the virgin's inseparable companion; and, if I am not mistaken, her sister-in-law Lisa, who is still alive, and the above-mentioned Alessia were also there at the time.

CHAPTER SEVEN

Saviour of Souls

───────────────●───────────────

YOU must believe beyond the shadow of a doubt, reader, that if I were to try to describe every single one of the miracles that the Lord performed through this holy virgin from the day I first met her, many of which I saw with my own eyes, I should have to write not one single volume but a whole series. But so as not to weary you, I have collected together a number of these miracles as best I can into a single chapter, as samples of all those which for reasons of brevity I shall have to pass over in silence. And since the spirit has precedence over the body, so spiritual miracles should come before those done to benefit bodies. I have therefore decided to narrate first the things that the Lord did through Catherine for the good of souls, and then I shall go on to those that concerned the health of people's bodies.

Although in my writings I try to keep as close as I can to the actual chronology of the events described, in this case I shall have to give that up, for to keep to my plan I may have to describe a miracle done by Catherine for the good of a soul towards the end of her life, before I report one performed much earlier for the good of the body; but it is after all fitting that more worthy things should come before those that are less worthy. However, although I intend to keep to this decision, I shall nevertheless make every endeavour to keep to the actual chronology within each separate group.

One thing is certain, and that is that some of her miracles, especially of a spiritual kind, remained so hidden and unknown that their only evidence is the revelation of them that she herself made to me and a few others; nevertheless they all have certain recognizable signs sufficient to convince devout believers of their genuineness.

Excellent reader, I want you to recall how, when the holy virgin's father Giacomo began to realize that his daughter was serving Almighty God with all her heart, he ever afterwards treated her with reverence and consideration, continually impressing on the minds of the people in the house that they were not to interfere with his daughter in anything she chose to do. Thus the love that existed between father and daughter increased daily: Catherine begged for her father's salvation in her prayers to the Lord, and her father rejoiced in the Lord because of his daughter's virtues and trusted in her merits and prayers to obtain his eternal salvation.

Time passed, and Giacomo's end drew near: he was taken ill and confined to bed. As soon as Catherine learned of this she at once had recourse to her accustomed prayer and turned to her Heavenly Bridegroom, pleading for her father to be cured. But she was told that Giacomo's time had come and that it was better that he should go.

Catherine then ran to her father's bedside and hastily reassured herself of the state of his soul, finding him resigned to dying and not avid for this life. For this she thanked the Saviour with all her heart. But, still not satisfied, she concentrated in spirit again, and begged the Lord, the fountain of all graces, that as He had allowed Giacomo to pass through this life without sin, so He would allow him to ascend to heaven without having to go through Purgatory. But she was told that in some way at least justice had to be maintained, it being impossible for a soul incompletely purged to enjoy the benefit of so much glory. The Lord said to her, "Although your father has lived an utterly blameless life as head of the family, and has always shown the utmost respect for me, especially in so far as you are concerned, nevertheless it would be against justice if his soul were not to pass through the fire. He has collected too much mud, and his soul has become stony with worldly concerns." Catherine said, "My most beloved Lord, how can I possibly bear to think that the soul of the one who brought me into the world, and fed me and brought me up with such love, and never in his life showed me anything but love, should be made to burn in that terrible fire? By all your goodness I beg and implore you not to let his soul issue from his body until you have purified it in some way or other, without making it pass through the flames of Purgatory."

Marvellously, the Lord God in a way accepted these human words and wishes, for Giacomo lost his bodily faculties, but his soul did not depart until the end of this pious and holy conversation, which went on for a long time, the Lord emphasizing the importance of justice and the virgin asking for grace. Finally, after persisting for a long time, the virgin said, "If grace is not to be had without justice being preserved by some means or other, let justice be done on me, for I am prepared to suffer for my father's sake whatever penalty may be decided upon by your goodness." The Lord took her at her word and said, "Very well then; for the love you bear me I accede to your request and will release your father's soul from all punishment; but as long as you live you will have to bear the tribulations I send you in his stead." Whereupon Catherine, full of joy, replied, "Lord, I accept your word; may it happen as you have ordained."

Thereupon she went to her dying father's bedside to comfort him, and filled him with joy by telling him that the Lord had guaranteed his salvation, and she did not leave his side until she had seen him breathe his last; and at the very moment when Giacomo's soul issued from his body, the virgin felt herself afflicted by a pain in the side which she carried with her for the rest of her life; there was never a moment when she did not feel it, as she herself, and her companions, told me on innumerable occasions, and as I and the others who were with her could indeed see for ourselves. But Catherine's patience did not give in to pain, as we shall shortly see; on the contrary, it triumphed over it.

What I have written here was told me in secret by the holy virgin herself when I was sympathizing with her about the pains she had to bear and trying to discover the cause of these obstinate afflictions. I must also relate that Giacomo had hardly breathed his last when the holy virgin's mouth curved into a laugh of great contentment and she said, "Blessed be the Lord! Would to God that I were like him!" And throughout the time of the funeral, while the others were weeping, she was unable to conceal her light-heartedness and joy.[1] She comforted her mother and brothers as though all the funeral business had nothing to do with her at all. She had seen that soul issue from the darkness of the body and fly immediately into the light of eternity, and this gave her an indescribable pleasure, especially because only a short time before, as has been narrated in the previous chapter, she had experienced what it meant to enter into that light. Her pains she accepted willingly, because she knew that they had gained this sublime glory for her father.

Do you see, reader, how wisely Divine Providence proceeded in this instance? Undoubtedly Giacomo's soul could have been purified and made worthy of glory in some other way, as for instance happened in the case of the soul of the thief who acknowledged the Lord on the cross; but God willed that the purification should not take place unless the virgin was prepared to accept the physical pain she had offered to endure, and this not for suffering's sake but to increase her own spiritual good. It was meet that Catherine, who loved her father's soul so dearly, should gain something through her love; and as she had loved his soul's salvation more than his body, so she too, through bodily pain, increased the salvation of her own soul. And so she always said that these pains were sweet to her—not without reason, seeing that they meant an increase of the sweetness of grace for her in this life and more glory in the next; from that point of view she could hardly call them anything but sweet.

The virgin told me secretly that for a long time after her father's death his spirit kept appearing to her almost continually, to thank her

---

1. Giacomo was buried on August 22nd, 1368, in the crypt of San Domenico.

for the gift it had received through her, and that it revealed many secret things to her, putting her on her guard against the Devil's wiles and preserving her from all evil.

Now that you have heard, dear reader, what happened to the soul of one who was just, listen to what happened to the soul of a sinner.

There was in Siena at this time, that is to say in the year of our Lord 1370, a certain Andrea di Naddino, a man very rich in worldly goods but very poor in the goods of the spirit. Living without any fear or love of God, he had been caught up in the trammels of sins and vices, and having in particular surrendered to a lust for gaming, he had become a horrible blasphemer against God and the saints.

In the December of the above-mentioned year, his own fortieth, he was attacked by a dreadful illness and confined to his bed, and, all the doctor's remedies proving unavailing, he advanced rapidly towards the death of body and soul, as, in his impenitence, he deserved.

The local priest, learning of his condition, went to see him, and reminded him that before he died he should ask pardon for his sins and, as the custom is, make his will. But being a man who had never in his life put a foot inside a church or had any respect for priests, he laughed at his adviser, and his advice. His wife and family in their anxiety for his salvation, and many other people who were religious and feared God, kept coming to him and trying to cure him of his obstinacy, but neither with the terror of hell-fire nor with the bait of God's mercy could they prevail upon him to confess his sins. He was heading straight for hell, with a load of sins on his back.

The parish priest, sad at the thought of his condition and fearing that he might die at any minute, went off to see him again at daybreak and repeated his advice to him and offered him more; but the wretched fellow still showed the same contempt for him and his words. Reduced to a state of final impenitence, he persisted in his sin against the Holy Spirit, which is not to be remitted either in this world or the next, and he was rightly on the way to the eternal fire.

All this came to the ears of the virgin's confessor, Fra Tommaso, who, saddened at the prospect of this soul's damnation, hurried off to Catherine's home to order her under obedience and as a matter of charity to implore the Lord in His mercy to deign to come to the help of this soul now on the point of eternal damnation.

Arriving at her home he found her in ecstasy, and it was not right for him to interrupt her in such intimate contemplations; and so, as he was unable to speak to her, or to wait, since night was coming on, he instructed one of her companions, whose name was also Catherine—she is still alive—to acquaint her with the facts of the unhappy case and his own wishes in the matter as soon as she returned to her senses. The companion humbly accepted the command and promised to carry it out, as she did.

The holy virgin remained in contemplation until five o'clock in the morning, and when she came back to her senses, her companion repeated all that the confessor had told her about praying for this soul continually as a matter of holy obedience. Immediately inflamed by the fire of charity and touched by compassion, the holy virgin turned to prayer, imploring the Lord not to permit the eternal death of this neighbour and fellow-citizen and brother of hers, who like her had been redeemed at the price of so much blood.

The Lord replied that the blasphemer Andrea's horrible iniquities had ascended as high as heaven, and added, "Not only has he blasphemed against me and my saints, but he also threw a panel that contained a painting of me with my holy Mother and others of my saints into the fire. Therefore it is only right that he should burn likewise in the everlasting fire. Let him be lost, daughter, for he deserves to die." But the virgin, prostrate at the feet of her sweetest Bridegroom, insisted with tears, "Most beloved Lord, if you look with utter strictness on our iniquities, who is there who can escape eternal damnation? Did you come down into the Virgin's womb and endure the atrocious torture of your death in order to punish us for our sins, or to annul them? Why speak to me of this unfortunate man's faults, when you bore all our faults on your most holy shoulders? Have I come to you to discuss justice, or to ask for mercy?

Remember, Lord, what you said to me when you laid upon me the destiny of bringing salvation to souls. In this world my one comfort is to see men turn to you, and for that I bear my separation from you calmly. If you will not grant me this grace, most unhappy am I, What am I to do? Do not cast me off, most merciful Lord! Give me back my brother, now engulfed in the abyss of his obstinacy."

From the fifth hour of the night until the break of day, Catherine, weeping continuously and without a wink of sleep, fought with the Lord for the salvation of Andrea's soul, the Lord adducing the many very grave sins for which justice demanded revenge, and Catherine reminding Him of His mercy, which had led to His incarnation and sufferings, and His promise to her about the part she was to play in the salvation of many souls. In the end pity had the better of the divine rights, and the inexhaustible fountain of mercy triumphed over justice. The Lord said to the virgin, "Sweetest daughter, behold, I have heard your prayers, and in a short time I shall convert him for whom you have so fervently prayed."

At the same hour He appeared to Andrea, who was in his agony, and said, "Why, dearest one, will you not confess the offences you have committed against me? Confess them all, for I am generously prepared to forgive them." On hearing these words, Andrea's heart was softened and he began to cry out loud, "Send for a priest, I want to confess. I can see the Lord and Saviour Jesus Christ telling me to confess my sins." Those present, hearing him speak in this way, were filled with joy, and hastily sent for a priest as he had bidden, and as soon as the priest arrived Andrea confessed his sins in full lucidity of mind and with endless grief, and made a fully detailed will. Then, in great repentance and resignation, he passed from this life to the life of heaven.[2]

---

2. Andrea died on December 16th, 1370. His wife was one of the Sansedoni family. His death is recorded in the San Domenico register as follows: "Andrea di Naddoni died on December 16th and was buried in the family vault which stands at the back by the cloister steps."

O Father of ineffable mercy, how great is your goodness, how profound your providence, how incomprehensible to us are your ways! You allowed this man to persist in his sins to the end, and seemed to be unconcerned about him, yet all the time you were not indifferent to him. Your servants, both men and women, went to see him, in vain it seemed, and then you inspired this virgin's confessor to order her to pray for him. You inflamed her heart to conquer with her poor tears yourself who are the unconquerable one, and, as it were, put your own omnipotence in thrall. Who was it but you yourself who infused such audacity into her? Who fired her with such sisterly compassion? Who gave her the tears to influence your clemency if not you yourself? You drew your bride towards you, that she in her turn might incline you to her way. Yours are the doings, O Jesus Christ, by which you glorify your Saints! To show how highly you esteemed your virgin bride, you revealed to her the danger threatening a man unknown to her, but a fellow-citizen and a Christian, and willed to bring assistance to him through the mediation of her you had chosen beforehand as your bride. Who, then, would not bind himself to you with the bond of love?

So far, reader, you have seen the great mercies of our God as revealed in a poor sinner freed by the virgin's merits; now you will see the same mercies more strikingly displayed in two sinners already well-nigh damned.

By order of the Chief Justice two malefactors were arrested in Siena, and for their heinous crimes condemned to a most cruel death: they were to be put in a cart, bound to a post, and tortured by the executioners in different parts of their bodies with hooks or red-hot pincers. Neither in prison nor on the point of being led out to die did they show any desire to repent of their misdeeds, nor would they confess to the priest. Moreover, when according to custom they were led through the streets of the city as a warning and example to others, instead of commending themselves to the prayers of the faithful they blasphemed against God and the Saints at the tops of their voices. Thus, from a temporal fire and temporal pains these miserable wretches seemed likely to end in eternal fire, suffering eternal pains.

But the Eternal Goodness, who wills that no one shall perish and never punishes the same fault twice over, determined to save these poor souls from hell through the virgin who was His chosen bride. Divine Providence therefore decreed that on that morning Catherine should have gone in search of greater quiet to the house of one of her spiritual daughters and companions named Alessia, who is now blessed in heaven with her, and Alessia lived in one of the streets down which the condemned men were to go.

During the morning Alessia was roused by the tumultuous shouts of the crowd, went to the window and looked down the street, and saw the cart approaching in which the condemned men were being tortured in the way described above. She hurried off to Catherine, saying, "Mother, look at this horrible sight just going past our door! A cart is going by with two men condemned to the torture."

At this news the holy virgin, prompted not by curiosity but by compassion, went up to the window too, and no sooner saw what was going on than in the twinkling of an eye she had disappeared and set herself to prayer. She told me later in confession that she had seen a tumultuous mob of evil spirits around each of the condemned men, burning their souls more painfully than the torturers were burning them outwardly with the red-hot pincers. Doubly moved to compassion, she immediately had recourse to prayer, eagerly imploring her Heavenly Bridegroom to succour and have pity on these two endangered souls. "My most merciful Lord," she said, "why do you show such contempt for your own creatures, made in your image and likeness and mercifully redeemed by your precious blood, and permit them to be tortured in the flesh, and tortured more cruelly still by the spirits of hell? The thief who was put on the cross with you was being punished for his misdemeanours, nevertheless he was so enlightened by you that while the Apostles were still in doubt he openly acknowledged you on the gallows and merited to hear it said, 'Today thou shalt be with me in paradise.' (*Luke* 23:43). Why did you enlighten him, if not to give the hope of forgiveness to all like him? You did not despise Peter who denied you, but looked upon him with eyes of mercy; you did not despise the sinner Mary, but drew her to you; you did not reject Matthew the publican, or the woman of Canaan, or Zacchæus, the prince of publicans, indeed you called them to you. I therefore beg you in the name of all your mercy to care for these two souls and succour them." And with these words she drew down to herself Him who willed to come down to her, and marvellously directed the inexhaustible fountain of mercy towards these two unfortunate men; for she was granted the grace to follow them in spirit. She accompanied them in spirit in fact for the whole of their journey right up to the city gate, weeping and praying all the while that their hearts might yield and be converted. The devils could see her and howled out openly, "If you don't stop, we and the spirits surrounding these two will find some way of tormenting you and making you a possessed woman." But Catherine answered, "Whatever God wills, I too will. I shall not stop doing what I have begun."

When the two unfortunate men arrived at the city gate the most merciful Lord appeared to them, all covered with wounds and dripping with blood, and asked them to be converted, promising them forgiveness. A ray of the divine light penetrated their hearts; they asked repeatedly for the priest, and confessed their sins to him with visible signs of grief. Then they turned their blasphemies into songs of praise, and making a public declaration that they deserved the punishments they were undergoing, and other far worse ones, went towards their death happily, as though invited to a wedding. Whereas at first they had responded to the executioners' tortures with blasphemies, they now redoubled their praises of the Lord, and proclaimed their conviction that they would arrive at glory through their very tortures, which were the proof of great mercy.

Faced with such a change of heart, those present were filled with amazement, and the torturers themselves were moved by the sight of such devotion and did not dare continue their cruelties. No one could explain this miracle or understand who could have interceded with God for those two most hardened souls. After it was all over the priest who had helped the two condemned men to stop being obstinate told the virgin's confessor, Fra Tommaso, all about it, and Fra Tommaso, when he had questioned Alessia, was able to establish that the two unfortunates had died just at the moment when the holy virgin had stopped praying and returned to her senses. Then, in confession, Fra Tommaso heard from her own lips all the details mentioned above, which were found amongst his notes. He adds that after the death of these two malefactors the holy virgin's companions heard her repeating for many days, "I thank you, O Lord, for saving them from a second prison." When Fra Tommaso got to know about this, he wanted to know what she meant by these words, and she replied that those criminals' souls were already in the glory of Paradise, because, although when they died they had gone to Purgatory, she had begged for their complete liberation.

This last event may seem to you slightly irrelevant, reader, because it did not take place under the eyes of human witnesses; but if you read Augustine and Gregory you will discover that this was a greater miracle than if those condemned men had died and come to life again. In the words of Gregory,[3] I will say that if their bodies had been resurrected, their newly dead flesh would have come to life again, but in this resurrection their souls came to life again to live eternally. Further, in the case of a bodily resurrection there is no obstacle to the divine power to be overcome, as there is in a way in the resurrection of the soul because of human free will. The person can still in fact will not to be converted; the result being that as a demonstration of God's power the conversion of the soul is held to be a much greater achievement than the creation of the whole world. St. Martin is rightly remembered because by the power of the Holy Trinity he merited to become the splendid means whereby three dead men were brought back to life. Again we read in the case of St. Nicholas, as a matter for great praise, that he marvellously freed three innocent men condemned to death. What are we to say

---

3. *Dialogues*, Part 3, chap. I.

then of our young virgin Catherine, who, entirely by her prayers, in a moment marvellously brought back to life two malefactors whose souls had been dead and destined for eternal death, and saved them from the everlasting fire? Is not this a greater and more stupendous miracle than the others I have mentioned?

Believe me, reader, I saw this virgin with my own eyes do many things for the benefit of the body, but they were as nothing compared with this. Here the Majesty of the Most High acted with power, and in a way truly superlative dropped the myrrh of his grace, graciously influencing and converting men given over to every kind of wickedness, hardened in their evil-doing and obstinate to the point of death, and reclaiming them to a final glorious salvation, when it was beyond anyone's power to bring them back to the faith or to hope for their salvation.

Another extraordinary conversion was obtained by the virgin, in the case of a person still alive.

There lived in Siena a certain Francesco dei Tolomei who by his wife Rabe had had many sons and daughters, the oldest of whom, Giacomo, had taken to a life of wickedness. Arrogant, worldly and viciously cruel, he had already killed two men, and he was so violent that even his own friends were afraid of him. He had no thought or fear of God, and in his completely unbridled way was going from bad to worse every day.

This man had a sister whose name was Ghinoccia, a woman entirely addicted to the pleasures of the world. Though she had retained her innocence, more from fear of what people would say than from fear of God, nevertheless she spent her life amidst vanities, making herself up and dressing up quite shamelessly. Their mother Rabe, who feared God and was afraid that her children would be damned, went to see the holy virgin, and begged her to have a word with them both, especially Ghinoccia, about the matter of their eternal salvation.

The virgin, with her great zeal for souls, was delighted to accept the task, and carried it out marvellously well, for as a result of her prayers and warnings Christ became so firmly impressed upon Ghinoccia's soul that she threw aside all the vanities of the world, cut off the hair that had been such a source of pride to her, and devoutly took the habit of the Sisters of Penance of St. Dominic. She spent the rest of her life, as I know for certain, in meditation and holy prayer, inflicting upon herself very harsh penances for which I occasionally found myself obliged to reprimand her.

Ghinoccia's sister Francesca followed her example, and she too took the habit; and it was splendid to see the two sisters, who had once loved the vanities of the world so much, now despising them so openly and utterly.

During the early stages of Ghinoccia's conversion Giacomo was out of Siena, but as soon as he got to know about the change in his sister's way of life he came rushing back to the city in a rage, with one of his younger brothers. On the way he kept threatening to tear the habit off his sister's back and to carry her off to the place where he lived outside the city, where she would have no one to encourage her to get up to such tricks. His young brother, inspired by heaven, said to him, "Giacomo, if you set foot in Siena you too will be converted and will confess your sins!" Whereupon the fellow began to curse the boy too in the most atrocious fashion, swearing that he would murder all friars and priests rather than go down on his knees before a single one of them. The youth merely went on repeating his prophecy, and the other his curses and threats; and so they reached Siena.

Giacomo rushed into his parents' home like a madman and made it clear that he would do terrible things if his sister did not get rid of that habit and come away and live with him. All this was not kept from the holy virgin. But his mother, Rabe, calmed her son down and asked him to wait till the next day at least.

When the morning came, she sent for Fra Tommaso, the holy virgin's confessor, who as though called to do so by God took Friar Bartolommeo di Domenico with him and went off to see Giacomo and spoke to him, but nothing would come of it. Meanwhile Catherine, who knew from God all about what was going on, was praying fervently for Giacomo's conversion. And what happened? What happened

When Catherine heard of this, she tried to get him to herself to talk to and so bring this unfortunate affair to an end, but Nanni avoided her as the snake avoids the charmer. In the end a holy man, a certain Friar William of England, of the Order of the Hermits of St. Augustine,[6] spoke to him, and got him to promise to go and see the virgin and listen to what she had to say; but he would not promise to do anything she told him. However, he kept his word and went to Catherine's house when I happened to be there, but he did not find her at home because she was out doing good to other souls.

While I was waiting for her, someone came and told me that Nanni was at the door wanting to speak to Catherine. I was glad to hear this, knowing how much the holy virgin wanted to see him, and I hurried down to tell him that the virgin was out and asked him to come in and wait for her. To encourage him I took him into her own austere little room; but it was not long before he began to grow impatient and said, "I promised Friar William to come here and listen to this lady, but seeing she's out and I'm a busy man I can't waste any more time. Please make my apologies to her and tell her that I have a lot of other things to attend to."

Seeing this and sad at the virgin's absence, I began to talk to him about the peace mentioned above, but he at once broke in. "See here," he said, "You are a priest and a Friar, and this religious woman is supposed to be a great saint, so I mustn't tell lies to you and I will tell you the whole truth; but don't imagine that that means that I have any intention of doing what you want me to do. It is true, I do stay in the background and disturb the peace now and again, and it is true that in this case the

---

6. William Flete, of the hermitage at Lecceto, was one of the Saint's most distinguished disciples. "He was a man of great penances," wrote Cristofano di Gano Guidini, "spending most of his time in the woods and only returning to the convent at nightfall. The only thing he drank was watered-down vinegar. Whence he was held in great reverence by the people. Now this man bad such a high opinion of the virgin that he almost made it a matter of conscience to touch the hem of her garment. He also used to say that people did not understand her and that the Pope ought to be glad to be one of her children, since the Holy Spirit was truly within her." He died in 1382.

whole thing would die down if I wanted it to; but that is not my idea at all, and it is no use preaching to me about it because I shall never agree with you, never. Let it be enough for you that I have told you what I have never told to another living soul, and don't bother me again!" I tried to answer him but he would not listen to a word I said.

At that moment God willed that the virgin should return home from doing good. The sight of her took Nanni aback and I was filled with joy. She greeted this man of the world with heavenly charity, then sat down and asked him why he had come. Nanni repeated word for word what he had said to me, insisting that he had no intention of mending his ways. Then the holy virgin began to point out the mortal peril he was in, and gradually she went after him, using words now biting, now sweet; but like a deaf adder he kept the ears of his heart tight shut against her. Realizing this, the virgin began to pray silently to herself and to ask for divine aid.

I saw what she was doing and turned to him, and, hoping for help from heaven, I began to talk, and by so doing kept him from going away. After a short while he said, "I don't want to be such a villain as to refuse you anything. I must go. I have four feuds; as to one of them [here he gave details], you can do what you like about it." Having said this he got up and made to go, but as he did so he exclaimed, "My God, how contented I feel in my soul from having said I shall make peace!" And he went on, "Lord God, what power is this that draws and holds me? I cannot go away and I cannot say no. Who has taken my liberty from me? What is it stopping me?" And with this he burst into tears. "I own myself beaten," he said, "I cannot breathe." He fell on his knees and said, weeping, "Most holy virgin, I will do as you say, not only as regards the enemy I told you about but with all the others too. I realize that the Devil has held me enchained; now I want to do anything you suggest. Tell me how I can save my soul from the Devil's clutches."

At these words the holy virgin, who had gone into ecstasy while she was praying, returned to her senses, thanked the Lord, and said, "O beloved brother, have you at last by the grace of God realized the mortal peril you are in? I talked to you, and you would not pay any attention; I spoke to the Lord, and He at once heard my prayer. So do penance for your sins, if you do not want to run into some new tribulation." To cut a long story short, Nanni with great grief confessed all his sins to me; through the virgin he was reconciled with all his enemies, and, following my advice, he was also reconciled with the Most High whom he had for so long offended.

A few days after Nanni had confessed, he was arrested by the Sienese authorities and put in prison. Finally a rumour spread that he was to be beheaded. When this news came to my ears I went in a state of great perturbation to Catherine and said to her, "Do you see? When this man was serving the Devil everything went well for him; now that he has returned to God, heaven and earth turn against him. Mother, I am afraid that this tender young shoot may be uprooted by this tempest and end up in desperation. Pray to the Lord for him! Protect him by your prayers during the time of his adversity, as with your prayers you saved him from the Devil!"

She answered, "Why are you getting so upset about him, when you should be pleased? If the Lord afflicts him with temporal punishments, you can be sure that he has forgiven him his eternal ones. According to the Saviour, the world first loved its own, but when He went out from the world, the world began to hate him. At first the Lord had destined this man for eternal punishment, but now in His mercy He has changed this into temporal punishment. Do not be afraid that he will give way to despair: He who saved him from the Devil will free him from prison too."

And it happened as she said. As a matter of fact Nanni was released from prison within a few days, though he had to suffer considerable loss of temporal goods. But the virgin was delighted about this, for she said, "The Lord has cleansed him of the poison that was infecting him."

Subsequently he was subjected to illnesses, and his devotion increased. By public deed he made a gift to the holy virgin of a magnificent castle of his about two miles out from Siena,[7] so that she could use it as a women's convent. Under special licence from Pope Gregory XI of holy memory, granted when I and all her other sons and daughters were present, she began to build a wall round it and turn it into a convent, calling it "Holy Mary, Queen of the Angels". The Supreme Pontiff's representative there was Friar Giovanni of the order of St. William of the monastery of St. Antimo, which I believe lies in the diocese of Chiusi.[8]

The transformation of this man's way of life was made by the Most High through Catherine, as I hereby testify. I was Nanni's confessor for a long time and I know that at least during the time of our acquaintance he did all he could to amend his life.

If to the facts clearly recorded I were to add all the other cases of conversion of the wicked, betterment and improvement of the good, or rather the well-disposed, courage infused into the weak, comfort given to the afflicted and troubled, spiritual warnings to those in danger, which the Lord performed through this venerable virgin His bride, I should have to write a whole series of large books. It is not possible for any man to remember the names of all the unfortunate people Catherine pulled back from the jaws of hell; all the hard-hearted sinners she brought back to belief; all the lovers of the world she taught to despise it, all the people tempted by every kind of temptation whom by her prayers and wisdom she saved from the wiles of the Devil; all those called by heaven whom she directed into the way of virtue; all those filled with holy intentions whom she helped to look for still greater graces; and lastly all she saved from

---

7. The castle of Belcaro.
8. Friar Giovanni di Gano da Orvieto was a man of holy life and one of the Saint's most devoted disciples. She herself called him "an angel on earth". It was his destiny to administer the last sacraments to Catherine and to assist her in her happy transit from this world to the next. He was the Abbot of Sant' Antimo. This abbey stood in the Val d'Orcia near Montalcino. It is said to have been built and endowed by Charlemagne for the Benedictines. In 1299 Pope Boniface VIII granted it to the Williamites, who held it until 1462, when Pius II created the diocese of Montalano and Pieviza and it came within the jurisdiction of that diocese.

the abyss of sin and by her labours and prayers bore almost on her own shoulders along the way of truth to the very end of their lives on earth. I can repeat St. Jerome's eulogy of St. Paula: "If all my bodily members were transformed into tongues, they would not suffice to describe the spiritual fruit produced by this virgin plant planted by the heavenly Father."

I have at times seen an endless stream of men and women coming down from the mountains and country towns around Siena, as though summoned by an invisible trumpet to see or hear Catherine, and I have seen them all stung with remorse not only by her words but at the mere sight of her and crying and sobbing over their own sins. They would run to the priests, including me, and confess with such compunction of heart that no one could doubt but that a great shower of graces had poured down upon them from heaven. And this did not simply happen once or twice, but again and again.

This was why Pope Gregory XI of happy memory, delighted and greatly encouraged by Catherine's rich harvest of souls, granted me and my two companions, by Apostolic brief, faculties equivalent to a bishop's, to absolve all who came to see the virgin and wanted to confess their sins; and the Truth who can neither deceive nor be deceived knows that we were visited by many people guilty of very serious sins, who had either never confessed before or had never received the sacrament of penance worthily. On many occasions both I and my two companions went without food until vespers and had still not heard all the people who wanted to make their confessions.

To make clear how far I was from responding to the success of this holy virgin's endeavours, I will let you know that so great was the crowd of people wanting to confess that I often felt tired and irritated because of the great amount of labour involved. But Catherine would be praying continuously, and like a true hunter of the Lord she would rejoice more and more whenever her prey was caught, and order her other sons and daughters to bear it to us, who were holding the net she had laid. It is difficult to give any idea of the joy that invaded her soul, and the sight of such happiness made such a powerful impression upon us that we forgot all about our tiredness.

This ends my account of the marvels that the Lord Almighty performed through this holy virgin for the good of souls. The chapter may seem a bit long to some readers, but not to me, because in fact I have left out such a lot.

Now it is fitting that we should pass on to the miracles that the virgin performed for the good of the body; but as this present chapter which has dealt with souls is already over-long, so as not to draw it out any further let us here draw it to a close.

CHAPTER EIGHT

An Incomparable Doer of Good

———————————•———————————

I AM about to tell a story that may seem beyond belief in our day, good reader, but nevertheless it was quite possible to Him to whom all things are possible.

Although the holy virgin's mother Lapa was a woman of great simplicity and uprightness of life, at the same time she had never been much concerned with the goods of the spirit; as a result of which she hated the thought that she would one day die, as will be seen clearly from the following story.

After her husband's death she was attacked by an illness that grew worse every day; whereupon the virgin consecrated to God had recourse to prayer, pleading with the Lord to deign to succour her who had brought her into the world and brought her up, and to bring her back to health. The answer she got from heaven was that it would be providential for her mother to die at this time, as this would prevent her from seeing the misfortunes that would otherwise befall her.

Having had this reply, Catherine went back to her mother and told her as gently as she could that if the Lord was disposed to call her to Himself she should resign herself without any feelings of sadness to His will. But Lapa, attached to life as she was, was horrified by the idea, and begged her daughter to pray to the Lord to get her better, and implored her never to mention the word death to her again.

The bride of Christ, saddened, indeed agonized, by this, fervently implored the Lord not to allow her mother to die until she herself was sure that her mother's soul was prepared to do the divine will. God in a way heeded the virgin's words, for, though the illness seemed to get worse from time to time, death did not dare to strike. Catherine thus became a mediator between the Lord and her mother. She begged the Lord not to take Lapa out of the world against her will, and at the same time urged her mother to consent to the Lord's designs. But though the virgin's prayers had succeeded to a certain extent in restraining the divine Omnipotence, her exhortations had no effect on her mother's weak soul. So the Lord said to His bride, "Tell your mother, who does not want to depart from the body now, that the time will come when she will ask for death with a great longing and will not be able to have it."

I, and many others with me, know that these words proved to be absolutely true, and there is no use trying to hide the fact. Right to the very end of her life misfortunes befell Lapa, with respect to both people and things, to all of which she was so firmly attached; so that she used to say to everyone she spoke to, "But why has God put my soul into my body askew, so that it cannot get out? So many of my sons and daughters, and nephews young and old, have died before me. Am I alone not to be allowed to die, despite the torture and affliction of all these miseries?"

To get back to our subject: Lapa remained true to her nature and did not confess or pay any attention to her soul. The Lord wanted to shine in His bride, and for her sake denied her things that earlier if she had prayed for them He would have granted. In fact, after delaying Lapa's death for a long time He suddenly permitted her to die without confession, in order to show how much merit the holy virgin had in his eyes. For Catherine raised her eyes to heaven and said, weeping, "Lord my God, are these the promises you made to me, that none of my house should go to hell? Are these the things that in your mercy you agreed with me, that my mother should not be taken out of the world against her will? Now I find that she has died without the sacraments of the Church. By your infinite mercy I beg you not to let me be defrauded like this. As long as there is life in my body I shall not move from here until you have restored my mother to me alive."

There were present at this death, and these words, three women of Siena whose names are given further on; they saw Lapa breathe her last, touched her dead body, and would even have started to do the things that always have to be done when someone dies, if they had not wanted to wait for the virgin, who was praying. As those who were once carrying the corpse to the sepulchre stopped when the Lord touched the bier, so, by inspiration of the same Saviour, those present did not move anything while the virgin was praying.

The virgin prayed, and the cries of her heart ascended to highest heaven; all her grief, united with her humble, copious tears, rose up before the eyes of the Most High; and then it was impossible that she should not be heard. And in fact the Lord of all comfort and mercy did hear her. Before the eyes of the three women present, Lapa's body suddenly began to move; her soul was restored and she again made the movements of a living person; and she lived to the age of eighty-nine, encompassed by many sorrows that came upon her—poverty, and the other misfortunes she suffered, as by the Lord's command had been foretold her by her daughter.

Eye-witnesses of the miracle were Caterina di Ghetto and Angela di Vannino, now members of the Sisters of Penance of St. Dominic, and also Lisa, the virgin's sister-in-law and Lapa's daughter-in-law, all of whom are still living and resident in Siena. All three saw Lapa expire after a serious illness lasting many days, saw her inanimate body, and the virgin praying, and also clearly heard Catherine's words when she said, "Lord, these are not the promises you made me." After a short time they then saw Lapa's body begin to move and return to life, and all its members perform their accustomed movements. Of the time she lived after that, there are a whole host of witnesses.

From all this, good reader, it can be seen what great merit the holy virgin must have had in the eyes of the Almighty, if He was prepared to save her father's soul from the pains of Purgatory and miraculously restore her dead mother to life. But in case you are tempted to imagine that this was the only miracle she performed for the good of the body, pay attention to those that are about to follow. But first I must assure you that what I have said about the Lord's words to the virgin I had from her when I was questioning her in private about her most intimate secrets, and the rest I found in the writings of her first confessor Fra Tommaso, who puts the miracle as having occurred in the October of the year of Our Lord 1370, in the presence of the witnesses already named.

Here is another miracle for you, which as to its time is more recent than the others; and since I had personal experience of it, therefore, apart from the person on whom it was performed, no one knows more about it than I do.

About seventeen years ago, we being now in the year 1390, I found myself under obedience in Siena, exercising the office of lector in the monastery belonging to my Order. While I was thus serving God to the best of my poor abilities, the plague of the groin, which has so often devastated the world in our day, broke out in Siena too, and it was so serious that men and women of all ages succumbed to it and within a space of two or three days passed from life to death, to the great terror of all.[1]

Our Order being founded on zeal for souls, I too was obliged to expose my life to the general danger, and day and night I visited the sick, often retiring for rest and recuperation to the hospital of S. Maria della Misericordia, which stands in the city, a thing which I was especially glad to do as its rector and head at that time was a certain Matteo,

---

1. The plague made its first appearance in Siena in May 1348. It was a real scourge. After that it made other appearances. In the epidemic of 1374 a great number of children died—in Catherine's family alone the servant, six of Bartolo's sons, and one of the Benincasa daughters; all of whom Catherine buried with her own hands, saying merrily, "Now I shall never lose them again."

who is still alive.[2] He was a man of praiseworthy life, highly esteemed by all, and he was very fond of Catherine in the spirit of charity. I loved him dearly, and still do, for the virtues that heaven had granted him. For the reason I have stated, and also for the sake of helping the poor people who were in such a miserable condition there, I was in the habit of seeing him at least once a day.

One morning after attending Mass in the monastery I went out on my visits to the sick and called in at the "Misericordia" to find out how the citizens who had been hit by the plague were getting on. As I went in I found Matteo being carried from the church to his own room by the brothers and clerks, like one dead. He had lost his usual colour and also all his strength and power of speech, for when I asked him how he felt he was unable to reply. I was very upset and I turned to the people who were carrying this very dear friend of mine and asked them what had happened to him. The reply I got was, "Last night, at about seven, while he was tending one of the sick, the plague attacked him in the groin and in a short time reduced him to the state in which you now see him." Upon hearing this I felt very sad, and I followed the company to Matteo's bed, where, as soon as he lay down, he recovered his spirits and called me over, and, as usual, confessed his sins.

Having given him absolution, I asked him how he felt and he said, "I have such a pain in my groin that it feels as though my thigh is breaking, and a dreadful pain in my head, which seems to have been split into four different pieces." After these words I felt his pulse and found he was suffering from a very high fever, whereupon I suggested to the people present that they should take a sample of his urine to a very good, conscientious doctor called Master Senso, who is still alive; and a little later I went off to see him myself.

---

2. Matteo di Cenni di Fazio was a Sienese nobleman of signal virtue, as Bl. Raymond testifies, and for that reason very dear to the holy virgin. He was made Rector of the Misericordia on September 1st, 1373.

The doctor, having tested the sample, decided at once that my friend had caught the plague, and also said that he had discovered fatal symptoms in the urine; and turning to me he said, "This water shows that there is blood in the liver, a common feature of this pestilence; and I am therefore afraid that the Misericordia will soon find itself without its worthy rector."

"Don't you think it possible for medical science to find some sort of remedy?" I asked. "Tonight," replied the doctor, "You can try purging his blood with cassia juice,³ but I have not much faith in it because the illness is so far advanced."

Made very melancholy by this news, I left the doctor and returned to the sick man, praying God to leave such an exemplary person in the world for all our sakes.

In the meantime the holy virgin had heard that Matteo had been struck down by the plague. As she was very fond of him because of his virtues, she hastened to see him, fired by charity and as though angry with the plague itself, and even before she reached him she started shouting from a distance, "Get up, Messer Matteo, get up, this is no time for lying in a soft bed!" At the words of this command the fever and the swelling in the groin and all the pain immediately disappeared, and Matteo felt as well as if he had never been ill at all. Nature had obeyed God through the mouth of the virgin, and at the sound of her voice his body had been restored to perfect health. Matteo got up as cheerful as a cricket, convinced that the power of God dwelt in the virgin, and went away rejoicing.

After the miracle, the virgin, to avoid being praised, hurried away; but as she was coming out of the house I came in, still very upset, and, not knowing what had happened, and imagining that Matteo was still

---

3. *Cassia*: a genus of plant of the Cisalpine family. The best known species in Europe is *cassia fistula*, from which is obtained what is commonly known as "cassia pulp", which is black, sweetish, astringent, and is used freely in a variety of homemade medicines. The small leaves of several species become senna pods, which are widely used as a drastic purgative by country people.

in the throes of the plague fever, I was so aggrieved when I saw her that I said, rather heatedly, "Mother, are you going to allow this man who is so dear and useful to us to die?" Whereupon, although she knew quite well what had happened, she answered most humbly, almost as though she was offended by what I had said, "What is this you are saying? Do you think I am God, to be able to deliver mortal human beings from death?" At this, being so unhappy, I said shortly, "You can say that to anyone else, but not to me, for I know your secrets, and I know that anything you ask the Lord for is always granted." Lowering her head, she gave a little smile, then, looking up at me with happiness written all over her face, she said, "Cheer up, he won't die this time."

At this my sadness left me, for I knew what power had been granted her by heaven, and leaving her I entered the invalid's room quite calmly and found him sitting on his bed, describing the miracle performed by the virgin with great satisfaction. I immediately told him that the holy virgin had assured me that he was not going to die of the plague, and he said, "Don't you know what she did for me by coming here in person?" I said no, and that she had only told me what I had just told him. Whereupon Matteo got up off his bed and described what I have related above.

To show still further how great the miracle was: the table was laid, and we all sat down to it, including Matteo. We ate food that was not for invalids but for people in the best of health, vegetables with raw onions. And he who had been unable to touch the lightest of foods ate with us; laughed and joked with us, when only a few hours before he had hardly been able to open his mouth. We were all in a state of delighted amazement, and kept giving thanks to the Lord for having granted us such an exceptional grace through the virgin, and we went on praising her to each other, absolutely dumbfounded by what had happened.

The other witness to this miracle besides me who is still alive is Friar Niccolo di Andrea, of Siena, a member of the Order of Friar Preachers; he was present that morning at all that I have described. It was also seen by all the people in the Misericordia, clerks and priests and a score and more of others.

Take care, reader, not to let yourself be deceived by the incredulity of those who are uncircumcised in their hearts and ears! (*Acts* 7:51). For those whose hearts have not been touched by God may say, "What is there exceptional about a man being cured of an illness, however serious it may have been? It is the kind of thing that is happening every day." I answer, what was there exceptional about the Lord curing Simon's mother-in-law, who according to the Evangelist had been taken ill with a high fever? Every day men are being cured of fevers, as high as you like. Why then does the Evangelist present it as a miracle? Listen, you unbelievers, who understand nothing except what concerns the senses! Listen to what the Evangelist says: "And standing over her, he commanded the fever and it left her. And immediately rising, she ministered to them." (*Luke* 4:39). You see what the sign of the miracle was: at the Lord's command, without any delay and without the help of any medicine, the fever disappeared, and she who was gravely oppressed by the fever at once arose without any remedy being administered to her.

So you can see quite clearly what happened in this case of ours, at least you can if your mind is not darkened and blinded. This holy virgin appears on the scene; in her breast the Lord lives; and this Lord, in the same way as He cured Simon's wife's mother, being not near her but far away, commands the fever and plague, and these without any help from nature immediately leave Matteo, who, getting up out of bed, begins to eat vegetables and onions with us, like a man in the best of health. So open the eyes of your minds and be not faithless but believing! (*John* 20:27).

As we have mentioned the Misericordia, I may be allowed to relate another extraordinary event that took place in that vicinity and was performed by the holy virgin even earlier than the one just mentioned. I first heard about it from Matteo when I was talking to him in the Misericordia itself.

I was told, then, by Matteo, who was the rector of the house, and Fra Tommaso, the virgin's confessor, and almost all the others who knew the things that Catherine had done, that a very devout woman who was also, if I remember rightly, one of the Sisters of Penance of

St. Dominic, had been living in the neighbourhood. Having heard of Catherine, and perhaps having seen her virtuous way of life, she had become friendly with her and always did as she suggested, following her example and venerating her with a devotion beyond words.

One day this woman was standing on the balcony of her house when, weighed down as it was with all the stuff that had been put on it, it opened under her feet and she went hurtling down along with everything else, and found herself cut and bruised among the débris. People ran up and dragged her out of the heap of wood and stone, believing her to be either dead or on the point of death, but, thanks be to God, when they managed to get her on to her bed, she was still alive and in fact revived a little; then, feeling herself to be all cuts and bruises, with shrieks and tears she began to signify to the people present where the pain was. Doctors were called, appropriate remedies applied, but the poor woman still could not move in the bed without assistance and was tormented by one pain after another.

When the virgin consecrated to God heard about this mishap, she felt very sorry for her sister and friend and went to see her and tried to comfort her, urging her to be patient. Seeing that she was suffering such agonies, she touched the parts that were hurting her as though soothing them, and the victim allowed her to do so because she was sure that only good could come from contact with her.

As the virgin's hand passed from one painful spot to another, the pain vanished. When she realized this, the woman begged Catherine to put her hand on one particular spot, which the virgin did willingly, for her one desire was to comfort her; and there too the pain vanished. Again the woman made her request and again the virgin responded, and one by one she touched all the places that were painful, and in a short time all the pain had gone; until the moment came when she who a little while before had been unable to make the slightest bodily movement began to turn this way and that, obviously quite recovered. But so as not to embarrass the virgin she said nothing until she had departed; then to everybody there, doctors and neighbours alike, she said, "Catherine, Mother Lapa's daughter, has cured me by touching me!" Everyone was absolutely amazed and gave thanks to the Creator for having given Catherine such power. It was as clear as daylight to them that the recovery could only have come about through the power of God. I got to know about this miracle from others, because it happened before I knew the virgin and before I went to live in Siena.

And now, to the glory of God and Catherine, let us pass on to the miracles that I myself saw and heard.

During the plague mentioned above, a certain hermit called Santi, a saint in name and a saint in deed, who had for a long time been leading an exemplary life of poverty in the city of Siena, fell a victim to it. The virgin learned of this and at once had him moved from his hermitage outside the city to the Misericordia, where she went to see him with her companions and ordered him to be given all the attention he required. Then, going up to him, she whispered softly into his ear, "Have no fear; however ill you may be you won't die this time." To us, when we kept asking her to pray for his recovery, she would not say a word; so that it seemed to us that she nevertheless felt certain that he was bound to die. This made us sadder than ever, for we felt united with Santi in his sufferings because of the friendship that bound us to him.

Santi got worse hourly, and we began to despair of his bodily health and to transfer our attention to the health of his soul. Finally he seemed to lose all his strength, and we waited sadly for him to breathe his last.

In the meantime the virgin of the Lord had returned, and she said again in his ear, "Don't be afraid, because you won't die." He already seemed to us to have lost the use of his senses, but he heard her perfectly and had more faith in what she said than in the death he felt to be so near. And in fact the virgin's words triumphed over nature, and the power of God, more certain than anything human and far beyond our human imagining, brought his well-nigh dead body back to life.

While we were waiting for Santi to breathe out his spirit and were preparing for his funeral, the time at which people generally die of the plague came and went and his agony kept us in suspense for several days.

In the end the virgin came back again, and whispered to the sick man, "I command you, in the name of our Lord Jesus Christ, not to die." It was no sooner said than done. The dying man revived, his strength returned, he sat up in bed and asked for something to eat; and in a short time he was completely recovered and lived for many years. He was present at the holy virgin's death and lived for a long time afterwards.

Santi—who was well named, for he was truly a "saint"—told us later what the virgin had whispered into his ear, and how he had felt the strength of her power holding back his spirit when it was about to issue from his body. He told everyone that it was no natural power that had cured him but the Divine Power alone, and added that he regarded the miracle as a real, genuine resuscitation. The sanctity of his life and his natural prudence guaranteed that he was to be believed in everything he said. For nearly thirty-six years he had been living an absolutely blameless life as an anchorite and he was held in the greatest esteem by all who knew him.

So far I have been speaking of others; now it is time for me to speak of the miracles that Catherine did for me.

The plague, as I have said, having broken out in Siena, I thought it incumbent upon me, for the good of souls, to expose myself to the risk of death, and I decided not to neglect any of the sick, even though, as is known, wherever the plague appears it infects the atmosphere and the people. I told myself that Christ was a good deal more powerful than Galen,[4] and grace more powerful than nature; I also saw that many people were leaving the city so that the dying were being left without spiritual advice or help; and so from charity, which obliged me to love the souls of my neighbours more than my own body, I made a firm

---

4. The Greek philosopher and physician, born in Pergamo in A.D. 131. At the age of twenty-one he went to Smyrna, where he attended the school of the celebrated anatomist Pelope. In 164 he arrived in Rome, and the fame of his learning was so great that he became Marcus Aurelius's physician. He died in 210.

decision, encouraged by the virgin, to visit as many of the sick as I could and comfort and instruct them. This I did, with God's help, and according to the grace granted me.

But I was almost alone in the big city, and many were the calls I had from the sick, so that I was always leaving the monastery and hardly had time to eat and sleep or even breathe.

One night, after I had had my usual brief rest, I was about to get up to say lauds, when I felt a great pain in my groin. Touching it with my hand, I found it was a swelling. I was so scared that I hadn't the courage to get up, and I began to think I was dying. I longed for the daylight to come, so that I could go and see the virgin before it got any worse. In the meantime the inevitable fever and headache came down upon me. Then I really did get worried, but I forced myself to finish saying lauds.

As soon as it was light I got hold of a fellow Friar and went as best I could to the virgin's home; but for the moment it was a fruitless journey as she was not there, having gone off to see someone else who was sick. I decided to wait for her but, being unable to stand up on my feet, was obliged to lie down on a bed that was there, urging the people in the house to send for her as quickly as they could; which they did.

When she arrived, and saw the state I was in, realizing what the matter was she knelt down by the bed and, putting her hand on my forehead, began to pray silently. I saw her go into ecstasy as on the other occasions, and waited for something unusual to happen for the good of my soul and body. I remained in this state of mind for about half an hour, and during this time I felt certain symptoms over my whole body which made me fear that I was going to die from suffocation by sickness, a thing that I had already seen happen to a number of people. But it did not happen; instead, it seemed as though something was being violently drawn out of me, through all my bodily extremities at once. Then I began to feel better, and bit by bit I recovered. Before the virgin returned to her senses I was quite better; I still, it is true, felt a bit weak, but that must have been a sign that the disease had been cured, or else that my faith was not quite solid enough.

As soon as the virgin of the Lord had obtained complete grace for me from her Heavenly Bridegroom, knowing that I was cured she returned to her senses and ordered a convalescent's meal to be prepared for me. This was done, I took the food from her own holy hands, and then she advised me to take a little rest, which obediently and gratefully I did.

When I got up, I found myself as well as if I had never been ill. Seeing that I was better, Catherine said, "Go and work for the good of souls, and give thanks to the Highest for freeing you from this danger." And so I returned to my accustomed labours, giving praise to the Lord for granting Catherine such power.

She performed the same kind of miracle again during the plague in the case of Friar Bartolommeo di Domenico of Siena, who was my companion at the time and is now Provincial of the Roman Province. This second miracle was greater than the first, because Friar Bartolommeo was attacked by the plague more seriously than I had been and in his case it lasted longer too. For reasons of space I shall not go into detail, being in a hurry to get on to others more widely known and, in my opinion, more important, although, for the same reason of space, I shall have to omit many of them.

However, dear reader, I must point out that the virgin of the Lord did not only perform these miraculous cures during the plague in her own city of Siena, but at other places and other times too, as, if you pay attention, you will discover from what I am about to say.

When the plague was over, many persons of both sexes, both religious and layfolk, and particularly a number of monks in Pisa who had heard of the virgin's great renown, had a great longing to see her and hear her doctrine, which was said to be marvellous, as it truly was. Being in many cases unable to undertake the journey, they asked her repeatedly, by letter or messenger, if she would go to Pisa. In their attempts to persuade her they assured her that her presence would mean a great harvest of souls to God's greater glory. Catherine, although she had always avoided going on any journeys, was touched by these oft repeated invitations and turned as usual to her Heavenly Bridegroom to ask Him in all humility whether or not she should go. Meanwhile, some of her friends tried to persuade her to go, others tried to persuade her not to.

After a few days, as she told me in secret, the Lord appeared to her as usual and told her not to waste any time, but to satisfy the desire of His servants and maidens in Pisa. As a true daughter of obedience, she humbly accepted the injunction, and after telling me about it and getting my consent she set off.

I went with her, with a few Friars of my Order, to hear confessions, for many of those who came to see her, after hearing her ardent words, would repent with all their hearts, and to prevent the age-old Enemy from snatching them from her grasp she would tell them to go off to the priest at once and make a proper confession. As they sometimes had to wait for lack of confessors, and she might be disappointed in her hopes of them, she was glad to have a few Fathers with her to administer the sacrament of penance. For this reason Pope Gregory XI of happy memory published a Bull giving me and two of my companions the equivalent of a bishop's powers to absolve anyone prompted to go to confession by hearing Catherine.

On arriving in Pisa the virgin was put up in the house of one of the citizens, Gherardo dei Buonconti.[5]

One day this Gherardo brought a youth of about twenty years of age home with him and introduced him to the virgin, asking her to pray for his health. He told her that he had been plagued almost continuously for eighteen months by quotidian fever; he had lost all his strength and there was no medicine that seemed to give it back to him. The young man's thin, pale face confirmed these words.

The virgin, moved to compassion, at once asked the youth how long it was since he had been to confession, and when he replied many years she said, "And that is why the Lord has willed that you should

---

5. Three Buonconti brothers were followers of the Saint—Gherardo, Tommaso and Francesco—and they very often accompanied her on her travels.

have this illness, because you have gone so long without purging your soul by making a holy confession. Dearest son, go and confess without delay, and spew up all the rottenness of the sins that have infected your soul and body." Then she called her first confessor Fra Tommaso, and put the sick youth in his charge, so that he could hear his confession and absolve him from his sins.

As soon as the young man had confessed he went back to Catherine who put her arm round his shoulders and said, "Go, son, with the peace of our Lord Jesus Christ, for I do not want you to suffer from the fever any more." Those were her words, and so it turned out, for from that moment he showed not the slightest trace of fever. There was hidden in the virgin the power of Him who no sooner spoke than the thing was done: He gave His command, and in a flash everything was created. (*Psalm* 32:9). Several days went by, and then the youth came back to see the virgin, quite cured, and before all the people present he said that since the miracle he had not felt out of sorts in any way at all.

I was myself a witness of this event, so that I can say with John: "And he that saw it hath given testimony: and his testimony is true." (*John* 19:35). Also present were Gherardo and his mother and the rest of the household; Fra Tommaso, the virgin's confessor and in this instance confessor to the sick man too; Friar Bartolommeo di Domenico, my companion then and now; and all the women who had come with the virgin from Siena.

The cured man himself spread the news of the miracle abroad in Pisa. Some years later I passed through the city and he came to see me, and I could hardly recognize him, he had grown so fat and strong; and giving thanks to God and the virgin again in the presence of all who were with me, he told me all about the miracle all over again, just as I have described it.

Another event of the same kind, if not more marvellous still because the malady was more dangerous, had taken place earlier in Siena.

There was a certain Sister of Penance of St. Dominic called Gemma, who was very fond of the holy virgin. She suffered from a complaint of the throat that doctors call quinzy. When the secretion began to descend from the head to the throat she failed to do anything about it and so aggravated the condition that the treatment that had at first seemed to do it good became absolutely ineffective. The inside of her throat, which was already constricted to begin with, was growing more constricted every day and threatening to suffocate the poor woman. As soon as she realized this she plucked up her courage and went to see the virgin, who at that time was living quite near by.

She found her at home, and speaking as best she could said to her, "Mother, I shall die if you don't come to my assistance." When Catherine saw how serious it was, she had compassion on the woman, who could hardly breathe, and putting her hand in faith on her throat made the sign of the cross over her, and cured her at once.

And so Gemma, who had come to her in tears and trembling, was able to go off home well and happy. Not to show herself ungrateful, she went to see Fra Tommaso and told him about the miracle, and he put it down in writing. I have taken this account from him.

Writing about these miracles that Catherine did for the good of the bodies of her relatives and friends brings others worth recording back into my mind, which I myself witnessed along with other people still alive.

When Pope Gregory XI returned to Rome from Avignon, the holy virgin came on ahead with her followers, of whom I was one. When we got to Genoa we stopped to wait for the Pope and the Roman Court, who intended to spend a few days resting there before going on to Rome. Catherine's stay in Genoa lasted for over a month. With us were two devout young men, natives of Siena, who used to take down her letters; they are still living virtuous religious lives. One of them is called Neri di Landoccio dei Pagliaresi, who now lives a solitary life almost like that of an anchorite. The other, Stefano di Corrado de Maconi, entered the Carthusian order as the result of an order that the virgin gave him on her death-bed; with the help of divine grace he has made such progress that in Italy a great part of his Order depends upon him and is ruled by his visits, exhortations and example. He has been Prior in one monastery after another, and at the moment is Prior to the Carthusians in Milan; he is known to everybody as a man of great energy and wisdom.

These two were witnesses with me and other men and women of almost all the miracles described in the second section of this book. But during our stay in Genoa the Lord through this virgin performed a miracle on these two people themselves.

While we were in Genoa, then, Neri was taken ill with a horrible complaint which made not only him but all the rest of us very unhappy. He was tormented continuously day and night by atrocious pains in his bowels; when the attacks came upon him he would howl piteously, and no bed could hold him. Being unable to stand upright, he would crawl round amongst all the beds in the room as though trying to escape from the pain; it was upsetting for him and for us too.

I spoke to the virgin about it and so did some of the others, but although she seemed sorry she did not take it upon herself to adopt her usual method of prayer to mitigate these sufferings, nor did she give us any reason to believe that she would soon have the sufferer cured. In fact she told me to call the doctors in and get him to have the usual medical treatment. She told me to do this at once; so I got hold of two doctors and we followed their instructions meticulously; but Neri, instead of getting better, got worse. I believe that this happened because the Lord willed to appear more marvellous in His bride. The doctors in fact continued to treat him, but as there was no improvement in his condition they told me that they had lost all hope of saving him. When I passed this news on to the Friars and the rest of the company at supper, Stefano, full of grief but full of faith too, got up from the table and went into the virgin's room. With tears in his eyes he threw himself at her feet and asked her humbly but impetuously not to let his brother and companion, who had come on this journey from love of God and herself, to be taken from the land of the living and his corpse left on foreign soil.

The affectionate virgin answered him like a fond mother: "My son, why lament and upset yourself? If God wants to reward your brother Neri for his labours, you should be happy about it, not upset." "Mother," he replied, "I beg you to listen to me and help him, for I am sure you can if you want to . . ." And, unable to hide her motherly affection, Catherine said, "I have tried to get you to conform yourself to the divine will, but as I see you are so cast down, remind me of it tomorrow morning when I go to Mass to receive Holy Communion, and I promise I will pray to the Lord. And you pray to God to hear me."

This promise pacified Stefano and the next morning he went and knelt before the virgin in good time before she went off to Mass and said to her, "Mother, I beg you not to let me be cheated of my desire." During Mass she received Communion and after the usual ecstasy came back to her senses. At once, turning to Stefano, who was waiting for her, she said, "You have obtained the grace you wanted." "Are you sure, Mother?" he said. "Will Neri get better?" "Of course he will get better," she said. "The Lord has given him back to us."

Stefano at once ran off to the invalid to encourage him in the Lord. In the meantime the doctors came along and discovered that he had taken such a turn for the better that they began not to despair and even admitted that he might be cured. Meanwhile Neri, in accordance with what the virgin had said, got better and better, until he was completely cured.

When Neri was quite well again, Stefano, partly as a result of over-work and partly because of his excitement during his friend's illness, incurred a high fever and vomitings, accompanied by a bad headache. He was obliged to take to his bed, and as we were all very fond of him we were all sorry and did our best to help him.

The virgin too, when she heard the bad news, was upset about it and went to see him. She asked him how he felt, and when she touched him and realized that he had a violent fever, she said in a sudden fervour of spirit, "I command you by the power of holy obedience not to suffer from this fever any longer." Marvellous! Nature obeyed the virgin's voice as though it had been the voice of the Creator Himself coming down from heaven, for without the help of any natural remedy, before the virgin had gone away from his bed, the fever had disappeared and Stefano was perfectly all right again.

As you may imagine, we were highly delighted to have our Stefano among us again, and we gave thanks to the Lord, who in the space of a few days had performed two such amazing miracles through His bride.

To these two miracles I shall add a third, which, though I did not see it with my own eyes as I was not there at the time, can be testified to by the person who was its subject, for she is still alive. I shall describe it as she described it to me. What she says can be guaranteed by other women still alive who were with the holy virgin at the time. The person concerned, then, is one of the Sisters of Penance of St. Dominic, a Sienese woman but not living in Siena, and her name is Giovanna di Capo.

Gregory XI had returned to Rome, and he summoned Catherine to Florence to negotiate the peace between himself and his rebellious sons—a task in which she was entirely successful, as will be explained in a separate chapter.

The infernal Dragon, the author and fomenter of all discord and the enemy of all unity, raised up so many scandals in the city, even against the bride of Jesus Christ, who was devoting all her efforts to procuring peace, that if I once began describing them I should never end, and we should get right away from our story. Nevertheless, all that happened as a result of the machinations of the virgin's enemies will be described in the promised chapter.

Well, then, while the holy virgin was in Florence at the Pope's request, the age-old Enemy raised up such awful scandals against her that a number of devout believers advised her to leave the city for a while, to give the furore a chance to die down. Prudent and humble as she was, Catherine accepted their advice, but said that, being under divine orders, she would never leave the city's territory until peace and concord had been achieved between the Supreme Pontiff and Florence. And so it turned out.

She was preparing to leave the city for a time and go to a place belonging to the Florentines when Giovanna unexpectedly fell ill. For no apparent reason one of her feet swelled up and she also had a fever. Handicapped as she was by these two complaints, she found it impossible to accompany the rest of the party. The virgin did not want to leave her behind on her own for fear that she might be insulted by some of the ungodly people in the city, and so she took to prayer, calling upon her Heavenly Bridegroom to help her and make some merciful provision for the event. The Lord did not suffer her to be in doubt for long.

The sick woman fell into a sweet sleep while Catherine was praying and when she woke up she found herself perfectly well again. She got up out of bed and prepared for the journey, and that same morning she was travelling along the road with the virgin and the rest of the party, more hale and hearty than she had been for years. The others, who had seen how she had been suffering, were full of amazement and gave thanks to Almighty God, who through His bride had performed miracles on the bodies of those who accompanied her.

I will relate another miracle which the Lord performed through Catherine in Toulon, a city in Provence, when we were on our way back from Avignon at the time of the Pope's return to Rome.

We had arrived in Toulon and put up at an inn. Catherine, as usual, retired at once to her room. We took good care not to tell a soul whom we had with us, but the stones, so to speak, had begun to publish abroad the news that the holy virgin was in the city, and first women, then men, began to arrive at the inn, asking where this holy woman was who was on her way to the Roman Court. Then the innkeeper gave the whole game away, and we could not deny it; and so we were obliged to allow the women at least to come in and see the virgin.

One of the women had a little boy on her back who was all swollen up, especially in his stomach; he looked an absolute monster; and all the women begged the virgin of the Lord to deign to take the child in her arms. At first, to avoid the world's praises, Catherine made a gesture of refusal; but then, overcome by pity and the people's faith, she consented. She had hardly taken the little boy in her arms when he began to expel wind, and his body was seen to go down and recover perfect health.

This miracle did not take place while I was there, but it was so widely spoken of that the bishop of the city sent for me, and when I had described the miracle to him he told me that the boy was this vicar's nephew. In fact he went on to ask me to get him an interview with the holy virgin, which I did.

I will end by saying that many more miracles, not recorded in this book, were indubitably performed by the Lord through His bride for the benefit of the body. But even the few that I have described should be enough, my good reader, to make you feel reasonably convinced that in Catherine lived Jesus, the Son of God and the Madonna, and the true author of all miracles.

And now, since this chapter is on the cure of bodily ailments, I should really discuss the cases in which people were freed from evil spirits, but as it has already gone on so long, and as the holy virgin manifested a special grace in these things, I have decided to end the chapter here and leave them all for the next chapter.

CHAPTER NINE

The Devil's Enemy

———————————•———————————

F ROM what we have said, dear reader, you will have been able to see
how the Heavenly Bridegroom lost no opportunity of demonstrating visibly the power He had granted His bride, the fact being that fire cannot be hidden nor can the tree planted near the running waters fail to bring forth its fruit in due season. (*Psalm* 1:3). The power, then, of our Lord Jesus Christ, or rather the Lord Jesus Himself hidden in our virgin's breast, appeared increasingly every day and in a variety of ways. Catherine pleaded to heaven for divine grace for all sinners, as we have explained in Chapter Seven; healed the sick or brought the dead to life, as we have shown in Chapter Eight; and commanded evil spirits, and cast them out of the bodies of the possessed. In these ways the things of heaven and earth and hell were subject to her, in the name of the Lord Jesus who lived in her. You will see this clearly if you attend to what follows.

There was in Siena a man known according to the custom of the place as Ser Michele di Ser Monaldo; he was a highly respected notary and clerk, who came to see me hundreds of times and told me all that I am about to write.

At an advanced age, being married with two young daughters, he decided, with his wife's consent, to devote himself to the service of God and to dedicate his daughters, who were unmarried, to Christ the Lord.

216

To this end he visited the convent of virgins in Siena dedicated to St. John the Baptist, and here he gave himself and all he had to God and St. John. He left his daughters in the company of the other enclosed nuns there, while he himself lived with his wife in the guests' quarters and for the love of God became the convent's bursar.

After some time had elapsed one of Ser Michele's daughters, Lorenza, who was about eight years of age, was, by one of God's just but inscrutable judgements, attacked and invaded by the Devil. When the age-old Enemy tormented her, and this happened frequently and in a very violent way, the whole community was frightened and upset, and the nuns finally decided that they had had enough of her and obliged Ser Michele to remove her from the convent.

As soon as Lorenza had been taken away it was discovered that the evil spirit that was plaguing her was in the habit of speaking a very elegant form of Latin through her mouth, despite the fact that the child knew nothing about that language, and could solve deep and difficult problems and reveal the sins and state of conscience of particular individuals; in fact it was quite clear, in many other ways too, that an evil spirit was for some reason incomprehensible to human beings being divinely permitted to torment the innocent girl.

The parents and relatives were naturally upset about this, and did all they could to find some way of driving the evil spirit out of the girl. They took her to visit the relics of various saints, hoping that their merits and power might drive the wicked spirit away. They had special faith in the blessed Friar Ambrogio,[1] of the Order of Preachers, who has been performing miracles for over a hundred years and had and still

---

1. Blessed Ambrogio Sansedoni was born in April, 1220, in Siena. When he was seventeen he became a Dominican. Because of his exceptional gifts, his superiors sent him to the University of Paris, where one of his masters was St. Albert the Great and one of his fellow students St. Thomas Aquinas. He taught in Cologne, was a graceful and effective preacher, a peacemaker between his city and Clement IV, and ambassador of peace in Florence, Pisa, Genoa and Venice. He died, after a life spent in the service of God and his neighbour, in March 1288.

has an extraordinary faculty for driving away unclean spirits—to such an extent, as I have seen many times with my own eyes, that his cappa or scapular, both of which are still preserved intact, are enough to drive evil spirits out of the possessed.

And so they took her to the church of the Friar Preachers, placed her on the blessed Friar Ambrogio's tomb, laid the above-mentioned clothing on her, and prayed for power to come down from the Most High to help the innocent child; but for the moment their prayers were not answered. The reason why Lorenza had to remain possessed in this way is in my opinion to be sought not in the girl herself, for she had not sinned, nor in her parents, whom I know to have been people of excellent lives, but rather, if I am not mistaken, in a permission granted by the Lord, who wanted to reveal Catherine's glory. Ambrogio too, already in the glory of the saints, gave honour through this miracle to the virgin who was still on her earthly pilgrimage, so that her powers should be manifested to the faithful even before she died.

Some people who knew Catherine advised Lorenza's parents to take the girl to her. They agreed at once and did so; but as soon as the holy virgin was told they were there, she said to those who had brought her the news, "Alas! every day I am tormented by evil spirits: do you think I want anybody else's?" Having said this, being unable to go out through the door without being seen by the people who had come to see her, she climbed up on to the roof and fled from that house secretly, so that it would be impossible for her to be found. And so, for the time being, the parents were left disappointed. But the more they saw of her humility and reserve, the greater their faith grew in the power of her sanctity, and they implored her with greater fervour than ever to help them.

Being unable to meet Catherine, for she had ordered her companions not to enter into conversation with them, they turned to her confessor, Fra Tommaso, knowing that the virgin was obedient to him in all things, and told him of their unhappiness, imploring him to order Catherine under obedience to help them in their great misfortune. Fra Tommaso was genuinely sorry for them, but knowing that he had no power whatsoever over the faculty of performing miracles, and knowing too the virgin's humility, he decided to adopt a ruse. One evening he went to the virgin's house[2] when she happened to be out, taking the possessed child with him as far as the oratory, and said to Catherine's companion who was in at the time, "When Catherine comes in, tell her that I order her under obedience to let this girl stay the night here and to keep her with her until tomorrow morning." And with these words he went off, leaving the little girl behind.

When, a little later, the virgin came in and found the child in her room, she realized at once that she was possessed by the Devil, and, with a shrewd suspicion that it was the child she had refused to see, said to her companion, "Who brought this little girl here?" When she heard what her confessor had said she saw that there was no way out and she had recourse to prayer, making the girl kneel down with her. She spent the whole night in prayer, in continual battle with the Enemy. Before daybreak the Devil was forced by the divine power to depart, much against his will, and he left the little girl without doing her any further harm.

Meanwhile the virgin's companion, Alessia, having realized what was afoot, told Fra Tommaso as soon as it was light that the girl had been freed from the Devil, and with Lorenza's parents he hurried to the virgin's cell, where, seeing the girl completely cured, they all with tears in their eyes gave thanks to God and the virgin. Having done this, they were about to take their daughter home when the virgin of the Lord, knowing by divine revelation that something would happen to the girl if they did, said to them, "Leave her with me for a few days: it will be good for her." To this they heartily agreed, and leaving their daughter behind went off in the best of spirits.

Then the virgin gave the girl holy instructions, taught her by word and example to pray often and devoutly, and forbade her to leave the house for

---

2. Catherine was at this time living in Alessia's house. To escape into peace and quiet she would leave her father's house and go and stay with her favourite companion and disciple, sometimes for months at a time.

any reason whatsoever until her parents came to take her away. Lorenza obeyed punctiliously and remained there, growing happier every day.

They were not in the virgin's own house at this time, but in Alessia's, which was not, however, very far from Catherine's.

On one of these days the virgin had to go to her own house with Alessia, and they stayed there the whole day, leaving Lorenza behind in the care of a servant; but after sunset, in the twilight before night fell, the holy virgin hastily called her companion Alessia to her and told her to get her cloak because she was going straight back to the house where she had left Lorenza. Alessia pointed out that at that hour it was not proper for two women to go through the city, but the virgin replied, "We must go, because the wolf of hell has got into our little sheep again after we had got her out of his mouth." With these words she went off, Alessia accompanying her.

When they arrived they found that Lorenza's appearance had changed completely; she was red in the face and in a kind of fury. As soon as the virgin saw her she said, "Ah, you infernal Dragon! How dare you invade this innocent little maiden again? But I have full confidence in the Lord and Saviour Jesus Christ, my Heavenly Bridegroom, that this time you will be driven right out and never come back again!" With these words she took the girl with her to the place where she prayed; stayed there for a while; and when she came out the girl was completely cured. Then the virgin ordered her to be put to bed. In the morning she sent for the parents and said to them, "Now you can take your daughter away with you, for her sufferings are over." And to this day that is true. As soon as Lorenza was better she went back to the convent, where, although it is now over sixteen years ago, she has continued in the service of God without having any more trouble.

This episode of the girl who was possessed I heard about from Fra Tommaso, Alessia, and also the notary Ser Michele, the girl's father, who venerated the virgin for the rest of his life as an angel of God. When he described the miracle his eyes would be full of tears. In the end, in my curiosity to know what exactly had happened, I questioned the holy virgin about it secretly, myself, especially because it looked as though that particular devil had been given licence to refuse to give in either to the relics or to exorcism. She told me that that evil spirit had been so obstinate that she had had to fight him all through the night until four o'clock in the morning, she commanding him in the name of the Saviour to be off, and he refusing with unprecedented stubbornness. After a long struggle, realizing that he would be forced to leave Lorenza, he said, "If I come out of here I will enter into you." Immediately the virgin had replied, "If the Lord wills it so, and I know that without His permission you can do nothing, God forbid that I should prevent you, or in any other way alienate myself from His will or set myself up against Him." Whereupon the proud spirit, struck amidships by such humility, lost nearly all the power he had over the little girl; but he still hurled himself against her, attacking her throat and causing changes and swellings there. Then the virgin placed her hand on the little girl's neck, made the sign of the cross, and so freed her from that affliction too.

There then, reader, is the story of the miracle, and how it happened, and the names of the people who witnessed it and later told me all about it.

Now I want to tell you about another one, which will make it even more plain that this holy virgin had received from God full power to drive out devils. As a matter of fact I was not present at this miracle myself, because at the time Catherine had sent me to see the Vicar of Christ, that is to say, Pope Gregory XI, about some matters concerning holy Church. It was told me by Friar Santi, the solitary whose miraculous cure has already been described, and Alessia and others who were with the virgin.

While the holy virgin was staying with a noble and remarkable woman, Monna Bianchina,[3] in the castle generally known as the

---

3. Monna Bianchina, of the noble Trinci family of Foligno, was the widow of Giovanni di Agnolino Salimbeni, who died in 1367. He was greatly respected, and his death was a great loss to the Republic.

Fortress,[4] where I too had spent occasional weeks in her company, it came about that one of the women there was invaded by an evil spirit and tormented so fiercely by it that the whole castle was discussing it. When the news finally reached Monna Bianchina's ears she took pity on her servant and waited for an opportune moment to ask the virgin to help her. Knowing how humble Catherine was, however, and how upset she got when she was made to discuss certain things, she arranged with her companions to have the possessed woman brought to her when she was with the virgin, so that when she saw what a wretched state she was in she might be moved to compassion and prevailed upon to free her from the devil.

On the day that they brought the woman before her, the holy virgin was involved in trying to reconcile two enemies and, to do this, was just about to travel some little distance. And so, when she was unable to avoid seeing the possessed woman, she immediately turned to Monna Bianchina and said, displeased, "May Almighty God forgive you, lady! Whatever have you done? Don't you know that I am always being tormented by devils? Why have you had her brought before me?" And turning to the woman possessed, she said, "But so that you, Enemy, will not hinder that blessed thing peace, put your head on this person's knees and wait there until I come back."

At this command the woman possessed meekly laid her head on the hermit Friar Santi's knees—it was he who told me that he was the one the virgin pointed out to the woman—whereupon the virgin of the Lord went off to accomplish her mission of peace.

In the meantime the Devil was howling through the mouth of the one possessed, "Why are you keeping me here? O, let me go away, I can't bear it any longer!" The people present kept saying, "Go on, then; the door is open!" And the evil spirit would answer, "I can't, because that accursed woman has bound me here." They asked him who he was

---

4. Tentenanno, in the Val d'Orcia. The castle ruins still give some idea of what this Salimbeni fortress must have looked like.

referring to, but he would not say the name, perhaps because he was unable to, and all he would say was, "That enemy of mine!" Then Friar Santi asked him, "Is she a great enemy of yours, then?" and he replied, "The greatest enemy I have in the whole world." The others, hearing him talking and howling like this, tried to calm him down and said, "Be quiet! Here's Catherine!" The first time they said this, he answered, "No, she isn't; not yet; because she is in such and such a place," and gave the name of the exact spot. They asked him what she was doing, and he replied, "As usual she is doing something I don't like." With these words, he shrieked out at the top of his voice, "Why do I have to stay here as though I was nailed to the spot?" But he did not succeed in making the woman move her head from where the virgin had commanded her in God's name to put it. After a little while he said, "Here she is; the accursed woman is coming back!" "Where is she?" they asked him. "She is not in the same place now," he replied, "she is in another." And a little later he said, "Now she is in such a place," and so he went on naming all the different places she was passing through. Finally he said, "Now she is coming in through the door of this house," and he was found to be telling the truth. When Catherine came into the room he began to howl, "O, why are you keeping me here?" And the virgin answered him, "Get up, you miserable creature, and be off with you at once; leave this creature who belongs to the Lord Jesus Christ alone and never again dare to torment her!"

Then the evil spirit, as he went out of the woman, left as it were sobs behind in her throat, and a swelling. The virgin put her hand to her neck, made the sign of the holy cross over it, and drove away the wicked spirit; and so, in the presence of all, restored the woman to perfect health.

As the poor woman was still aching and stunned from the violence of what she had gone through, the virgin held her up for a time with her arms, letting her lean against her breast; then she got the others to give her something to eat so that she could go home fully recovered. And this was done.

After resting for a while she was able to open her eyes again, and finding herself surrounded by so many people in her mistress's house she said, "Who brought me here? When did I get here?" They told her that she had been possessed by a spirit; and she went on, "I can't remember a thing. But I can feel all my bones aching, as though I had been beaten all over my body with a hard wooden stick." Then she humbly thanked her liberator and went back home, walking all by herself, whereas only a little while before she had been carried into someone else's house.

Present at this miracle, besides Monna Bianchina, who is still alive, were Friar Santi, the holy virgin's companions Alessia and Francesca, her sister-in-law Lisa, and about a score and a half of other people of both sexes, whose names I cannot give as I have no record of them.

Many more miracles involving victories over evil spirits than are recorded in this chapter were performed by the Lord Jesus through this holy virgin, His bride. Those that are recorded, however, dear reader, should be sufficient to enable you to appreciate how great was the gift of driving away evil spirits that the virgin had received from heaven; she having already, helped by the grace of God, gained a complete victory over them by fighting with all her might against their malice.

Here I end the chapter.

CHAPTER TEN

Prophetess

———————•———————

T HE things that I am about to relate, reader, will no doubt seem absolutely impossible to you, but the Truth that cannot deceive or be deceived knows that I have experienced them so many and many a time that I am now more certain of them than I am of any human actions, even my own.

There dwelt in Catherine a prophetic spirit so perfect and continuous that it was plain that nothing remained hidden from her of the things concerning herself, or the people who shared a joint life with her or turned to her for help in matters concerning the good of their souls. It was impossible for any of us who were with her to do anything of any importance, either good or bad, when she was away, without her coming to know of it; as we frequently, indeed continually, learned from experience. The extraordinary thing was that again and again she would tell us our own most intimate thoughts, word for word, as though they were in her mind, not ours. I know from my own experience, and confess it before the whole Church Militant of Christ, that on various occasions she reprimanded me for certain thoughts that were passing through my mind; and, I am not ashamed to admit it as it is to her greater glory, if I tried to get out of something by lying she would say, "Why do you deny it when I can see quite clearly that you think such and such?" And she would end with some sound advice on the particular subject, and then illustrate it by her own example. This, as I have said, often happened to me; may He who knows all things be my witness!

But let us turn to the actual facts, and, not to put the cart before the horse, let us begin with the things of the spirit.

There was in Siena a soldier of aristocratic family, an expert in the handling of arms, known to all as Messer Niccolo dei Saracini. After spending his life in various parts of the world serving in the army, he had at length returned to his own land and devoted himself exclusively to the day-to-day affairs of his own home, where he lived quite contentedly, and the notion of death was very far from his mind. But the eternal, almighty Goodness, who wills that no man shall perish, inspired his wife and some others in his family to try to persuade him to go to confession and do penance for whatever evil he had done during the wars and in the battles in which he had been for so long engaged. But as he was a man entirely absorbed in the things of this world, he laughed at this sound advice, and, turning a deaf ear to those who urged him, paid no attention at all to the health of his soul.

Just at this time the holy virgin was gaining great renown in Siena for her powers, especially for the miraculous conversions she was achieving amongst even the most hardened sinners. It was known, in fact, as a matter of experience, that after anyone, even the most hard-hearted, had talked to her, even if he had not gone away converted, which happened in many cases, he would at least go off intending not to sin again in the same way.

These conversions were known to the people who were trying to get the old soldier to think about his salvation; and when they realized that they were not getting anywhere, they tried to persuade him to at least have a word with Catherine. But Niccolo treated the whole thing as a joke.

"What interest have I got in that little woman?" he would say. "What good can she do me in a hundred years?" At which his wife, who knew the holy virgin personally, went to see her and told her about her husband's obstinacy and implored her to pray to God for him.

One night the holy virgin appeared to the old soldier in a dream and told him that if he wanted to avoid eternal damnation he should pay attention to what his wife said. When he woke up he said to his wife, "Last night in a dream I saw that Catherine you have talked about so often: I really must speak to her and find out if she looks like the person who appeared to me."

Then the good wife, in a state of great delight, went to the virgin, thanked her, and asked her when she would see her husband. What more need be said? He went, talked to her, was converted to the Lord, and promised to go and see the virgin's confessor, Fra Tommaso, as soon as he could, and confess his sins, as indeed he did, thanks to the grace granted him.

After he had made his confession, this soldier, whom I already knew, met me one morning when I was on my way back to the monastery from the city and asked me where he could find Catherine. "I believe she is in church," I said. "Will you please take me there," he said, "and arrange for me to talk to her about a number of things that are on my mind?" I gladly consented, and we went into the church.

Calling one of the holy virgin's companions, I asked her to tell her what the soldier wanted. Catherine immediately got up from praying, came up to him and greeted him warmly. The soldier, after making a great bow, said, "Lady, I have done as you told me. I confessed my sins to Fra Tommaso and he gave me a good penance, which I intend to carry out in the way he said." "You have done an excellent thing for the good of your soul," the virgin replied, "but now you must see that you don't repeat any of your past actions, and from now on you must be a soldier of the Lord Jesus Christ as formerly you were a soldier of the world." Then she added, "Sir, are you sure you told him all the wrong things you have done?" When the man replied that he had made an absolutely clean breast of everything he could remember, she said to him again, "Think the matter over and make sure you have not left anything out."

As he repeated once again that he had definitely told everything, she took her leave of him and let him go off for a moment. Then she suddenly got one of her companions to call him back, and said to him once again, "Ransack your conscience and try to find out whether you may not have left one of your past sins out." When once again he insisted that he had told everything, she took him aside and reminded him of a certain sin which he had committed very secretly when he was in Apuleia. When the soldier heard this he was astounded, and then, confessing that it was true, said that he had truly forgotten it. He asked for a confessor, and confessed this sin. Having seen this miracle, he could not stop relating it and in a way preaching about it to anyone who would listen to him, saying like the woman of Samaria, "Come and see the virgin who has told me of the sins I committed in distant parts." "Is Catherine a prophet as well as a saint, then?" "Of course she is," he would reply, "because she reminded me of a sin that no one in the world knew of apart from myself!"

From that moment Niccolo was always in the virgin's company and obedient to her, as a pupil stays with his master and obeys him: I saw this myself.

How necessary this conversion had been for him, was shown by the fact that not long afterwards he was surprised by death. In fact he was taken ill and ended his life on earth in the same year, and so, well prepared, passed over to the Lord.

Consider in the first place, reader, the miracle of the apparition, then the prophetic revelation, and lastly the way the Lord through the holy virgin achieved the ultimate salvation of a man who had been obstinate in his sins and allowed us to see it. But attend to what follows; and you will see how the virgin's prophetic presentiment was united with aid miraculously given from heaven through her.

Many years ago, before I had the good fortune to know Catherine, I lived in the castle of Montepulciano, in charge of a convent of nuns subject to my Order.[1] I was there for about four years. During my stay

---

1. The convent in question had been founded by St. Agnes of Montepulciano by permission of Ildobradino, Bishop of Arezzo, who at that time had jurisdiction over Montepulciano. The first stone was laid in 1306. Pope Eugenius IV later transferred the

I had only one Friar for my companion as there was no friary in the town and I was always glad to see anyone who came from any of the friaries round about, especially people I was friendly with.

On one occasion the virgin's confessor, Fra Tommaso, and Friar Giorgio Naddi,[2] now a Master of Sacred Theology, decided to come over from Siena to see me for one of our talks on spiritual matters. So as to get back as quickly as possible to the virgin, whom Fra Tommaso had in his constant care, they borrowed horses from some citizens of their acquaintance, and on the way, when they were about six miles from the castle, they decided to rest for a while and give their horses a breather; so, unwisely, they stopped. The district was infested with brigands, who did not exactly rob everybody who came along, but when they saw someone alone and unprotected they were quite willing to carry him off into a secret place and there relieve him of all he possessed, and perhaps murder him so that their misdeeds would not come to the knowledge of the authorities.

On this day these worthies happened to be at an inn, when they saw the two Friars going by all on their own. Whereupon ten or twelve of them immediately set off, going ahead unseen by side paths while the two were resting, and stopped to wait for them at a narrowing in the road. As soon as the Friars reached this spot, the brigands, armed as usual with swords and lances, accosted them violently, and without more ado knocked them brutally down off their horses, and then, when they had robbed them of all they possessed, dragged them half-naked into a thicket in the middle of the woods. From a number of signs that

nuns to the San Paulo monastery in Orvieto and replaced them by Dominican friars, who built the monastery and entered into possession of it on March 15th, 1472. Raymond went to Montepulciano towards the end of 1363 and during his stay there wrote his *Life* of St. Agnes, finishing it on April 20th, 1366, the anniversary of her death.

2. Friar Giorgio Naddi had entered the Dominican Order as a youth and soon distinguished himself by his virtue and intellect. He taught in the monasteries in Florence and Siena and became a noted preacher. In 1378 he was elected Master of Theology at the General Chapter in Bologna. He died on December 5th, 1398. In 1378 he was in charge of the "Mantellate" in Siena and drew up a list of them.

passed furtively between them the Friars realized that they intended to murder them and bury them in that hidden spot so that no one would ever know.

Fra Tommaso, seeing their all too expressive gestures, grew more and more certain of the danger that threatened, and convinced that prayers and entreaties and promises not to breathe a word about the affair would only get them dragged off into the bushes more quickly than ever, he raised his mind to the Lord, all human help lacking, and, knowing how welcome and acceptable to the Lord His daughter and disciple Catherine was, turned in his thoughts to her, saying, "O sweetest daughter, virgin consecrated to God, come to our aid in this tremendous danger!"

He had not finished saying these words when one of the robbers, in fact the one standing nearest to him, who seemed to be the one who was to murder them, suddenly burst out with the words, "Why should we kill these good Friars, who have never done us any harm? It would surely be a great sin! Let us let them go in the name of the Lord! They are good men and won't say a word!" With these words they all found themselves in such agreement that they not only spared the Friars' lives but gave them back their clothes and horses and what they had stolen from them, with the exception of a small amount of money; and then they set them free.

The two Friars reached me the same day and told me what had happened, just as I have described it.

When Fra Tommaso got back to Siena, he discovered—as he relates in his writings and told me by word of mouth—that at the very hour, in fact at the very moment that he had prayed for help, the virgin had actually said to the companion who was with her at the time, "My father is calling me, and I know that he is in great distress," and had got up and gone off to the place where she was accustomed to pray.

I have no doubt that even as she said those words she was praying for him and that the miraculous transformation in the brigands was due to the power of her prayers, and that she did not stop praying until the two Friars had got their things back and been set free and were on their way again.

Have you noticed, reader, how perfectly the virgin's soul possessed the spirit of prophecy? Invoked from a distance of twenty-four miles,[3] she at once heard the invocation and hastened to bring help to those in danger. Again, consider what a great help it is to have a friend endowed with angelic vision, who can know things from a distance and is nourished by divine power so that she can give assistance in all misfortunes and help in times of need. From this you may conclude what the holy virgin can now do in heaven, if she could see and do so much when she was on earth.

To the deeds already mentioned I shall add another of which I was myself a witness along with Friar Pietro di Velletri of my Order, who is now head confessor in the Lateran Church. This next deed will show quite clearly to anyone who gives it his attention that the holy virgin was indeed filled with the spirit of prophecy.

It took place in the days when, as a result of the wickedness of many Italians, nearly all the cities and lands that belonged by irrefutable right to the Roman Church had rebelled against the Roman Pontiff, Pope Gregory XI. The year was 1375.

The holy virgin was in Pisa with me, when news came through of the latest insurrection of the city of Perugia.[4] She was staying in a hostel recently opened on the premises of certain poor buildings looking out on to the square, which lies in front of the church and the Pisan monastery belonging to my Order. On hearing the news, I reflected bitterly that Christians had lost all their fear of God and respect for Holy Church, and, consequently, their fear of being excommunicated, and of usurping not only the rights of others but the rights of the Church of Christ itself. I went in my state of dejected preoccupation with Friar

---

3. Apparently the distance in Roman miles between the point at which the attack was made and Siena.
4. Perugia fell to the enemies of the Holy See on January 1st, 1376.

Pietro di Velletri to the hostel where Catherine was staying, and with tears in my eyes, and in my soul, gave her the news. The virgin grieved with me, and had sad things to say about the loss of souls and this grave scandal in the Church of Christ.

But then, seeing me too disposed to tears, she said, "But calm yourself! It's nothing to cry about! What you see today is milk and honey compared with what will follow." At these words, not certainly because of any pleasure I felt, but because of a sadness and bewilderment stronger than ever, my tears stopped and I said, "Mother, what worse ills can lie ahead, when today we see Christians losing all devotion and respect for Holy Church, paying no attention to her censures and acting publicly as though they no longer believed in her? The only thing left now is to deny the faith of Christ."

"Father," she answered, "this is what layfolk are doing at the moment, but you will soon see that churchmen are capable of even worse things." Even more astounded, I said, "Alas! Even the churchmen will rebel against the Roman Pontiff then?" "You will soon see what happens," she answered, "when the Pope tries to do something to reform the scandalous way they live. They will cause a scandal throughout the whole of God's Church, and the consequent schism will split the Church, and torment it like a plague of heresy."

These words left me like one stunned, and I asked her again, "Mother, shall we have a heresy then and real heretics?" She replied, "Not a real, genuine heresy, but a kind of heresy, yes, because there will be a sort of split in the Church and throughout Christendom. So be prepared to have to suffer this, for you will find yourself witnessing what I have said."

I did not answer, but I could see quite clearly that she was ready to say a lot of other things but refrained from doing so, for fear of increasing my unhappiness. But I confess that with my feeble intelligence I was unable to fathom what she meant, for I imagined that those things were to take place in the time of the Supreme Pontiff Gregory XI, who was reigning at the time. When he died he was succeeded by

Pope Urban VI, and I had almost forgotten this prophecy when I saw the present schism begin to develop in the Church. Then I saw all that Catherine had predicted coming true, and, castigating myself for my lack of brain power, I sighed for the moment when I should be able to see her and speak with her again.

The Lord granted me this when, at the beginning of the schism, the holy virgin came to Rome at the request of Urban VI. Then I reminded her of what she had said to me in Pisa years before, and she, remembering it quite clearly, said, "As I told you then that that was milk and honey, so I tell you now that this is child's play compared to what you will see later, especially in the territories on the border," and she referred to the province of the Kingdom of Naples and the lands adjoining the Roman province. And what she predicted came true, as heaven and earth can witness.

Queen Joanna is still alive; but the disasters that beset her and her kingdom and her successor and all who came to her from the most distant countries, and the extent of the ruin in her lands, are known to everyone.

Now you can understand, reader, unless you have lost all understanding, what fullness of prophetic spirit was in the virgin, when nothing of importance in the future was hidden from her.

But so that you will not say, as Achab did of Micheas, (*3 Kings* 22:18) that Catherine always prophesied evil and never good, I shall bring before you all the virgin's purest treasure, both old and new, and after the bitter, here comes the sweet.

After she had foretold the things just described, when she was in Pisa, I said, curious to know more, "Tell me, dearest mother; but what will happen to the Church after all these disasters?" And she answered, "After all these tribulations and miseries, in a way beyond all human understanding, God will purify Holy Church by awakening the spirit of the elect. This will lead to such an improvement in the Church of God and such a renewal in the lives of her holy pastors that at the mere thought of it my spirit exalts in the Lord. The bride who now is ugly and ill-clothed will then, as I have told you often before, be most beautiful, adorned with precious gems and covered with the diadem of all the virtues. All the faithful will rejoice to be honoured by such pastors, and even unbelievers, attracted by the sweet odour of Jesus Christ, will return to the Catholic fold and be converted to the true Pastor and Bishop of their souls. Give thanks to the Lord, therefore, who after the tempest will give His Church a period of splendid calm." These were her very words.

Knowing that Almighty God takes more pleasure in offering us the sweet than the bitter, I firmly hope and trust that as the evils which Catherine predicted have already turned out to be true, so the good things will indubitably prove true too. Then it will be known to all the people of Israel, from Dan to Beersheba, that Catherine, the virgin of Siena, was a true prophetess of the Lord.

But it is not sufficient for me to state the truth; it is also necessary, as we are speaking of her true prophecies, to rebut the rabid ignorance of certain people, who, not having the slightest idea what they are talking about, have the temerity to speak ill of her prophetic words and put out libels and lies against her sanctity. To give verisimilitude to their slanders, most of them say that Catherine said that "the holy universal journey of the faithful to the parts beyond the seas"[5] was to follow soon, and that she would take part in it herself with her followers. And they say that several years have now gone by since she departed this life, and many are those who have followed her to heaven—one hopes— and that all these will certainly never take part in the "journey". From this they conclude that the holy virgin's words are not to be regarded as prophetic but to be despised, if anything, as idle chatter.

Some of these people, the worst of them, try to make out that not only the holy virgin's words, but even her works, are of a kind to be despised, and should on no account be included in the catalogue of the saints.

---

5. *I.e.* the Crusade. This had been started by Gregory XI in 1373, who ordered many people, especially Dominicans and Franciscans, to enrol in it.

Such calumnies I feel obliged to rebut, first by demonstrating the false bases on which these slanderers build their arguments and then explaining, according to my small amount of understanding and the light that I hope the virgin will implore the Lord to vouchsafe me, how her prophecies are to be understood. In this way two things will be brought out into the light: their slander and their lies.

I cannot deny that Catherine always wanted the "holy journey" to take place and that she laboured greatly to bring it about. This was indeed the main reason for her going to Avignon to see Pope Gregory XI: to prevail upon him to order the "holy journey"; as she did. I myself am a witness to this, since I saw and heard and was present at all the things she devised to bring this about.

I have never forgotten one occasion when she was discussing the question very animatedly with the Pontiff, and I was there listening to what was being said because I was acting as interpreter between the Pope, who spoke Latin, and the virgin, who expressed herself in her own Tuscan tongue; and the Pope said, "It would be better for us to get peace between the Christians first, and then order the 'holy journey' afterwards."

Whereupon Catherine retorted, "There is no better way to bring peace to the Christians than by ordering the 'holy journey'. All those armed people who at the moment do nothing but make war amongst the faithful will be glad to go and serve God professionally. There will be very few so far gone in wickedness that they will refuse to give glory to God through the profession they find so much pleasure in, or who will not be glad to wipe out their sins in such a way. If there is no spark, the fire goes out. Thus, holy Father, you will have many advantages at one fell swoop. You will bring peace to the Christians, who want peace, and by losing them you will save people loaded down with their sins. If they obtain victories, it will be your gain as against the other princes in Christendom; if they die in battle, you will have saved their souls from the brink of damnation. So that there will be three distinct gains: peace between Christians, repentance on the part of the soldiers, and the salvation of great numbers of Saracens."

Good reader, I have related this so that you may realise how zealously the holy virgin laboured for the "holy journey."

Having said this, I now say, in the teeth of all the liars, that Catherine never, never, never, in private or in public, affixed any times to the future events that she predicted. On the contrary, I always found her very reserved about this; and even when I questioned her about some of her statements I was never able to find out any exact times. She left everything in the hands of Divine Providence.

It is true that she often liked to talk about the "holy journey", and that she urged and encouraged as many people to go on it as she could. It is true that she hoped the Lord would look down upon His people with eyes of mercy and lead many believers and unbelievers to their eternal salvation along that particular way. But that she ever said when the "holy journey" would take place, or that she herself would take part in it with her followers—no one but a liar could say such a thing! Some may perhaps seem to have heard her say that the "holy journey" should be proclaimed soon, or something like that, but if so they misheard her. And because a long time has now gone by and there is still no talk of proclaiming any crusade, they pretend to be scandalized!

Now that I have shown how mistaken these murmurers are, you will see, good reader, if you have followed what I have said attentively, that the holy virgin could say with her Heavenly Bridegroom the words that the Evangelist Matthew reports as having been said by the Saviour to the disciples of John the Baptist after He had referred them to His miracles: "And blessed is he that shall not be scandalized in me." (*Matt.* 11:6). And why should Jesus have connected being scandalized with miracles if not because the nature of wicked men is such that, egged on by their own malice, they are scandalized by God's goodness and His marvellous works? In the same way, these other people, not understanding a thing that the holy virgin said or did, find reasons for being scandalized where they should in fact be edified.

Even supposing Catherine had said that the "holy journey" was to take place soon, can these people genuinely maintain that she was mistaken? Are they forgetting, for instance, that John the Evangelist relates in the Apocalypse that the Lord said to him, "Behold, I come quickly," (*Apocalypse* 22:12) which some interpret as referring to His Second Coming? Yet what He said was absolutely true! I beg you: listen to what Augustine says in his commentary on the Psalm *Noli Aemulari*. He says, "What is 'slow' to you, is 'quick' to God. Unite yourself to God, and 'soon' He too will unite Himself with you." (*Comm. on Psalm* 36:1). Hear too what the Prophet says: "Her time is near at hand and her days shall not be prolonged." (*Isaias* 14:1).

Thus, because of your shortsightedness, it may seem to you that the Lord is taking too long, but He certainly will not take too long! Now let us go on and see with what enthusiasm the Prophets promise the Lord's coming: they announce it as though it is imminent, so that Habakkuk can even say, "For as yet the vision is far off and it shall appear at the end and shall not lie," (*Habakkuk* 2:3) and yet many hundreds of years went by before the prophecy was fulfilled.

What reason can these people have, then, for finding fault with the virgin Catherine because ten or twelve years have gone by, when they find both Old and New Testament prophets announcing such high mysteries hundreds of years before they actually took place after having stated that they would be fulfilled shortly? If they really intend to say that Catherine was mistaken because twelve years have gone by, they must also admit that the prophets too were mistaken, to the extent of hundreds of years!

And I wonder what these people would have said if Catherine had announced that a King or Pope prostrate upon a bed of sickness was to die and then he had got better, as happened in the case of Isaias with King Ezechias. (*Isaias* 38:1–8). And if she had announced that some city was to be destroyed, as Jonas did about Nineve, and then this had not happened, as indeed it did not happen: how much fun would they have made of that! And yet these holy prophets were not mistaken: they could not be mistaken, inspired as they were by the Truth that neither deceives nor can be deceived! How in fact the Truth can be reconciled with a prediction that is not fulfilled the Doctors of the Sacred Science explain by saying that it is sufficient for a prophecy to be regarded as truthful if the prophetic word agrees with the disposition of the second-ary causes, which God Himself reveals to the prophet and wills to reveal through him.

This is clearly seen in the case of King Ezechias, who was undoubt-edly seriously ill and in such a condition was certain to die, though he himself perhaps hoped to be cured by natural remedies. This is what the prophet announced to him—*i.e.* that he could not avoid death by any natural means; but he did not rule out the possibility that the divine Omnipotence might miraculously cure him, as in fact it did, as a result of his tears and devout prayers. Isaias was therefore right to tell him that in the conditions in which he actually found himself he was bound to die; but in saying this he did not exclude the possibility that he might be saved from death by some other means.

The same thing is to be said about Jonas, (*Jonas* 3:4) who predicted that the city of Nineve was to be destroyed and gave forty days as the limit. By this way of speaking Jonas meant to show how serious the sins of the Ninevites were, and what kind of judgement and condemnation they deserved; but this did not mean that the Holy Spirit meant to say that the punishment would be carried out whether they did penance or not.

From what we have said it should be perfectly plain that the words of prophets, especially those we have mentioned who were united to God by other holy works, are to be received with great reverence, but interpreted prudently; and the same is true in our own case. Who is to say that the holy virgin did not foresee that the "holy journey" would take place many years after her death, helped by the mediation of her merits and prayers, which are certainly more effective now that she is in heaven than they were when she was on earth? Who knows whether she was not chosen by God to be present, not in the body but in the spirit, to animate and support those who in His good time were to take part in the "holy journey"? It would be no new thing, indeed, for the Eternal; for, though He can do all things Himself, nevertheless He rules and governs us through the ministry of creatures He Himself chooses, and leads us by human means to the end that has no end.

Let this suffice, reader, for the evil tongues concerned; and now let us pick up the thread of our story again.

When we discussed the miracles, we said that the dignity of the spirit is above that of the body, and concluded that miracles performed for the benefit of the spirit should come before those done for the good of the body. Coming now to prophecies, those that were concerned with the good of the soul seem to me to be the ones more worthy of consideration, and I shall therefore go on now to describe one which was sufficient to induce the person who received it to report it immediately.

When I had the good fortune to get to know Catherine, there was in Siena a young man—who is still alive: his name is Francesco dei Malavolti—who came of a very noble family but was far from noble in his way of life. Left without parents too early in life, he had taken to very bad ways indeed, and although he should have felt obliged to abstain from frivolity through having married a young wife, nevertheless he was unable to give up these wicked ways of his.

A friend of his, one of the holy virgin's followers, feeling sad about the state he was in, occasionally tried to get him to come and hear what she had to say, and brought him to us. He was affected by the experience and for a little while gave up his former habits, but could not manage to achieve any permanent improvement. He often used to come with us to see Catherine and found delight in her salutary teaching and good examples, but would then return to his old vices, especially gaming, for which he had a great weakness.

The holy virgin often used to pray for him, but, seeing him relapse into his old ways again and again, one day she said to him severely, "You often come and see me, but then, like a frantic bird, you fly back to all your old vices; go on flying then, wherever you like, but in the end with the Lord's help I will trap you and stop the beating of your wings for ever." These words were clearly heard by Francesco and all the others who were present.

Before they were proved true the virgin passed from this life, and with Francesco returning to all his worst habits there seemed to be no chance of ever getting him to improve. But the holy virgin did more for him in heaven than she had done by her admonishments when she was on earth.

Catherine's death was followed by those of Francesco's wife, his sister-in-law, and others who had stood in the way of his salvation; then, turning in upon himself, he forsook the world and with great devotion entered the Order of the Brethren of Mount Olivet,[6] in which by the grace of God and the merits of the virgin he still continues. He recognizes so clearly that he obtained grace through Catherine's prayers and the prophecy she made to him that he tells everyone about it quite openly, and he has told me the whole story many and many a time, giving thanks to God and the holy virgin.

Finally I will relate something that was made manifest by the Lord in my presence, but which could be better described by Dom Bartolommeo di Ravenna, a devout and wonderfully wise Carthusian who was then, as he is now, Prior of the island of Gorgona, which is about thirty miles from the port of Pisa.

This Bartolommeo had grown very fond of the holy virgin because of her marvellous knowledge and wonderful deeds, and he had implored her again and again to set foot on the island at least once to meet his monks. By hearing what she had to say, he said, they would be instructed in holiness. To this end he had also written to me, asking me to do all I could to persuade Catherine to accept his invitation.

One day the holy virgin decided to make the journey, and with her went almost a score of men and women. The night we arrived, the prior lodged Catherine and her women companions in a house about a mile from the monastery, and us men he entertained in the monastery itself.

---

6. On being left a widower he had intended to enter the military order of the Knights of St. John, but the virgin appeared to him and advised him to become a monk of Mount Olivet. This he did, and after leading a life of penance in that Order for twenty-two years he died in 1410.

Early the following morning he took all the monks to see her, and entreated her to say a few words of instruction to them. At first she declined, saying that she was an ignorant and incapable woman, adding that it would be more fitting for her to hear the word of God from them instead. In the end, however, persuaded by their reiterated requests, she began to speak, saying what the Holy Spirit suggested to her. She spoke about all the different kinds of temptations and illusions with which the Enemy can afflict solitaries; the way to avoid falling into his traps; and how to achieve complete victory over him; and she said all this so well and in such an orderly fashion that she filled me and all the others with amazement.

When her speech ended, the Prior turned to me admiringly and said, "Dearest Fra Raimondo, you know that it is one of our rules that I am the only person who hears these monks' confessions, so that I know whether they are advancing in virtue or not. Well, I tell you, if the holy virgin had been their confessor and not I, she could not have spoken better or more appropriately to every single one of them, for she left out nothing essential and yet wasted no time over irrelevances. From this I can see, quite seriously, that she is full of the spirit of prophecy and that the Holy Spirit speaks in her."

In conclusion, I know—know for certain—that besides the prophecies related above Catherine also predicted many things about me personally; though I am not acquainted with all of them. I shall not go into these, because I might be suspected of being biased about them, and am content to leave them to be told by some of her other sons and daughters.

She also predicted some grave punishments for the persecutors of Holy Church, but these I shall keep to myself because of the wickedness of the people of today, so as not to excite the malice of wicked tongues against her glorious memory.

I end the present chapter and go on to relate things of a different kind.

CHAPTER ELEVEN

Even Inanimate Things Obeyed Catherine

————————————•————————————

T HE first law of justice is that anyone who is perfectly obedient to God shall himself be obeyed by all things. I have therefore decided, my dear reader, to introduce into the present chapter a number of events which will show you quite clearly how Catherine, being obedient to the Creator, was obeyed by created things.

In the days before I made the holy virgin's acquaintance, when she was living in Siena, a young widow of the name of Alessia became so fond of her that she could not live without her. This led her to adopt the habit the virgin wore, and, so as to be as near her as possible and able to enjoy her company, she left her own house and rented another near to where Catherine lived. Whereupon the virgin of the Lord, to avoid the distractions in her own home, started staying at Alessia's for a few days at a time, and occasionally for weeks and even months.

During one of these years there was a great famine in Siena and most people were obliged to buy old wheat that had been kept in store and gone mouldy, for it was impossible to find any of the good sort, no matter how much you were prepared to pay. Like everyone else Alessia had to buy this kind of wheat or go hungry. At harvest time good new wheat came on to the market, and though Alessia still had some of the bad wheat left in the bin, when she got to know that there was new wheat about she decided to throw the old away and have bread made from the fresh wheat, which she had already bought.

As the holy virgin was staying with her at the time, Alessia told her what she was thinking of doing and said, "Mother, this wheat makes sour bread, so as the Lord has had compassion on us I have decided to throw the little that is left away." The virgin answered, "You want to throw away what the Lord has given us for our human food? If you won't eat it yourself, at least give it to the poor—they haven't even that." But Alessia replied that it would be on her conscience if she gave sour bread to the poor, and said she would rather give them a good supply of bread made from the good wheat. So the virgin said, "Get the water ready and bring me the flour you're thinking of throwing away, because I would like to make some bread for the poor of Jesus Christ myself." And she suited the action to the word.

First she mixed the bit of mouldy flour with water, then she went on to make the loaves—and she produced so many and at such high speed that Alessia and her servant, who were standing there watching, were absolutely amazed. In point of fact the number of loaves that Catherine with her virginal hands presented to Alessia to put on the trays could not have been made with four or five times as much flour as she had used, nor did they smell sour as the others had done that had been made with the same flour. They were sent into the bakehouse, and as soon as they were baked were sent back into Alessia's house. At the virgin's request they were served at table, and the people at dinner found nothing wrong with them; in fact they remarked that they had never before eaten such sweet bread.

The virgin's confessor, Fra Tommaso, got to hear of this, and with a few Friars who were interested and other devout people went off at once to see Catherine and investigate the affair, and they were all absolutely dumbstruck when they saw how much bread had been made from that small amount of flour, and how much sweeter it was to taste.

To this dual wonder was added a third, when Catherine ordered the bread to be generously distributed amongst the poor and given in abundance to the Friars; for no other bread was eaten, yet the bin remained almost full.

Thus the Lord performed three miracles with this bread through His bride; first He took the mouldiness and sour smell away from the flour, then increased the amount of dough, and finally multiplied the number of loaves in the bin, so that, as we have said, although the loaves kept on being given away for several weeks, they never seemed to come to an end. On seeing this, some people were moved by God to keep pieces of this bread as though they were relics; and there are still people alive today who have them in their possession, even though the miracle happened nearly twenty years ago.

The first time I was told about this miracle my curiosity was aroused, and I determined to find out more about it. I asked Catherine herself to tell me in detail how it happened, and what she told me was this. "I was seized with a desire to show that nothing that the Lord has given us should be despised, and I was also prompted by compassion for the poor; I therefore went enthusiastically to the flour box, but suddenly found my most sweet Lady Mary in front of me, accompanied by many angels and saints. She ordered me to go on with what I intended to do, and so great was her courtesy and piety that with her own most holy hands she began to make the bread with me, and by virtue of those holy hands the loaves increased in number. The Madonna herself gave me the loaves as she made them, and I passed them on to Alessia and her servant."

"Then it wasn't surprising, Mother," I exclaimed, "that that bread seemed so sweet to us all, seeing that it had been made by the perfect hands of the holy Queen, in the bin of whose most sacred body, so to speak, the Trinity made the Bread that came down from heaven to give life to all believers."

Just think, reader, what this virgin's merit must have been, if the Queen of Heaven deigned to assist her in making bread for her sons! In doing this the Mother of the Son of God wanted us to realize that while she could give us good material bread she could also offer us the spiritual bread of the word of salvation. It was for this reason that we all involuntarily called the virgin "Mother"; because to us she was indeed a mother, who day by day, without tears or fuss, brought us to birth through the womb of her mind until Christ was formed in us, and fed us with the bread of her life-giving holy doctrine.

And now, since we are on the subject of the multiplication of loaves, keeping to the same line of thought and forgetting all about chronology for a moment, I will go on to relate things that happened towards the end of her life.

There are at present living in Rome two Sisters of Penance of St. Dominic; one is called Lisa, and she was the wife of one of the holy virgin's brothers, and hence her sister-in-law, and the other is Giovanna, of the Capo family. Both are Sienese women, and they accompanied the virgin when by order of Pope Urban VI of happy memory she went to Rome. Catherine stayed in the Colonna district, with a considerable number of sons and daughters whom she had generated in Christ and was instructing in the ways of holiness. These people had come to her from all over Tuscany, almost against her will: some to make the pilgrimage and visit the holy places, others to obtain special graces from the Supreme Pontiff, and all for the sake of enjoying the sweetness of Catherine's conversation, which filled them with ineffable joy. It must be added that the Supreme Pontiff, on Catherine's suggestion, had summoned a number of servants of God to Rome, and Catherine with her love of hospitality had gladly lodged them all in the house in which she was staying.

Despite the fact that she had no worldly possessions or gold and silver, and was thus obliged, along with her most intimate friends, to beg even for her food, nevertheless she would have been ready to accommodate a hundred of these pilgrims as soon as one. Her heart had such trust in the Lord that it never occurred to her that One so liberal might fail to provide for everyone who came along. The result was that on this occasion there were never less than sixteen men and eight women living as guests in her house, and sometimes the total number was over thirty.

The holy virgin had herself given orders that each woman should have a week looking after the household affairs, so that the others could attend to the things of God or go on the pilgrimages for which in fact they had come to the holy city; and things were proceeding according to plan, when the week came along in which Giovanna di Capo was supposed to be doing the housekeeping. As all the bread they ate had to be begged for daily, the holy virgin had arranged that when the weekly housekeeper saw that they were coming to the end of their supply she should tell her the day before, so that she could send one of them out to beg some, or go herself. This week God permitted Giovanna to forget this instruction, and one evening there was no bread: she had not warned the virgin about it, nor had she gone out in search of any.

When dinner-time came along there was hardly enough bread in the bin for four people. Giovanna, realizing her negligence, went to the virgin feeling miserable and ashamed and told her about her oversight and the lack of bread. "May Almighty God forgive you, sister," said the virgin. "Why ever have you brought us to this pass, after the order I gave? Our family is hungry, and it is late: whatever shall we do to find bread for everybody?" Giovanna answered that they had reached this pass through her forgetfulness and that as she was the guilty one she should be punished; but the virgin said, "Tell the servants of God to come and sit down at table." At this Giovanna said again that there was not enough bread and that there would not be enough for even one piece each; but Catherine replied, "Tell them to begin with the little there is, until the Lord provides for them." And having said this, she went off to pray.

Giovanna carried out the order and shared the small amount of bread out between them all, and being hungry, as they were, and weak from the effects of the daily fast, they all fastened on to their own piece with avidity, convinced that it would be finished after one mouthful. But instead, what happened? They went on eating, and nevertheless that small amount of bread remained as much as it was at first; each person made a meal of it, and yet there was always bread on the table.

And no wonder, for this was the work of Him who with five loaves satisfied the hunger of five thousand people! They were all astounded, and kept looking at one another in amazement, asking each other what the virgin could be doing. The answer came that she was praying fervently. Whereupon the people at table, all sixteen of them, burst out together, "This prayer of hers has brought us bread from heaven, for we have all had enough to eat, and the small amount of bread that was on the table has not gone down but has, if anything, increased!" When the supper ended there was enough bread left on the table for all the nuns, who also had quite enough to eat; then a large proportion of it was given by order of the virgin to the poor.

Another miracle of the same kind was described to me by Lisa and Giovanna, who witnessed these things. It happened in the same year and in the same house, during a week in Lent when Francesca, one of the Sisters of Penance of St. Dominic, was in charge; she was one of the virgin's inseparable companions, and I believe her to be now in heaven with her.

I cannot pass over in silence a similar miracle which happened to me after Catherine passed into the other life. As witnesses of what I am about to say, I can quote all the Friars who were in the Siena monastery at the time.

Five years ago,[1] needing to take the natural baths that are near the city, I betook myself on medical advice to the monastery, and there, after repeated requests from her sons and daughters, I began to write this life. I remembered that the virgin's head, which I had arranged to have brought over from Rome,[2] was still not being exhibited to the public or had had a solemn reception, despite the fact that when the mortal remains of the people of this world are transported from one place to another they are always received by the people and clergy with

---

1. Raymond is known to have been at the Vignoni baths in April 1384.
2. Raymond transported Catherine's body from the place of its first burial in the Church of the Minerva on October 3rd, 1383. On that occasion he separated the head from the body and entrusted Fra Tommaso della Fonte and Friar Ambrogio Sansedoni, his fellow monk and Provincial of Terrasanta, with the task of taking it to Siena.

lighted candles and solemn prayers. It therefore occurred to me—and perhaps the idea was not entirely my own—to arrange for the head to be given a solemn reception by the Friars as though it had just arrived, and for the Friars to sing the psalms that are usually performed on such occasions, since no special prayers can be said until the Roman Pontiff has inscribed the person concerned in the catalogue of the Saints.

This was indeed done one morning, to the great satisfaction of the Friars and the people, especially her spiritual sons and daughters, and to celebrate the occasion I invited all her special sons to lunch, and ordered an extra plate of meat for the Friars.[3]

When the divine office ended and it was time for lunch, the Friar who was in charge of the larder went in a very unhappy state to the Prior to tell him that it contained at a pinch enough bread for half the Friars at the first table but not for the guests, who numbered about twenty. The Prior decided to make sure for himself, and when he saw that it was indeed so, he at once sent this Friar and the virgin's first confessor, Fra Tommaso, to a number of houses belonging to friends who were very devoted to the Order, to collect enough bread for everybody.

Off they went, and as they were a good time coming back the Prior had enough bread brought out for the guests who were with me, so that they should not have to wait any longer; this meant that very little was left in the larder. Then, seeing no sign of the two Friars, he ordered the community to sit down at table and begin with the bread that was still left. To cut a long story short, either in the bin, or on the table, or somewhere or other, those loaves by Catherine's merits multiplied miraculously to such an extent that both the Friars at the first table and those at the second were able to eat as much as they liked and there was still more left to be taken back to the larder. To think that there were about fifty of these Friars, whilst there was hardly enough bread on the table for five!

---

3. The solemn procession bearing the sacred head took place on May 5th, 1384. It was at this time that Raymond began to write St. Catherine's *Life*.

We were half-way through the meal when the two Friars returned from their search, and they were told to put the bread they had collected aside for another time as the Lord had already provided abundantly.

After lunch I was sitting with the guests discoursing at length on Catherine's virtues when the Prior came along with some of the Friars and told everybody of the miracle that had taken place. When he finished I turned to the guests, all sons of the virgin, and said, "Our mother did not want to let this day of her festival go by without performing a miracle for us, of the kind that was almost a usual occurrence when she was alive; for frequently when she was with us she performed this miracle. She wanted to show us that our ceremony has pleased her and that she still lives amongst us; therefore, let us give thanks to her and to Almighty God."

When I had said this, perhaps by inspiration from heaven, it came into my mind how St. Dominic too when he was alive had twice performed the miracle of the loaves; thus Catherine, as a specially perfect daughter, showed herself to be in all things like her spiritual father.

Moreover, the Lord performed many other marvels through His bride by way of natural things: by way of flowers, in which the flowering virgin took such great delight; household utensils that got lost or broken; and other inanimate objects—miracles that I must omit for the sake of brevity. I must not, however, miss out one that was witnessed by me and a score of others, who spread the news of it throughout the whole of Pisa.

As was said in the previous chapter, with reference to her spirit of prophecy, Catherine was in Pisa in the year of our Lord 1375, and when she first arrived there she was put up with the rest of the party in the house of Gherardo dei Buonconti. On one day during her stay there she was so weakened by an ecstasy more powerful than usual that we expected her to die at any minute.

Fearful at the thought of losing her so soon, I tried to find some remedy that might possibly revive and sustain her—not meat, or eggs, or wine or any other of the usual restoratives, for she detested these so much that there was no hope of getting her to take them—but I begged her to allow me to put at least a little sugar in the fresh water that was her usual drink; whereupon she at once retorted, "You want to get rid of the little life I have left and make me die, for all sweet things are death to me."

So Gherardo and I puzzled our brains to find some remedy for her extreme weakness.

I remembered a successful method I had seen in similar cases, of bathing the sick person's wrists and temples with a certain kind of wine, known as *vernaccia*; and I said to Gherardo, "Since we can't get her to take anything internally, let us see what that will do." At once he answered, "A friend of mine who lives near by usually has a bottle of *vernaccia* in the house; I will send someone to ask him for it, and he will be delighted to send it me."

Off the servant went, and after telling this friend about the virgin's indisposition he asked him on Gherardo's behalf for a decanter of *vernaccia*. The man—I can't remember his name—answered, "My dear fellow, I would give you a whole barrel for my friend, but it has been empty for three months and at the moment there isn't a drop of *vernaccia* in the house. I am deeply sorry. So that you can tell my friend that I am telling the truth, come and see." And he took him into the cellar. He showed him the barrel, and the servant could see at once that it must have been dry for some time, but to make quite sure that it was empty the owner went up to the vessel and pulled the spigot out of the hole that is made in the middle to let the wine through, so that the servant could see quite clearly that there was nothing inside. But he had no sooner pulled the bung out than a generous gush of *vernaccia* poured forth and began to make a pool on the floor. Amazed by this miraculous happening, he closed the hole up again and summoning all the men and womenfolk in the house asked them whether any of them knew who had filled the barrel up with wine. They all swore that it had been empty for three months and that it would have been impossible for anyone to put any kind of wine into it without their knowing.

The news spread round the neighbourhood and everyone believed that it was the result of a miracle.

The servant returned in a state of high delight and wonderment with the decanter full of wine and told us what had happened. Whereupon all Catherine's sons, exulting in the Lord, gave thanks to her Heavenly Bridegroom who could perform such miracles.

The whole city was agog about the miracle; and when Catherine was able to leave the house a few days later and went to see a Patriarch who had just come to the city, an Apostolic Nuncio, everyone was in such a state of excitement when she arrived that even the tradespeople shut up their shops and ran off to see her, saying, "Who is this person who doesn't drink wine herself and yet is able to fill an empty flask with it?"

The saint was upset by all the noise and could hardly bear it; then, realizing what it was all about (as she told me herself in confession), she wept miserably and took refuge in prayer, saying, more or less, what follows: "O Lord, why have you willed to inflict upon your little servant the pain of seeing herself mocked by everyone? All your other servants can live amongst people, but not I. Who asked your goodness for the wine? Inspired by your Grace, I have long deprived my body of wine and now wine is making a butt of me. By your infinite mercy I beg you to have pity on me and dry all the wine up and put an end to this chattering."

The Lord heard her prayer and, as though He could not bear her to be unhappy, added a second miracle in my view greater than the first. After the empty bottle had been miraculously filled, and a great number of citizens were drinking it out of devotion, it suddenly went as sour as vinegar, and whereas in the first place it had been doubly pleasant to the taste it now became undrinkable because of the thickness of the lees. And so both the householder and the people who came to sample it were obliged to keep quiet about it, and were shamed into saying nothing about what they had at first been telling everybody. Even we who were the holy virgin's sons blushed when we heard about the change that had taken place; but Catherine, happy and content, gave thanks to her Heavenly Bridegroom for freeing her from the praises of men.

Now, reader, reflect a little while on these marvels of God, which the senseless man comprehends not and the foolish cannot understand.

The Lord performed a great public miracle without Catherine's prayers, in fact without her knowing anything about it; then, moved by her prayers, He destroyed what He had done. Why was this? What was the point of two such contrary acts? Was it perhaps, as the virgin's slanderers suggest, that the first miracle was an illusion created by the Devil, and that this was proved by the wine's going bad? Even if we assume that this was so, these same slanderers can still not draw any conclusions against the virgin's sanctity from it. For in fact she was entirely outside the first miracle and knew nothing about it; so that if there was any illusion about it, it was not her fault in any way, for she was not involved in it either by word or by deed; and if the Lord revealed the deception, as a result of her prayers, it was a clear sign of acceptance and love, since He would not allow the Enemy to take her in. Therefore from either point of view Catherine's slanderers are bound to acknowledge her sanctity.

But, cheerfully dismissing the tittle-tattle of the Pharisees, who even had bad things to say about Our Lord Jesus's miracles, let us concern ourselves with giving greater glory to our Creator, and according to our modest capacity for seeing let us try to look into the depths of His judgements and purposes.

If I mistake not, the Most High willed to show how much He loved his bride when, unknown to her, He miraculously produced the wine that was being sought on her behalf. So when the virgin heard about the miracle she could echo her Bridegroom's words to the people, "This voice came not because of me, but for your sakes." (*John* 12:30). In other words: "By this miracle the Lord willed to make known to you, not to me, how well disposed He is towards me. I do not need miracles to know this, but you do, because when you have seen them you will have more concern for the state of your souls. Then, as in this life I must always be afraid of becoming proud over the greatness of the gifts granted me in the way of revelations and miracles, I begged the Lord to free me from the danger of vainglory, and the Lord accepted my prayer and provided for both you and me at the same time: for you with the first miracle and for me with the second . . ."

If anyone still wants to object that the second miracle was the negation of the first, let him tell us how and through whom the bad wine got into that little cask, which had been absolutely empty. The fact is this: where there had been nothing, something was found. Who put it there? By the will of Almighty God we have a further motive for praising Him!

However, if the friends of the Devil want to attribute God's work to him, let them do so; but don't let them defame Catherine. There were two miracles, one that took place without her knowledge, and another that came about as a result of her prayers. In neither case can she be calumniated, for she did not come into the first at all, and in the second she got what she wanted. Now I think myself that in the first miracle the Lord wanted to show how acceptable Catherine was to Him, and in the second how subject to Him she was in her profound humility; in the former He willed to give us a motive for honouring her, in the latter He willed to give us a motive for imitating her; first He showed us with what grace she was adorned, then with what wisdom she was filled; for where humility is, there is wisdom. (*Prov.* 11:2).

If St. Gregory in the first book of the *Dialogues*[4] puts the virtue of patience above marvels and miracles, who can fail to see that the second miracle, which was performed through the virtue of humility, without which there can be no wisdom, greatly exceeds the first? But men of the world cannot understand these things; which is not surprising, since, as the Apostle says, the wisdom of the flesh is not subject to the law of God. (*Rom.* 8:7).

If I tried to describe one by one all the other miracles that the Lord performed on inanimate things through His bride I should have to compile several books. But, not wishing to tire my readers, I will end the chapter.

---

4. Bk. I, Ch. XII.

CHAPTER TWELVE

Love of the Holy Sacrament

———————————•———————————

GOD knows, good reader, I shall be glad to come to the end of this account of Catherine's life—especially because of my other occupations, which besiege me on all sides. But so many, and so beautiful, and so typical, are the things that invade my mind when I think back on her life that I am pricked by conscience and constrained to go on and on; and so against my own will I see this book growing larger and larger under my very eyes.

All who were acquainted with Catherine will know as I do how especially great was her devotion to the most holy body of the Lord, so much so that as a result of her receiving it so frequently a rumour spread through the people that Catherine communicated daily and lived in perfect health without taking any other food. Though this was not absolutely true, I believe that the intention behind what was said was good—to give honour to God, who is always admirable in His saints. The truth is that she received the Sacrament not every day, but frequently, and always with great devotion; and some wiseacres, who can best be described as Philistines rather than Christians, complained about this.[1] I took up the cudgels against these people, and they had

—————————

1. In the early Church the faithful communicated every day, but subsequently, as Christian

nothing to say in answer to my arguments, being in fact quite crushed by the custom and teaching of the holy Fathers and Holy Church.

The fact is that according to the teaching of Dionysius, as set out in his book on the *Hierarchy of the Church*, it is quite clear that in the early Church, when the fervour of the Holy Spirit was high, the faithful of both sexes fed on the most holy Sacrament every day. Luke too seems to say the same thing in the Acts of the Apostles, when he refers to "breaking bread" and adds, at one point, "with gladness"; (*Acts* 2:46) which cannot be satisfactorily accounted for unless it is a reference to the Sacrament. If, too, the fourth petition in the "Our Father", the request for our daily bread, is taken to mean this Sacrament, it is clearly hardly a laughing matter, but something to be accepted with heartfelt devotion. Furthermore, as a proof of this daily communion by the faithful, our holy mother the Church, not without reason, has introduced into the Canon of the Mass a prayer for those who communicate with the priest: "We most humbly beseech thee, almighty God," it runs, "command these things to be carried by the hands of thy holy angel . . ." and then comes, "that as many of us as, by participation at this altar, shall receive the most sacred body and blood of thy Son . . ." The holy Fathers themselves teach that it is not only lawful but meritorious for any member of the faithful who is not stained by mortal sin to take this health-giving Sacrament.

Who then can forbid someone who is living a holy Christian life from acquiring this merit frequently? I personally have no doubt that it would mean doing such a person the greatest injury, as serious as refusing him the memorial of the Lord's Passion, and the viaticum for his final pilgrimage.

Let this be the answer to those who say that it is not lawful for any member of the faithful, even the most perfect and devout, to feed frequently on the Body of the Lord, and to those ignoramuses who maintain that it is enough to communicate once a year. I have a higher

fervour cooled, the custom of frequent reception or the Holy Sacrament declined.

opinion of what the Holy Scripture tells me than of any reasoning based on probabilities.

To prove their stupid assertions some of these aforementioned wiseacres, who have no feeling or knowledge of Holy Scripture, rake out a text from St. Augustine in which he refers to the custom of feeding every day on the Sacrament of the Eucharist, but without either praising or condemning it:[2] as though to imply that receiving it is a good thing but that it may sometimes be harmful, thus leaving everything to the divine judgement which sees all things, and not daring to give a definite opinion of his own. But if the wisest of Doctors will not hazard an opinion on this point, I cannot understand how the people who quote his words can have the temerity to lay down the law.

In this connection I remember a retort that I once heard the holy virgin give to a bishop who used this passage from St. Augustine to condemn people who communicate daily. The virgin said, "If St. Augustine does not blame them, why, my lord, do you want to blame them? By quoting him you set yourself up against him."

Thomas Aquinas, the famous saint and Doctor of the Church, replying to the question whether it is fitting for the faithful to receive this Sacrament frequently or daily, says that frequent reception increases devotion in the person receiving it but sometimes reduces his feeling of reverence:[3] every member of the faithful, he says, should have devotion and reverence for so adorable a Sacrament, and if he knows that frequent reception of it reduces his reverence for it, then be should abstain from it for a while and then he will receive it more reverently; on the other hand if he feels not a lessening but an increase of reverence, he need have no qualms, because there is no doubt that a well-disposed soul gains a great grace in partaking of this inestimable Sacrament. That is the great Doctor's opinion and teaching and it was also the holy virgin's, for she communicated frequently, but sometimes, again, she

---

2. *De Ecclesiasticis Dogmatibus*, cap. 53.
3. *S. Th.* III, Qu. 80, art. 10.

would abstain—even though she nearly always felt the desire to unite herself with her Bridegroom through this Sacrament, as a result of the ardent love that drew her to Him whom she had seen and loved, and in whom she firmly believed, and on whom she centred all her affections.

She desired this so much that when she was unable to satisfy her longing for Communion her body suffered more than if it was being tormented with the most frightful pain or burdened by many days of fever. All this was the result of the spiritual sufferings that were inflicted upon her both by the Friars' unimaginative superiors and the nuns' prioresses, and sometimes even by those who were more closely acquainted with her.

One of the reasons why Catherine got on better with me than with those who had been her confessors before me was in fact precisely because I did all I could to satisfy her in this matter, notwithstanding the objections raised by those who wanted to deprive her of Holy Communion. The result was that when she wanted to communicate, and saw me, she developed the habit of saying, "Father, I'm hungry! For the love of God, give my soul its food!"

Pope Gregory XI of happy memory, to content this longing of hers, published a Bull that granted her the right to have a priest at her disposal to absolve her and administer Communion to her and also to have a portable altar, so that she could hear Mass and receive Communion whenever and wherever she liked.

After these words of explanation I should like to describe a miracle shown only to me, though not through any merit of my own. For the glory of His name, I believe that the Lord must have wanted me to know how dear Catherine was to Him, for she herself chose me as her confessor, and often, despite my unworthiness, I administered Holy Communion to her. I realize that if it was not for the sake of the honour of God and this virgin it would not be right for me to divulge certain things, which, as it is, conscience obliges me not to omit.

You must know, then, reader, and this time I beg you to pay special attention to my words, that after our departure from Avignon and arrival back in Siena Catherine and I went one day to see some servants of God who lived outside the city,[4] as a sort of change and recreation in the Lord.

On the morning of the feast of St. Mark the Evangelist[5] we returned to the city, and when we entered her house, it being past the hour of Terce, she turned to me and said, "Father, you know I'm hungry!" I knew all too well what she meant and I replied, "It is almost past the time for celebrating now, and I am so tired that I could hardly get ready to say Mass properly." For a while she was silent, but then, unable to restrain her longing, she said again that she was very hungry. Wanting to please her, I went to the chapel that had been installed in the house by permission of the Supreme Pontiff, and there, after confessing her, I put on the sacred vestments and said the Mass of St. Mark. Having consecrated a host especially for her and consumed the body and blood of the Lord, I turned as usual to give her the general absolution and then I saw that her face had become like an angel's and was sending out bright rays of light: I could no longer recognize her, and in fact thought to myself, "That isn't Catherine's face," and then thought again, "But of course, Lord, this is your faithful, acceptable bride." With these thoughts in my mind I turned back to the altar and said mentally, "Come, Lord, to your bride." I cannot explain why I said this, but I had no sooner formulated that thought than before I could take hold of the host it moved of its own accord, and I saw it quite clearly come towards me, rising to a height of over three fingers, until in fact it reached the paten I was holding in my hand. I cannot remember whether it came to rest on the paten itself or whether I put it there, for what with the brilliance of the virgin's face and then this second miracle I was absolutely dumbfounded; however, although I cannot say for sure, I believe that it rose of its own accord.

---

4. There were three monasteries around Siena, all Carthusian: at Pontignano, Maggiano and Belriguardo.
5. April 25 th.

God, the Father of the Lord Jesus Christ, is my witness that I am not romancing. If anyone, considering my failings, and, alas, the far from perfect life he sees me leading, is inclined to disbelieve what I say, let him remember that the Saviour's mercy embraces both men and beasts of burden and that God's secrets are revealed to great and small. Let him also recall the words spoken by the Truth, when He said, "For I am not come to call the just, but sinners," (*Matt.* 9:13) saying, too, to those who despised sinners, "Go then and learn what this meaneth, I will have mercy, and not sacrifice."[6]

With these excuses, which can be applied to all sinners, I defend myself, then; and I shall therefore be forgiven by the just and the servants of God. I know that they will forgive me, because the servants of God are merciful. If others prefer to condemn me, that is their affair. Whether I stand or fall, it is the Lord who will judge me. He knows when I lie down and He knows when I get up; He searches and judges, for He is the Master. He knows that I am telling the truth. And I will never believe that I was the victim of an illusion fostered by the Devil, in connection with such an adorable, awesome Sacrament; in fact I know with absolute certainty that I saw that sacrosanct Host move and come towards me without being touched, while I was simply saying in my mind, "Come, Lord, to your bride." May those who want to believe this, believe it, and give glory to the Lord; those who do not, will, I am sure, see the day when they will have to acknowledge their error. Let us pass on to other things.

Since I have undertaken to relate things known to me alone, I shall include another miracle which in my view is no less surprising and memorable. This will show, at least to those who believe me, how much the Lord our Saviour was pleased by the desire that burned in Catherine's soul to receive the adorable Sacrament. If I am not mistaken, this miracle happened before the one already related; but there is no point in bothering about the actual date—it is the truth of the event that concerns us.

6. *Ibid.*

I was in Siena under obedience to my Order, exercising the office of lector. I had known the virgin for a little while and, as I have said, was doing all I could to satisfy the desire she had for frequent Communion. Being sure of me, whenever she wanted to receive the Sacrament she turned to me with more confidence than she did to the other Friars in my Order.

One morning she had a great longing to partake of the Body of the Lord, but was obliged to remain at home because of nasty pains in her sides and other complaints she suffered from. These did not lessen the longing she felt, however; in fact they only served to increase it, so that, hoping from one moment to the next that they would pass off, she sent one of her companions to me, just as I was going into the church to say the conventual Mass. This companion said to me, "Catherine begs you not to say Mass yet, because she is too ill to come at the moment and she wants to receive the Sacrament this morning if she possibly can." I gladly agreed to this, and went into the choir instead.

I said my office and went on waiting. At about the hour of Terce the virgin of the Lord came into the church to satisfy her longing, but without my knowing it. Her companions saw how late it was and knew that after she communicated she went into ecstasy for three or four hours and that it would then be impossible to move her from wherever she was, so thinking that this would mean that they would be unable to close the church at the accustomed time and that this might make some of the more ignorant of the Friars grumble, they advised her not to receive Communion. She, humble and tactful as usual, did not have the hardihood to contradict them, and agreed.

But the longing she felt was too strong, and she had recourse to prayer. Kneeling down at a pew at the back of the church, she began to implore her Heavenly Bridegroom passionately, that as He had lovingly inflamed this longing and she could not have it satisfied by human means He would satisfy it Himself.

Then God, who always contents the desires of His servants, mercifully and miraculously heard His bride. I of course was unaware of what was going on and imagined that the virgin was still at home. When she had decided not to communicate one of her companions came to me and said, "Catherine has sent me to ask you to say Mass whenever you like as she can't come to Communion today." At this I went into the sacristy, put on the sacred vestments, went off to an altar more or less at the top end of the church, which, if I remember aright, is named after St. Paul the Apostle, and began to say Mass. The virgin was the whole length of the church away from me and I did not know she was there.

After the consecration, when I had said the *Pater Noster,* following the Church's ritual, I began to break the sacred Host first into two, and then one of the two parts into two more, but at the first break it split not into two parts but three, two big ones and one little one, and the little one, as far as I can remember, was about as big as a kidney bean. I have no doubt, however, that the true Sacrament was in that little part. I saw the particle quite clearly jump out of the chalice over which the Host is broken, and it seemed to me to fall on to the corporal, for I noticed that it flew down below the chalice towards it; but after that I lost sight of it.

I decided that I could not see it because of the whiteness of the corporal, and went on to break the other half of the Host. Having said the *Agnus Dei* and consumed the sacred Species, as soon as my right hand was free I put it on the corporal on the other side of the chalice to where I had seen the particle fall and felt with my fingers, touching one part of the corporal after another, but I could not find it. Much saddened by this, I went on with what I was doing, and when I had consumed the Sacrament I started searching again, touching and feeling every bit of the corporal; but though I went on doing this most carefully for a long time I could not find anything. This made me sadder than ever, and I was almost in tears, but I decided to go on with the rest of Mass, so as not to keep the faithful waiting, and then look for it all over the altar when I was calmer and the others had gone away.

So, when the faithful had departed, I made a careful search of the corporal and the whole of the altar, but my eyes failed to alight on anything remotely resembling the particle. As there was a big painting with pictures of the saints in front of me, I could not believe that the particle had fallen behind the altar, although I had seen it fly in that direction; however, to make quite certain, I looked on both sides and finally on the ground with the utmost care, but I could see absolutely nothing.

In my state of perplexity I determined to ask the Prior of the monastery, a learned God-fearing man, for his advice; and so I carefully covered the altar, called the sacristan, and told him to let no one come near it until I came back. Then, upset and out of breath, I went into the sacristy and took off the sacred vestments, intending to go straight to the Prior and hear what he had to say about the matter.

While I was in the sacristy I received a visit from a close friend of mine, the Prior of the Carthusians at Belriguardo,[7] Dom Cristoforo, and he asked me if I would tell Catherine that he wanted a word with her. I told him to wait awhile as I had one or two things I wanted to see my Prior about at once. He answered, "Today is a solemn fast day and I have to get back to the monastery at once. As you know, it is many miles from the city, so for the love of God be as quick as you can, because I must speak to Catherine about a matter of conscience without more ado." So I told the sacristan again, "Don't move from here until I come back; and don't let anyone go near the altar." And I went off with Dom Cristoforo to Catherine's house.

Her parents told us that she had gone to the Friars' church some time before and had not returned. This surprised me, and the Prior and I redirected our steps to the church. When we got inside I saw her companions at the lower end of the church, and at once asked them where the virgin was. They replied that she was there, kneeling in one of the pews, and that as usual she was in ecstasy. As I was still on edge about the fragment of Host I begged them to rouse her gently, because we were in a great hurry.

---

7. The Charterhouse at Belriguardo, three miles from Siena, had been founded in 1347 by Nicolo Ciunghi.

When the holy virgin returned to her senses the Prior and I sat down to talk to her. Preoccupied as I was with all that had happened, I at once began to tell her about it as briefly as I could, making no attempt to conceal my distress. She, smiling a little as though acquainted with the whole story, said, "Did you look everywhere?" and when I answered that I had, she went on, "Why are you so upset about it then?" And having said this she could not restrain another smile. This did not escape my notice, but I said nothing. Meanwhile the Prior of Belriguardo told her what he had come about and, having received an answer from her, went off.

Then, heartened by her first response to my words and with a suspicion of the truth, I said, "Mother, truly I believe it was you who took that bit of my Host." With a smile she said, "Don't say it was my fault, Father! It was someone else, not me! Anyway, as far as that fragment is concerned I warn you that you will never see it again." I made her tell me plainly all she knew about the matter, and she said, "Father, don't get upset about that fragment, for, to tell you the truth—as one must to one's confessor and spiritual father—it was brought to me, and when it was offered to me by Jesus Christ I took it. My companions did not want me to receive Holy Communion today in case anyone complained about it, so, to avoid upsetting them and scandalizing others, I turned to my most kind Bridegroom, and He appeared to me and in His mercy offered me the fragment that He made you lose, and I received it from His most holy hands. So rejoice in Him, for nothing dreadful has happened to you, while I have had such a gift given me that I could sing the Lord's praises in thanksgiving all day." On hearing this, my sadness was changed to joy, and my doubts were put at rest.

Meanwhile I was thinking the matter over and saying to myself, hadn't I clearly seen the fragment fall on to the corporal? And yet I had not managed to find it. There had not been any breath of wind nor could there have been, for the altar was under cover, and in any case there was no wind blowing, either inside the church or out; and even if there had been I would easily have seen which way the fragment went because I was watching it carefully. There had been no wind of any kind about,

I had seen it fall, and I had clearly seen which way it fell; then I had lost sight of it and been unable to find it anywhere, even after looking for it three times over, with a care that would have discovered the tiniest grain of mustard seed. I went on thinking and it occurred to me that when I had been telling the virgin about the unhappy state I was in she had not, as she usually did, shown the slightest sign of compassion for me but in fact had been smiling, and when I had told her that I had lost a piece of consecrated Host she had not shown any emotion about it at all but still smiling had said, "Have you not looked for it carefully and been unable to find it? Why be upset about it then?" This and other indications gave me such a feeling of assurance that I lost all my doubts about the matter and all thought of going on looking for that fragment of Host.

I have written this about the marvellous things I saw the Lord perform through the merits of this holy virgin, in connection with the adorable Sacrament, so that I shall not be accused by God or men of being ungrateful or neglectful.

Now let us pass to other things that I have heard in this connection from others.

Many reliable persons who used to be at Mass when the virgin received the Body of the Lord have assured me that they have seen the consecrated Host detach itself from the priest's fingers and fly into Catherine's mouth; and they also say that they have seen it go out of my fingers as I was offering it to her. To tell the truth, I never noticed this; but what I did notice was the noise the sacred Host made as soon as it went into her mouth: it sounded as though a stone had been thrown into her mouth from a long way off.

Friar Bartolommeo di Domenico, Master of Sacred Theology and the present Provincial of the Roman Province of my own Order, said that when he gave the virgin Communion he felt the two fingers with which he held the sacred Host drawn towards her mouth. I do not either affirm or deny these assertions, but, considering the foundation of these graces, leave the devout reader's own judgement to decide what importance is to be accorded them.

Many other things have already been related, and there would be no point in repeating them here; so let us end our discussion of the miracles connected with this Sacrament and pass on to a brief account of the miracles that happened in connection with relics of the saints. This will bring us to the end of the second part of Catherine's life.

It was revealed to this holy virgin, as she herself told me and her other confessors, that she would find herself in the company of Blessed Agnes di Montepulciano in heaven and have her as a companion in the eternal bliss. This had made the virgin long to visit her relics, as a sort of first pledge in this life of the everlasting companionship she was to enjoy with her in the next.

Now, reader, since you will know nothing about the sanctity of the virgin Agnes, and therefore will have no way of estimating the value of the miracles that I am about to describe, I must tell you something about her.

In obedience to my holy Order, I lived as Rector for over three years in the monastery that housed Agnes's virginal body. By collecting together a few writings that I found in one place and another there, and talking to four nuns who had been contemporaries of hers and were still alive, I wrote a story of her life which I will here briefly repeat. This will help to give you some idea of her virtues and her great sanctity.

You must know then, that though Agnes's name is not inscribed in the catalogue of the Saints,[8] her birth was announced as a blessing with such grace by the God of all mercy that when she was coming forth from the womb the bedroom in which her mother lay was seen by all the people present to be full of lights, which vanished as soon as the child came into the world. In this way it was revealed to them what great merit the new-born child was to have in the eyes of God.

During her earthly life, in which she was adorned with increasingly

---

8. St. Agnes di Montepulciano, who was born in 1268 and died in 1317, was canonized by Pope Benedict XIII on December 10th, 1726.

wonderful virtues, she founded two convents,[9] in the second of which she now rests in peace. It was there that during her lifetime she became famous for a great number of striking miracles, the number of which increased after her death and became known throughout the world.

One that took place after her death concerned her holy virginal body, which, though it has never been buried, is still incorrupt today. The people of Montepulciano decided to embalm it and preserve it in view of the miracles that Agnes had performed during her lifetime; whereupon from the tips of the dead woman's lingers and toes a precious liquid began to be distilled, and it was collected by the nuns and kept in a glass vase. This liquid, which has the colour of balm but which I believe to be far more precious than balm, is shown to the public. By this Almighty God willed to reveal that Agnes's virginal body, which could miraculously produce balm itself, had no need of any natural balm.

At her passing, which took place in the depths of the night, all the children who had been put to bed by their parents shouted out, "Sister Agnes has just died and is a saint in heaven!" and when day broke a crowd of young girls were inspired by God to gather together, refused to have any grown women with them, got themselves candles, lit them, and went in procession to the convent to present the virgin with their virginal offerings.

The Lord performed other great miracles through Agnes in the sight of all the people of those parts, and for this reason her feast is celebrated with special honour every year, when many great wax candles are devoutly offered to her.

Catherine, wishing to go and venerate Agnes's corpse, came and asked permission from me and her other confessor, like the true daughter of obedience that she was, and then set off. We followed her to see what would happen, and to see whether the Lord would perform any miracle at this meeting between two such privileged brides of His.

---

9. The two convents founded by St. Agnes are to be found at Proceno, about five miles from Aquapendente, and Montepulciano.

Arriving at her destination before we did, Catherine at once entered the convent buildings, and, in the presence of nearly all the nuns, and the Sisters of Penance of St. Dominic who had come with her, went devoutly up to Agnes's body, knelt down at its feet, and began to lower her head devoutly to kiss them; but in the sight of all the people present, without injuring Catherine as she bent down, the lifeless body, without a word of a He, raised one of its feet up to her; whereupon Catherine, humbling herself more than ever, bent over still further, and gradually the virgin Agnes's foot returned to its original position.

Here I feel obliged to mention one special point: Agnes raised one foot only, in full view of those incredulous witnesses—and not without reason. For in point of fact if she had raised both it might have been thought that as her body was lifeless and rigid a chance pressure upon the upper part of her body had naturally or accidentally caused an upward movement of the feet; but as one foot only rose this made it quite clear that what happened was outside the range of natural possibility, something that could only take place through divine power, not through any possible deception.

I have my reasons for introducing this point, for when we who were following Catherine arrived at the castle of Montepulciano the next day we found everyone talking about the miracle that had been performed through the merits of these two virgins by their Bridegroom. There were however some nuns in the convent—only a few—who had been present at the miracle and yet slandered the work of God like Pharisees, saying, "By the power of Beelzebub, the prince of devils", etc. (*Luke* 11:15). So as I had been put in charge of this convent by my Provincial, according to the custom in the Order I summoned all the nuns together in chapter and, under the rule of holy obedience, made a careful investigation into the miracle. All the people who had been present at it confirmed it. I then called one of the critics up before me and asked her whether it had all happened as the others had said it had. At once she said quite voluntarily in front of everyone that everything had indeed happened as the others had said it had—but then she went on to say that the blessed virgin Agnes had had a quite different intention in performing this miracle from the one we imagined her to have had. "Dearest sister," I answered her, "we are not interested in hearing your idea of what Agnes's intention was: you are not her adviser or secretary! All we want to know is whether you saw the miraculous raising of the foot." And she said she had.

For her calumny I then gave her a penance that I regarded as appropriate in the light of my zeal for the Lord, and the need to give the others an example. I say this to confirm what happened.

Some time later the virgin Catherine returned again to the convent with two of her nieces,[10] who were to enter the service of the Most High.

On this second visit to blessed Agnes's body, another miracle happened that is worth recording.

As soon as she arrived at the convent, then, and set foot inside it, her first thought was to go and venerate the body of the blessed Agnes, followed by her companions and some of the nuns. When she came into the presence of the corpse she did not go towards the feet this time, but, radiant with joy, went up to the head. Perhaps in her humility she wanted to avoid any second miraculous elevation of the foot, or she may have remembered the Magdalene, who first anointed the Saviour's feet with ointment when He was sitting at table and then sprinkled it on His head. Bending down, she lowered her face close to Agnes's, which was wrapped in a silk cloth threaded with gold, and remained in that position.

A long time passed, and then she turned to her companion and sister-in-law Lisa, the mother of the two girls she had brought to the convent, and said to her, joyfully, "Can't you see the gift she has sent us from heaven? Why are you so ungrateful?" At these words Lisa and the others, raising their eyes, saw very fine, perfectly white manna coming down like rain, in such abundance that it made Agnes's body and

---

10. The daughters of Lisa, the wife of Bartolommeo Benincasa.

Catherine herself, and all the other people there, quite white, and Lisa was able to collect handfuls of the grains.

Not without reason did this appear in this place, for the miracle of the manna had been very common with Agnes, especially when she prayed. I remember describing in my life of her how the daughters she was instructing in the ways of the Lord, ignorant of what was happening, saw her get up from prayer with her cloak all white and tried to shake it off until she gently stopped them.

Agnes, knowing that Catherine was one day to be her companion in heaven, through this her accustomed miracle was beginning to accompany her and honour her on earth. Quite rightly, too, for this manna, with its whiteness and the fineness of its grains, represents to those who understand these things purity and humility, the two virtues that shine out most brightly in these two virgins. All this I know from these two lives, and not through any merit of my own have I recorded it, but by the Saviour's mercy.

Witnesses of this miracle were Catherine's companions, including Lisa, who is still alive, and many nuns belonging to the convent, who stated on their honour to me and the Friars that this was how the thing happened, describing it and assuring us that they had seen it all with their own eyes. Many of them have now passed on to the next life, but their testimony I can well remember, as can the Friars who were with me at the time. Lisa, indeed, showed a number of people the manna she had collected, and made a present of it to them.

In truth, infinite are the amazing things that God revealed through His bride Catherine whilst she was amongst us, and not all are set down in this book. Those that can be read here have been written to the honour and glory of the Divine Name and for the good of souls, and also that I may not be found ungrateful for the gift given me from heaven. May God keep me from burying the talent that is meant to be used profitably, and enable me to return it to Him with some increase—the fruit of gratitude.

So I end Part Two of this book, and begin on Part Three, in which

I shall speak of Catherine's death, and of the miracles performed both then and thereafter; and, with this number Three, may praise and glory be rendered to the Holy Trinity for ever and ever. Amen.

PART THREE

CHAPTER ONE

The Marvellous Ambassadress

———————— • ————————

T HE old Synagogue, seeing the rise of the Church and the flight of
    an espoused soul to Christ the Lord, says in astonishment, "Who
is this that cometh up from the desert, flowing with delights, leaning
upon her beloved?" (*Cant.* 8:5). This question, which we can apply
to the last part of the story of Catherine's life, will show clearly that
the result and ultimate purpose suggested in the quotations prefixed to
Parts One and Two are perfectly achieved in this, Part Three.

According to the prophet, a thing is good if its ultimate purpose
is good. The Lord, again, tells us to judge a tree by its fruit. And the
ultimate comes first, because the thing which is the last to appear is the
first in the intention of the Agent, being the purpose which moves the
Agent himself to act.

From all this any intelligent person will understand that this third
part of our book, which contains the ultimate holy purpose and final
result of all our holy virgin's work, sets the final seal and crown on Parts
One and Two.

Certainly, the words quoted suggest the beauty of all Catherine's
virtues and her extraordinary excellence, in the wondering question,
"Who is this?" We are further made to realize that the strength of her
spirit was such that in flight she was lighter than the highest of flying

things, when the words go on, "that cometh up from the desert, flowing with delights." Finally we may see that by the intensity of her affection and eternal friendship the Lord was united to her, when it is said, "leaning upon her beloved."

The first of these things is shown in Part One, which describes the very special graces with which the virgin was enriched by the Lord during her childhood and early adolescence, and in the miraculous marriage described in the final chapter.

The second is shown in Part Two, which contains an account of her sublime virtues and virtuous deeds, all of which lead to the conclusion that Catherine, filled with divine love, had by the grace of God arrived at such a high degree of virtue in this vale of tears that even before she reached the end of her life she had all but achieved her aim within the world of time, having run forward with the utmost speed to gain the heavenly reward.

Being so closely associated with her, I was able to see at first hand how, as soon as she was freed from the occupations in which she was engaged for the good of souls, at once, one might almost say by a natural process, her mind was raised to the things of heaven; so quick was her soul to fly up into the heights! This is not surprising, in view of the fact that this movement was caused by an ever-burning fire that always ascends towards higher things—that is to say, the fire that the Lord came to kindle on earth and willed should burn ever more brightly. This became as clear as daylight when, as related in the sixth chapter of Part Two, Catherine's heart was split from top to bottom by the vehemence of God's love and her soul was separated from her body; a thing which I cannot remember reading about as ever having happened to anyone else.

In Part Three, which follows on from the other two, it will be clearly seen how at the end of her life, Catherine, made like her Heavenly Bridegroom in sufferings, united to Him, leaning upon Him, glorious from her victory over this wicked world, ascended into heaven in bliss and glory.

Though to the eyes of the foolish she may have seemed to die, and people of the world may fail to understand the glory she now enjoys, nevertheless, reposing peacefully with the Heavenly Bridegroom she had loved with all her heart, Catherine showed by signs and wonders, as we shall see particularly in the course of this third part of the book, with what glory she had been received in heaven. My good reader, I must tell you that when, in an endeavour to bring peace between the shepherd and his sheep, this holy virgin was sent by Pope Gregory XI of happy memory to the city of Florence,[1] which had rebelled against the Church, she had to endure many unjust persecutions. These reached such a pitch that one Devil's hireling rushed madly out upon her with a naked dagger, and would certainly have killed her if the Lord had not come to her rescue. Despite all this Catherine would not leave the city until Gregory died and was succeeded by Urban VI, who made peace with the Florentines.

Only when the peace pacts had been made public did Catherine return home, and then she applied herself with all diligence to compiling the Book[2] which she dictated in her native tongue under the inspiration of the Holy Spirit. She had asked her secretaries, who were used to taking down the letters she sent to various places, to take care not to miss anything when she was taken up into one of her customary ecstasies and to write down carefully whatever she said. They obeyed her faithfully, and the result was a book overflowing with deep, life-giving thoughts revealed to her by the Lord, which she spoke in her native tongue. The most extraordinary thing is that she only spoke when as a result of the raptures her senses seemed to be quite dead.

During all the time she was in ecstasy her eyes could not see, her

---

1. Catherine went to Florence on the Pope's orders in the December of 1377 and remained there until peace was made, *i.e.* until July 1378. Gregory XI died on March 27th, 1378, and Urban VI was elected Pope on April 9th of the same year.
2. The *Book of the Dialogue with Divine Providence*. Catherine dictated it in ecstasy, and it was written down by three of her disciples in turn—Barduccio, Stefano de Maconi and Neri di Landoccio.

ears could not hear, her nose could not smell, her tongue could not taste, nor could she feel anything with her hands. And yet in this state she could dictate this book; which shows that it was not composed by any natural powers but by the power of the Holy Spirit working within her. I think anyone who reads this book carefully and gives his serious attention to the things revealed in it will be of the same opinion.

While Catherine was in Siena dictating this *Book of the Dialogue*, Pope Urban VI, who had got to know her in Avignon when he was Archbishop of Acerenza and had formed a very high opinion of her, knowing that I was her confessor, asked me to write to her and ask her to come to Rome to see him. I wrote to her at once, but she replied very prudently, "Father, many of our citizens and their wives and also some of the nuns of my own Order are quite scandalized by all the journeys—too many, they say—that I have hitherto made to one place and another, saying that it is not right for a religious virgin to travel about so much. I myself am quite sure that I have not done anything wrong by undertaking these journeys, because wherever I have gone it has been in obedience to God and His Vicar and for the good of souls; still, to avoid giving further cause for scandal, I propose for the moment to stay where I am. But if the Vicar of Christ insists that I come, let his will be done and not mine. In this case, make sure that his will is set down in writing, so that the people who are inclined to be scandalized may see quite clearly that I am not going off just because I want to."

When I got this letter I went to see the Pontiff and prostrating myself at his feet told him the whole story. He asked me to send Catherine an order to set out at once, under holy obedience, which I did.

So Catherine, like a true daughter of obedience, immediately set out for Rome,[3] accompanied by a great number of men and women. There would have been many more too if she had not stopped them. Those who went with her put themselves in the hands of God's providence by voluntary poverty, preferring to go on pilgrimage with the

---

3. Catherine went to Rome in November 1378.

virgin and beg for their food rather than stay at home where they lacked for nothing—except that they would have been deprived of her sweet and wholesome company.

The Supreme Pontiff was clearly delighted to see her again and asked her to say a few words of encouragement to the Cardinals, especially with regard to the Schism, which had then just begun.[4] The virgin urged them with many arguments, which she expressed most felicitously, to be strong in constancy. She showed that divine providence is always with us, above all when the Church has to suffer, and ended by telling them not to be afraid of the schism that had just begun and to do the things of God and to fear no one.

When she had finished, the Pontiff, comforted by what she had said, echoed her words, and turning to the Cardinals said, "You see, brothers, how reprehensible in the eyes of the Lord our fears are. A mere woman puts us to shame. I call her a 'mere woman', not out of disrespect, but with reference to her sex, which in itself is weak, and also for our own instruction. By nature she should be fearful, even when we feel perfectly confident; instead of which it is we who are fearful, while she presents us with the most heartening arguments. This is shameful indeed!" And he went on, "Of whom should the Vicar of Christ be afraid, even if the whole world were against him? Christ is stronger than the world, and it is not possible that He should abandon His Church."

---

4. The "Great Schism". In 1378, on the death of Gregory XI, the seventh successive Pope of French nationality, the people of Rome banded together and clamoured to the Cardinals assembled in conclave for an Italian Pope. The person elected was the Archbishop of Bari, Bartolomeo Prignano, who took the name of Urban VI. Five months later the same Cardinals, dissatisfied with Urban's strict methods, assembled again, first in Anagni and then in Fondi, pronounced the Roman election null and void, and elected a new pontiff in the person of the Cardinal of Geneva, who called himself Clement VII. Clement set himself up in Avignon, supported by France, Spain, Scotland and Sicily, whilst the rest of Christendom remained under obedience to the Bishop of Rome. This scandalous state of affairs lasted from September 20th, 1378, to July 26th, 1424, when at the Council of Constance Martin V was elected Pope and peace was restored to the Church.

With these words the Supreme Pontiff heartened himself and his brothers, and committed the holy virgin to the Lord, granting her and those who accompanied her many spiritual favours.

A few days went by, and then the Pontiff decided to send Catherine, together with another virgin called Catherine[5]—the daughter of the blessed Bridget of Sweden,[6] whose name has recently been included in the catalogue of the Saints by Pope Boniface IX—to Joanna, Queen of the Kingdom of Sicily.[7] At the Devil's instigation, this queen had rebelled against Holy Church and was supporting the Schism and the schismatics. It was hoped that the two virgins, who were well known to Joanna, would make her renounce her great errors.

As soon as our virgin was told of the Pope's wish, she bowed to the yoke of obedience and agreed to set out. The other Catherine, however, the Swedish one, would not hear of it, and in my presence refused point blank. I must confess that I too, small of faith as I was, had great doubts about the wisdom of the Pope's decision. It seemed to me that the good name of these holy virgins was a very delicate thing, which could be tarnished by the merest trifle. The queen whom they had been asked to go and see, egged on by the followers of Satan—and there were plenty of them around her!—could easily have ordered unprincipled men to do them some injury on their way and stop them from ever reaching her, whereby we should both fail in our purpose and they lose their good name.

---

5. St. Catherine of Wadstena, the daughter of St. Bridget, died in 1383 and was entered in the Roman martyrology on March 24th.
6. St. Bridget was born in Sweden in 1302. In 1344, on the death of her husband, she founded the Order of the Saviour. She had ecstasies and revelations and preached penance above all things. She died in Rome on July 23rd, 1373.
7. Joanna of Naples, born in 1324, was the daughter of Carlo of Angiers, Duke of Calabria, and Marie of Valois, the daughter of Charles of Valois. She had four husbands but no heir, her only son dying in childhood. Catherine wrote many letters to Joanna trying to get her back to the right path, but in vain. At the beginning of Urban VI's pontificate Joanna supported him, but she soon changed. In 1380 she was excommunicated as a schismatic, heretic, blasphemer and conspirator against the Pope; Charles of Durazzo took her throne from her, and then, on May 22nd, 1382, had her strangled.

I imparted these thoughts of mine to the Pontiff, and after reflecting on them he replied, "You are right: it would be better for them not to go." When I told the virgin this she was listening to me lying down on her bed, but she suddenly stared at me and interrupted me, almost shouting, "If Agnes and Margherita[8] and other holy virgins had thought of things like that they would never have gained the crown of martyrdom! Haven't we a Heavenly Bridegroom, who can free us from the hands of the ungodly and keep our purity intact even in the midst of a shameless mob of men? Your arguments are quite worthless and were suggested by lack of faith, not prudence." On hearing this, although I felt inwardly ashamed of my imperfection, nevertheless I was overjoyed by her great virtue and full of admiration for the constancy of her faith.

The Pontiff, meanwhile, had decided that the journey should not be undertaken by the two virgins and I did not mention the matter to anyone else.

I have told this little story so that every reader can see what degree of perfection Catherine had reached.

After this the Holy Pontiff decided to send me into France,[9] in the belief that his Legates would be able to prevent the French king Charles,[10] who had begun to fall into error, from siding with the schismatics. But the journey was to prove fruitless, as Charles had a heart harder than that of the Pharaohs.

When I learned of the Pontiff's wish I mentioned it to the virgin, who although she was sad at the prospect of not having me with her

---

8. Stefano di Corrado Maconi, who came from a noble Sienese family, was one of the virgin's most distinguished disciples, and also her secretary. After taking the Carthusian habit he soon became Superior and by order of the Pope was for a time General of the Order in Italy. He died at an advanced age in 1424 and was honoured with the title "Blessed". He wrote an account of Catherine's death.

9. St. Agnes, a Roman virgin, was martyred in Rome during the persecution by Valerian in 258. St. Margherita, a virgin and martyr of Antioch, is remembered in the Roman martyrology on July 20th.

10. In November 1378 Urban VI ordered Raymond and his Friars to preach the crusade against the schismatics and on the 21st sent him as Papal Legate to the King of France.

persuaded me to fall in with the Pope's wishes without delay. Amongst other things she said, "Take it for certain, Father, that he is the true Vicar of Christ, whatever the slanderous schismatics may say. I want you to undertake to preach and defend this fact, as you have a duty to work for the truth of the Catholic faith." Though I had been quite certain in my own mind about this all along, nevertheless I found her words heartening in my determination to labour against the schismatics who denied it, and to this day I still labour as hard as I can in the defence of the true Pontiff. The memory of her words is truly a great comfort to me in times of sadness and discouragement. And so I followed her advice and bowed my neck to the yoke of obedience.

A few days before I set off,[11] Catherine, foreseeing what lay ahead, wanted to talk to me about the revelations and consolations she had had from the Lord, and our conversation took place privately, though there were other people there at the time. We spent several hours together, and at the end of this long talk she said, "Go; and God be with you; for I don't think we shall ever again in this life have such a long conversation as we have had today." And so it turned out! I set off, and she remained behind, and before I got back she had ascended into heaven; and true it was that I could no longer enjoy her holy conversation!

When I went on board ship Catherine came along with me in person—I believe it was to say a last farewell—and when we pushed off she knelt down and prayed, and then, with tears in her eyes, made the sign of the cross towards us, as if to say, "You, son, go under the safe protection of the sign of the Holy Cross; but in this life you will never see your mother again."

Everything went splendidly. The sea was infested with pirates, but we reached Pisa without interference, and then, still untroubled, went

---

11. Charles V, known as "the Wise", was born in 1337. He supported the Schism for political reasons, for France had certainly no reason to be pleased with the prospect of siding with the Avignon Pope. Charles died in 1380, a few months after Catherine, and seems to have repented of his support of Urban VI.

on and landed at Genoa, despite the fact that we passed a great number of ships belonging to the schismatics, all on their way to Avignon. Continuing our journey overland, we arrived at Ventimiglia, and if we had gone on we should have fallen into an ambush prepared for us by the treacherous schismatics, whose first desire was to kill me,[12] but God willed that while we were resting in Ventimiglia one of the Friars of my Order, a native of those parts, sent me a letter saying, "On no account go beyond Ventimiglia, because there are snares laid for you; if you fall into them no one will save you from death." When I had read the letter, on the advice of the companion the Pope had given me I turned back and remained in Genoa.

From there I sent word to the Pontiff of what had happened and asked him what I should do. He answered that I was to stay where I was and preach the crusade against the schismatics in Genoa. This meant that my return was delayed, and during this time the holy virgin happily ended the course of her life, which was crowned, as we shall see, with a wonderful martyrdom.

From that time onwards I could no longer be an eye-witness of the things that happened to her, and all that I write now has been collected together from three sources; from the letters she frequently sent me during this time, to keep me acquainted with what she was doing; from what I have been told by men and women who were with her until the end, and who after her death saw the marvellous things that the Lord performed through her; and also from the writings of some of her more highly educated sons, who left various notable things in writing, both in Latin and the native tongue, so that everyone should know about them.

But in case I may seem to be simply misleading my readers by mentioning these people in a merely general way, I shall give their names, both the men and the women, separately. These are the people to be believed, not me! I knew them all, and they are all, as perfect imitators of Catherine's example, trustworthy reporters of her actions.

---

12. Raymond left Ostia in December 1378.

Here are their names. I will begin with the women, as these were with Catherine practically all the time.

Alessia of Siena,[13] one of the Sisters of Penance of St. Dominic, though she was one of the last to put herself under Catherine's guidance, was nevertheless in my opinion the most perfect of all of them in the virtues. She had married a learned nobleman, but had soon been left a widow and though she was still young she despised the pleasures of the world and the flesh and grew so fond of the virgin that she could not bear to live without her. On the virgin's advice she sold all her goods and distributed the proceeds to the poor, and imitating her mistress, fasted, watched, mortified her flesh with many penances, and gave herself continually to prayer and contemplation. She was so assiduous and perfect that if I am not mistaken the holy virgin revealed her most intimate secrets to her towards the end and desired that after her death the others should accept her in her stead and take her as their model.

As soon as I got back to Rome I found her still alive there, and she told me a great number of things; but after a little while she died and followed her whom she had so much loved in the Lord. Alessia was my prime source of information about what had happened while I was away.

The second of these women is Francesca,[14] a most religious woman, united to God and Catherine in truest affection. Upon being left a widow she had at once taken the habit which the virgin had adopted and had consecrated her three sons to the service of God in the Order of Preachers, directing them to heaven, as I myself can testify, before she died, for their subsequent lives were exemplary, as I well know. They ascended to heaven during the plague, not without a miraculous intervention on the part of the Highest in answer to the virgin's prayers, as I remember having related in Part Two of this Life, in the chapter

13. Because he was the Pope's Legate, and to prevent him from detaching Charles from the Schism.
14. She had been the wife of Niccolo di Francesco dei Saraceni. She died soon after Catherine.

describing the miracles performed for the good of souls. Francesca, like many others, gave me much information; she died shortly after Alessia.

The holy virgin's third companion was Lisa, who is still alive.[15] She is well known in the city, especially in her own district. Of Lisa I shall say no more, as she is still alive, and also because she was the wife of one of Catherine's brothers. I should not like the unbelievers to be able to cast doubts on her evidence, though as a matter of fact I have always found her to be the kind of woman who does not tell lies.

After Catherine's death I came across a number of men who had been present at her passing, but I shall name only four whom I know to be renowned and full of virtue. Two of these are already in heaven with her; the other two are still alive on earth. I mention them by name to confound the unbelievers, and also so that I may give a few details about each one of them in particular.

The first was a certain Santi,[16] a man saintly in deed as well as in name, so much so that we used to call him Brother Santi. He came originally from Teramo, and for the Lord's sake he had left his parents and his home town and come to Siena, where for thirty years and more, if I am not mistaken, he led an utterly blameless life as an anchorite, guided by books and by devout men of religion. He was an ageing man when he first met the "pearl beyond price", that is to say the virgin Catherine; whereupon he gave up the quiet of his cell and his habitual way of life to follow her, not only for his own benefit and to help other

---

15. Also known as Lecca. She was the widow of Clemente Gori, a Sienese nobleman. The Siena death register mentions three sons of Francesca's: Friar Ambrogio, a deacon, who died on January 14th, 1374; Friar Taddeo, also a deacon, who died in the S. Maria Novella monastery in Florence in 1374; and Friar Bartolommeo, a priest, who died on October 2nd, 1378. She also had a daughter, Giustina, who became a Sister of Penance of St. Dominic in Montepulciano. Francesca died in Rome on February 15th, 1383, and was buried in the church of the Minerva.

16. Lisa, the daughter of Golio di Pietro dei Colombini, was the wife of Bartolommeo, Catherine's eldest brother. She had two daughters who became nuns in the Montepulciano convent. She was still alive when Raymond finished his *Life* of Catherine in 1395. She died in about 1400.

people but also because he was attracted by the signs and miracles that seemed to be happening every day both in himself and in others. He used to say that he found more quiet and peace of mind, and made more progress in virtue, from being in Catherine's company and listening to her teaching than he had ever done in the solitude of his cell—especially in the virtue of patience, for he suffered a great deal from a painful affliction of the heart, and he learned from the holy virgin to bear it with patience and joy; for which he gave thanks to the Highest. Santi gave me a great deal of information about things that happened while I was away. He too went to rejoin his mistress in heaven during one of my later absences.

The second was a Florentine, young in years but old in wisdom, and one, in my opinion, decked with the flowers of all the virtues. His name was Barduccio.[17] Forsaking his parents, brothers and native land, he accompanied the holy virgin to Rome and remained with her until her death. It was discovered later that Catherine loved him more tenderly than all the others; I believe that this was on account of his virginal purity. There is no wonder that one virgin should love another virgin. When Catherine died, she told Barduccio to turn to me and put himself under my direction. I believe that she ordered this knowing that he had little time to live. For shortly after the virgin's death Barduccio was attacked by the malady that doctors call phthisis, and though he seemed to improve from time to time he finally died of it. Thinking that perhaps the Rome air did not agree with him, I sent him to Siena, but within a short time he gave up his spirit to Christ. Those who were present at his death tell me that at the end he looked upwards and began to smile happily, and died with this smile on his lips. The signs of that joyful smile remained even after death. This must have been because he saw coming towards him, joyful and clothed in glory,

---

17. Fra Santi had become a disciple of Catherine's after the death of his intimate friends, Bl. Giovanni Colombini and Bl. Pietro Petroni. Though old, he followed her everywhere, even to Rome, where he was present at her death, dying there a year later himself.

her whom in this life he had loved with sincere purity of heart. He too told me of many things that had happened in my absence, and I believe him absolutely, as though I had seen the things with my own eyes, for I know beyond a shadow of a doubt that he was a youth of great virtue.

The third of these men is still alive: he is Stefano dei Maconi, of Siena, whom I have already mentioned.[18] I shall not attempt to laud him here, since he is still on earth, and no one should be praised while he is alive. For its information value, however, I will say that he was one of the virgin's secretaries, and that he wrote down from her dictation most of her letters and the greater part of the Book. He was so enthusiastic about Catherine that he left mother, father, his three brothers and his native city, and accompanied her wherever she went. When the virgin was in her last agony she called him and said, "Son, it is God's will that you shall entirely forsake the world and enter the Carthusian Order." Like the good son he was, he received the command devotedly and obeyed it scrupulously. It is clear from the facts, and becomes clearer every day, that these words came from the mouth of the Highest, for I cannot remember ever having seen or heard of anyone entering an Order and making such remarkable progress in the virtues.

As soon as Stefano was professed he was made Prior, and fulfilled the office so satisfactorily that he kept on being re-elected. At the moment he is Prior in Milan and Visitor to many of the monasteries of his Order. His name is held in high honour. As he was present at the time, he wrote down things that happened during the virgin's passing, and he has since told me more fully by word of mouth. He also witnessed almost the whole of Catherine's life, so that I can say with John the Evangelist, "And he knoweth that he saith true;" (*John* 19:35) that is to say, he, Stefano, a Carthusian, knows that Raimondo, of the Order

---

18. Barduccio di Pietro Canigiani had got to know Catherine in Florence when she went there to make peace between the Florentines and the Pope in 1377. From then on he was always with her and acted as her secretary. After her death he became a priest. He contracted consumption, and Raymond sent him to Siena, where he died on December 8th, 1382.

of Preachers, who, unworthy and undeserving though he is, has written Catherine's Life, is speaking the truth.

The fourth and last of the men who have told me all they know is also still alive: he is Neri (or Ranieri) dei Pagliaresi,[19] of Siena, the son of the late Landoccio. After the holy virgin's death he began to live the life of an anchorite, and still does so. Along with Stefano and Barduccio he used to take down her letters and the Book, but he had become one of Catherine's followers before them, leaving his father, who is still alive, and relatives, to do so. As he was acquainted with the holy virgin's actions over a long period, I have mentioned him and appeal to him as a witness to this Life along with Friar Stefano the Carthusian.

All these men and women gave me, either by word of mouth or in writing, information about what happened while I was away, before Catherine's death and during her agony and passing.

Dearest reader, now that I have put you in a position to believe what I say, I end the present chapter.

---

19. Neri di Landoccio Pagliaresi, a Sienese nobleman, was another of the virgin's secretaries and one of her first disciples. In Caffarini's *Supplement* he is described as *"vir mirabilis"*. He died on March 8th, 1406.

CHAPTER TWO

The Martyr

————————•————————

A FTER I had left the bride of Christ at the Pope's behest (as I have explained above), Catherine remained behind in Rome, and there marvellous things took place which deserve to be included in this story. Some I have already related, and the rest I shall describe now, particularly the ones that will demonstrate to the faithful the splendid sanctity of her happy ending, which will form a sort of introduction to her entry into glory.

The holy virgin, then, seeing such a succession of evils cropping up in the most beloved Church of God as a result of the abominable Schism which she had foreseen, and seeing too that the Vicar of Jesus Christ was being so to speak suffocated by the endless persecutions that he was obliged to endure, wept day and night and prayed unceasingly to the Lord to restore peace to the Church. And the Lord was pleased to comfort her, for a year before she died, on the very same day that, a year later, she was to ascend into heaven, He gave His holy Church and the Supreme Pontiff a twofold victory. The castle of St. Angelo, which until then had been in the hands of the schismatics, was re-taken, and the armed men who had been ravaging the whole countryside for the schismatics were entirely suppressed, the leaders being taken prisoner and many put to death.

The Pontiff, who had been unable to return and live near the Church of the Prince of the Apostles because of its proximity to the castle, on Catherine's advice now went barefoot to the church, followed by a great concourse of people, devoutly giving thanks to the Highest for all these benefits; and Church and Pontiff began to breathe a little more freely, to the no small satisfaction of the holy virgin.

All too soon, however, her sorrows returned, for the old Serpent, being unable to succeed in one way, tried another, this time more crude and dangerous. Having failed in his efforts with the foreigners and schismatics, he made another attempt through the friends and household of the Faith, and began to sow discord in the city between the citizens and the Pontiff. Things finally reached such a pass that the people even began to threaten to kill the Pontiff.

In this crisis Catherine, bowed down with grief, turned ardently to prayer, and with all her soul asked her Heavenly Bridegroom not to permit such a crime. While she was praying, as she later wrote and told me,[1] she saw in spirit the whole city a prey to devils who were goading the people on to commit this parricide, and they besieged her, shrieking out in fury, "Curse you! You are doing everything you can to stop us. But we shall make you die a horrible death!" She paid no attention to them, however, but went on praying fervently, imploring the Lord, for the honour of His own name and the good of His Holy Church shaken by all these storms, to bring the devils' tricks to nought, to preserve His Vicar from harm, and to refuse to allow the people to commit their monstrous crime.

Once the Lord answered her as follows: "Let this people who daily blaspheme My Name descend to these depths of wickedness, so that afterwards I may wreak vengeance upon them for their heinous crime and destroy them. My justice will not allow me to endure their

---

1. Of Catherine's letters to Raymond seventeen are extant (Gigli 87–103). The one mentioned in this chapter is No. 102: a letter which Tommaso describes as "the words of a daughter and mother, woman and martyr".

iniquities any longer." Despite this the virgin continued to plead with Him fervently in the following words, or others of a like kind, "O most merciful Lord, you know how savagely your Spouse whom you redeemed with your own blood is being torn to pieces throughout almost the whole world. You know too how few helpers and defenders she has; nor can it be hidden from you that her enemies desire the death and dishonour of your Vicar; if what you have said should take place, it would be a very great disaster not only for the people of Rome but for all Christian people and the whole Church. So, Lord, mitigate your wrath, and abandon not your people, whom you redeemed so dearly."

If I remember aright Catherine continued this contest for several days and nights, to the great fatigue and weakening of her already weak body; she pleading again and again, the Lord speaking of justice, and the devils besieging her howling. Her prayer was so fervent, she wrote to me, that, to use her own words, if the Lord had not encircled her body with strength as a hoop is put round a barrel to keep it together, it would certainly have broken down and gone to pieces.

At the end of this arduous conflict, which caused her indescribable torment, the virgin triumphed and obtained what she wanted. To the Lord, who kept on insisting on the requirements of justice, she replied, "Very well, Lord, since there is no getting away from your justice, do not, I beg you, refuse your servant's prayers on that account: visit upon me the punishment deserved by this people. For the honour of your Name and your holy Church I will gladly drink the chalice of passion and death—which, as you yourself know, I have always desired to drink, ever since with the help of your grace I began to love you with all my mind and heart." At these words the divine voice speaking in her mind was stilled; but the silence was proof that the virgin had obtained what she asked for.

In fact from that moment the clamouring of the people gradually died down, until it finally died away altogether. The person who felt the weight of this was the most virtuous virgin, because those hellish serpents, having by divine permission obtained power over her body, vented their rage upon it with such cruelty that, as eye-witnesses have told me, no one who had not seen it would ever have believed it.

Her poor body, now weighed down with every kind of infirmity, was reduced to mere skin and bone and seemed not to be alive but already devoured by the grave; nevertheless she went on walking about, praying and working, seeming to everyone a walking miracle rather than a creature of nature. The torments increased continuously, and consumed her body before one's very eyes. This, however, did not make her stop praying; on the contrary, she gave herself to prayer more fervently than ever and for even longer periods.

The sons and daughters she had generated in Christ who were with her all the time could see the visible signs of the punishment that was being inflicted on her by the infernal enemies, but they were unable to do anything to help because they could not set themselves up against the divine will, and also because even though the virgin herself was failing in bodily resources she was nevertheless eager and happy to suffer more. I was told by those who were with her, and the same thing was repeated in the letters she wrote to me, that the more she prayed the more violence she had to endure.

These torments, she wrote and told me, also included the devils' terrible voices, for as their final affliction they would howl at her, "Accursed be you, who have never stopped persecuting us! But the day will come when we shall have our full revenge on you. You send us away from here, but we shall take you right out of the world!" And these threats were accompanied by blows.

From Sexagesima Sunday[2] to the next to the last day of April, when she passed into heaven, the holy virgin endured this martyrdom, which increased from day to day.

During all this time, as she wrote to me, an extraordinary thing was happening. Because of the pains in her sides and her other complaints, she was in the habit of waiting until Terce to hear Mass; but

2. January 29th.

throughout the whole of this Lent she went to the Church of St. Peter, Prince of the Apostles, every morning, and there after she had heard Mass she remained for a long time in prayer, not returning home until it was time for vespers. When she was in the house she had to lie down in bed, and anyone seeing the state she was in would have sworn that she would never be able to get up again; but as soon as it was light she would be up, and, making her way along the street called Via del Papa,[3] where she lived, between the Minerva and the Campo dei Fiori, she would hurry to St. Peter's, covering a distance that even a person in the best of health would have found tiring.

However, finally called by heaven, she was confined to her bed for a few days, until, on the day already mentioned, she rendered up her spirit to Christ. It was about the hour of Terce on April 29th, a Sunday, in the year of Our Lord 1380, on the feast of St. Peter the Martyr of the Order of Preachers.

Thereupon many extraordinary things happened, which we shall briefly describe in the following chapters. Here I end this chapter.

---

3. Today known as the Via di Santa Chiara.

291

CHAPTER THREE

For Christ Alone

────────────●────────────

A S the life of this holy virgin drew towards its end, the Lord gave
many signs of the glory which, after all the fatigues and languors
she had endured, He was shortly to grant her in heaven—a glory pro-
portionate to the graces with which He had enriched her on earth. One
of the signs by which the Lord revealed the perfection of her soul to
those who wished to know it was this, that her desire to be freed from
the bonds of the body and united with Christ increased daily, for only
in her heavenly home could she come to a clear view of the Truth that
on earth she could see only in a glass darkly. And this desire of hers
became all the stronger, the greater the supernatural light that was shed
down into her soul from above. Thus, nearly two years before she died
such brightness of light was revealed to her from heaven that she felt
constrained to spread it abroad by means of writing, begging her secretaries to be on the alert to take down whatever issued from her mouth
as soon as they saw that she was going into an ecstasy.

In this way there was composed within a brief space of time a certain book, which consists of a Dialogue between a soul that asks the
Lord four questions, and the Lord Himself who replies to the soul and
enlightens it with many useful truths. At the end of this book are to
be found two passages that I consider worth introducing here, to show

the reader that the above-mentioned desire really did exist in the mind of this blessed virgin. And perhaps it is not unfitting that I should refer to these two passages, for the natural tendency of all movement is towards some desired end. John the Evangelist says that the Lord Jesus loved to the absolute limit, and there can be no one, however deficient in knowledge of the sacred sciences, who does not know that the first Truth is the universe's final end.

Meanwhile, so that no one will imagine that to the teaching or prayer that I take from the book I have added anything of my own, I call upon the first Truth itself to be my judge and witness.

These two passages I have transposed into Latin from the native tongue in which they are written in the book, adding nothing of my own and changing nothing; on the contrary, I have tried to keep to the same order of words, and have made every effort, in so far as is allowed by the Latin syntax, to translate word for word, though strictly speaking this cannot always be done without adding some kind of interpolation, a conjunction or an adverb for instance, that is not in the original. But this does not mean that I have tried to change the meaning or add anything; it simply means that I have tried to achieve a certain elegance and clarity of utterance.

The two passages I shall reproduce consist of an epilogue, to be found at the end of the book, which gives in a few words the whole gist of the book itself, and a prayer which the virgin herself dictated upon the completion of the work, from which it can be seen how greatly she desired to be freed from the body and united to Christ.

The holy virgin, then, relates that the Lord God, the Father of Our Lord Jesus Christ, after speaking at great length about obedience, towards the end of the Dialogue spoke to this soul in the following words:[1] "Now, dearest, most beloved daughter, I have satisfied your

---

1. These form the last two chapters of the *Dialogue*. The book is divided up as follows: Introduction, Chapters 1–8; On Discretion, Chapters 9–64; On Prayer, Chapters 65–134; On Providence, Chapters 135–153; On Obedience, Chapters 154–167. The

desire to know all about the subject of obedience. If you remember, in the beginning you implored me—as I made you do, to develop the fire of my charity in your soul—you asked me, I say, for four things. The first was for yourself, and I have satisfied you by enlightening you with my Truth, showing you how you may come to know the Truth which you desired to learn, and how, with the light of faith and the knowledge of yourself and me, you may arrive at the knowledge of the Truth.

"The second request you made was that I should have pity on the world. The third was for the mystical body of my Church; you begged me to do away with darkness and persecution and asked me to punish you for their iniquities.

"With regard to this, I explained that no punishment inflicted in finite time can of itself make satisfaction for any crime committed against me, who am in fact infinite. Nevertheless, the punishment can make satisfaction if it is joined with contrition of heart and the soul's desire. How this comes about, I have already explained to you. I also said that I will have pity on the world, showing you how mercy is proper to me. Thus, through the great pity and love I have for man, I sent the Word, my only Son—whom, to give you an absolutely clear idea of this, I described to you by comparing Him with a bridge going from heaven to earth; and this referred to the union of the divine and human natures that is achieved in Him.

"To enlighten you further about my Truth, I showed you again how this bridge rises in three stages, that is to say, the three powers of the soul. And I made another comparison, as you know, by imagining these three stages as different parts of His body, the first being His feet, the second His side, and the third His mouth: which I used to represent the three states of the soul—the imperfect state, the perfect state,

---

whole book revolves round four petitions addressed to the Heavenly Father by the virgin, imploring mercy for herself, mercy upon the world and peace between Christians, and for the reform of the Church. The passage from the book given here by Raymond occurs in Chapter 166.

and the most perfect state of all, in which the soul arrives at the excellence of unitive love. And in each state I showed you what things take away imperfection, and the way that leads thither, how to distinguish between true spiritual love and the secret wiles practised by the Devil. And I spoke to you of the three kinds of punishment meted out by my clemency in these three states. One I described to you as being suffered by people on this earth, before they die. The second takes place at death and concerns those who die in mortal sin and without hope—of whom, in narrating their miseries to you, I said that they followed not the bridge but the Devil's way. The third form of punishment will take place at the Last Judgement; and I told you something of the pains of the damned and the glory of the blessed, when everyone will have his own body restored to him.

"I also promised you, and promise you again, that as a result of all the sufferings undergone by my servants I will reform my Spouse. I asked you to endure these sufferings, complaining of the iniquities of wicked ministers with you, and, showing you the excellence in which I have established these ministers, spoke of the reverence that I look for and desire from layfolk towards them. Answering you further, I explained how there was to be no lessening of reverence for them notwithstanding their failings, and how much any such thing was displeasing to my will. I spoke to you too of the virtues of those who live like angels, mentioning in this connection the excellence of the Sacrament of the Altar.

"As, when I was speaking to you of the three above-mentioned states of soul, you wanted to know about the different kinds of tears and whence these arise, I explained this to you by equating the different kinds of tears with the different states of the soul. And I told you that all tears come from the fountain of the heart, and, in an orderly way, I explained why this is so. I also spoke to you about four kinds of tears, and about the fifth that leads to death.

"I also answered your fourth request, in which you begged me to provide for a certain particular case that had occurred. I explained it all to you, and spoke to you at length about my providence, both general and particular, from the creation to the end of the world; describing how I made and make everything according to my absolute divine providence, giving or permitting all that you receive, tribulations and consolations, spiritual and temporal: all for your good, that you may be sanctified in me and my Truth fulfilled in you.

"My Truth was and is this, that I created you to have eternal life; and this Truth I revealed to you through the blood of the only begotten Word, my Son.

"Finally I satisfied your desire, and the promise I had made you, that I should tell you about the perfection of obedience and the imperfection of disobedience, and whence it arises, and what it is that prevents you from being obedient. I presented this to you as the key to everything else, and so it is. I also told you about the kinds of obedience that are appropriate to the perfect and the imperfect, religious and layfolk, speaking of each one separately in turn; describing the peace that comes from obedience, the war that comes from disobedience, and how the disobedient deceive themselves, adding in explanation how death came into the world through the disobedience of Adam.

"Now I, the Eternal Father, the supreme eternal Truth, end by saying that in the obedience of my only begotten Son and Word you have life. And as all inherit death from the first old man, so all who bear the key of obedience draw life from the new man Christ, sweet Jesus, whom I gave you as a bridge after the way to heaven had been disrupted. Pass through this sweet straight way, the way of clear straight Truth, with the help of the key of obedience, and then you will pass through the darkness of this world without offending against me, and at last will open heaven with the key of my Word.

"Now I ask you and my other servants for tears; for it is through tears and continual humble prayer that I will have mercy on the world. Run mortified along this way of Truth, so that you may not be accused of dawdling, for more will be expected of you than ever now that I have shown myself to you in my Truth.

"Take care never to emerge from the cell of self-knowledge, but in that cell both spend and store the treasure I have given you. For this treasure is a doctrine of Truth, founded on the solid living rock of Christ, sweet Jesus; and this doctrine is clothed in light, which banishes darkness. Clothe yourself in this, most beloved daughter—in Truth."

Then that soul, having seen with the eye of her mind and recognized the Truth and the excellence of obedience in the light of the most holy Faith, having heard it with feeling and tasted it with affection and ineffable longing, gazing into the divine Majesty gave thanks unto Him, saying:

"Thanks be unto you, Father, who have not despised me your handiwork, or turned your face away from me, or looked with scorn upon my desires. You who are the light have not ignored me because of my darkness; you who are Life have not ignored me though I am dead; you are a Doctor, and have not despised me despite my grave infirmities; you are Eternal Purity, and have not despised me, full as I am of dirt and manifold miseries—you who are Infinite, while I am finite; you who are Wisdom, while I am all stupidity.

"Despite these and all the other infinite evils and innumerable failings in me, you have not despised me, nor have your wisdom, your goodness, your clemency, your infinite good scorned me; on the contrary, with your light you have given me light. Through your wisdom I have come to know the Truth, through your clemency I have found charity and love of the neighbour. Who constrained you to this? Not any virtue of mine, but your charity alone.

"This same love constrained you to enlighten the eye of my mind with the light of faith, so that I should come to know and understand your Truth, revealed to me. Grant, O Lord, that my memory may be enabled to retain your blessings, and my will burn in the fire of your charity—and may that fire cause blood to spring in my body, that with it, with the love of the Blood, and with the key of obedience, I may open the gate of heaven. This same thing I ask for every reasonable creature, one and all, and for the mystical body of your holy Church.

"I confess, and do not deny, that you loved me before I existed, and love me now ineffably, like one maddened by excess of love.

"O Eternal Trinity! O Deity, who by the union of the divine nature gave such value to the blood of your only begotten Son! You, eternal Trinity, are a deep sea, in which the more I seek the more I find, and the more I find the more I seek for you. You satisfy insatiably; for you satisfy the soul in the abyss of yourself, in such a way that the soul always remains hungry; and hungering for you, O Eternal Trinity, the soul longs to see you in the light of your light. As the heart longs for the fountain of living water, so my soul longs to be freed from this body of darkness and to see you in Truth as you are. For how long yet is your face to be hidden from my eyes?

"O Eternal Trinity, fire and abyss of charity, henceforth dissolve the cloud of my body. The knowledge you have given me of yourself in your Truth constrains and compels me to desire to leave the weight of this body behind, and makes me eager to surrender this life for the praise and glory of your Name, because I have tasted you and seen with the light of my mind into your light, your abyss, O Eternal Trinity, and the beauty of your creature: seeing myself in you, I saw myself made in your image, having had infused into my mind, O Eternal Father, your power and wisdom, the wisdom that belongs to your only begotten Son. The Holy Spirit that proceeds from you, Father, and your Son, has given me the will by which I am enabled to love. You, Eternal Trinity, are the creator and I am your handiwork. With your light I have come to realize that in the creation that you made of me in the blood of the only begotten Son you have fallen in love with the beauty of your handiwork.

"O abyss! O eternal Deity! O unplumbed sea! What more can you give me, when you have given me yourself? You are an ever-burning fire; consuming and never consumed; consuming with your heat all the soul's self-love. You are fire, annihilating all cold, enlightening the mind with your light, the light with which you have enabled me to recognize your Truth. You are the light above all light; who with your light give to the eye of the mind such abundance and perfection of supernatural light that even the light of faith grows clearer—the faith in which I see that my soul has life; and in this light I receive you, light. For in the light of faith I acquire wisdom, in the wisdom of the Word your Son; in the light of faith I grow strong, constant, persevering; in the light of faith I acquire hope, that you will not forsake me along the way; this light teaches me the way to go, and without this light I walk in darkness. Therefore, O Eternal Father, I ask you to enlighten me with the light of the most holy faith.

"Truly this light is a sea that feeds the soul, until it is entirely immersed in you, O Sea of Peace, Eternal Trinity! The water of this sea is clear and calm, and so it brings, not fear, but knowledge of the Truth. This water is transparent and reveals things that are hidden: and so, where the most abundant light of your faith abounds, the soul is as though made certain of what it believes. This sea, as you, Eternal Trinity, have made me see, is a mirror that the hand of love holds up in front of the eyes of my soul and shows me in you, as your creature. In the light of this mirror you are shown to me, and I recognize you, the supreme and infinite good: the good above all goods, blissful, incomprehensible, beyond price; the beauty above all beauty, the wisdom above all wisdom, for you are wisdom itself. You, who are the bread of angels, have given yourself with the fire of love to men; you are the vesture that covers my nakedness, and you feed us who are hungry with your sweetness, for you are all sweetness and nothing in you is bitter.

"O Eternal Trinity, in the light that you gave me, and which I received with the light of the most holy faith, I have come to know you, who by your many wonderful explanations have made clear for me the way of great perfection, so that not in darkness but with your light I may serve you and be a mirror of a good and holy life, and rise up from my own miserable life in which until now I have served you always in darkness.

"I did not know your Truth, and therefore I did not love you. Why did I not know you? Because I did not see you! Because I did not see you with the light of the most holy and glorious faith! Because the cloud of self-love obscured the eye of my mind! But you, O Eternal Trinity, with your light dissipated my darkness. O who can ever ascend to your height, and give thanks to you for the unbounded gifts and great benefits that you have bestowed upon me for the doctrine of truth that you have taught me? This doctrine is undoubtedly a special grace, beyond the general grace you give to other creatures. You willed to condescend to my need and the need that others feel, that subsequently they might be mirrored within you too.

"But do you, O Lord, answer for me yourself; do you, who have given, give satisfaction and response for your gifts by infusing into me the light of grace, so that with this same light I may give thanks to you. Clothe, clothe me, let me be covered by you, Eternal Truth, so that I run this mortal life in true obedience and in the light of the most holy faith."

These are the holy virgin's words, which I have translated into Latin as best I can, preserving, in so far as the Latin allows, her very words.

If, reader, you reflect on all this, you will venerate the excellence of this holy virgin, not only for her way of life, but also for her teaching about the Truth, which is a most wonderful thing for a woman to achieve. And if you think back to the things related earlier, you will realize how passionately she must have longed to be freed from the bonds of the body and united with Christ.

Catherine realized, at that time especially, that it is better to be united with Christ, the Good who is the end and perfection of all goods. From this time onwards the desire grew continually in her, until she finally obtained all she desired; from her marriage to Christ when she was a girl (as described in the last chapter of Part One), she passed on to the nuptial union of the spirit after she had left the body.

But for an account of her passing, let us go on to a new chapter.

CHAPTER FOUR

The Virgin's Spiritual Testament and Passing

———————————————•———————————————

THE witnesses mentioned above have informed me, as do the writings that I have here with me and the words that are fixed in my memory—all of which make up for what I was unable to see and hear myself—that as soon as the virgin felt the hour of death approaching, perhaps not without an explicit revelation, she gathered around her the whole family that the Lord had given her who had accompanied her to Rome.

She delivered a long memorable speech to them, encouraging them to persevere in virtue, and touching on certain special points that I have found written down and signed by those present. I consider this a suitable place to mention these points.

Her first and fundamental principle was that people who wish to begin to serve God must rid their hearts of all that kind of love into which the senses enter, not only for people but for any kind of creature whatsoever, and that they must seek for God the Creator single-mindedly and wholeheartedly. The heart, she said, cannot be entirely given to God unless it is delivered from all other affections and is simple and open and free from double-mindedness. She also said that from her childhood days her one aim had been to labour towards this end. She said, further, that she had realized that the soul cannot reach this perfect state, when it can give its heart to God completely, unless it prays; and she showed that prayer must necessarily be founded upon humility, and not derive from any belief in his own virtue on the part of the person praying, who on the contrary should always recognize that of himself he is nothing. She went on to say that she had always done all she could to practise prayer and to make it a continual habit, as she had realized that it strengthened and increased the other virtues, whereas without it they weakened and withered away. And so she urged her auditors to persevere in prayer, which she said was of two kinds, vocal and mental, and she taught them that they should devote themselves to vocal prayer at certain fixed times, but should always be praying mentally, either actually or habitually.

She said again that in the light of faith she had seen quite clearly that everything that happened to herself and everyone else came from God, and not from hatred but from the great love that He has for His creatures. From this she had conceived a love for God's commandments and ministers and had learned to obey them promptly, firmly believing that their orders always came from God, either for her own salvation or for the sake of an increase of virtue in her soul. She added that to acquire purity of mind it was necessary for people to refrain from judging their fellowmen and from gossiping about what they do, and to have regard only for God's will for them. This led her to say a great deal about not judging people—for any reason whatsoever—that is to say, not saying anything in contempt or condemnation of them, even though we were to see them committing sin with our very own eyes. If, again, we were to discover that someone had committed a fault we should have compassion on them, pray to God for them, and not treat them with scorn or contempt.

She said that she had always had great hope and trust in Divine Providence, and urged her listeners to do the same, saying that she had learned from experience that this Providence was great and unlimited. In this connection she reminded them that when they had been with her they had sometimes experienced this too, on occasions when the Lord had miraculously provided for their meals, and she added that this same Divine Providence never lets anyone down who trusts in it and that it would be with them always in a special way.

These and other instructions the holy virgin gave her people, ending her discourse with the Saviour's own precept and exhorting them humbly but repeatedly to "love each other". She said this to them again and again, in a voice that was itself sweet and loving: "Love each other, O my dearest children; love each other!" If they truly loved each other, she said, they would show that they really had been her spiritual children, and had wanted to be; and she would remain in contact with them and do all she could to show them that she was still their mother. Furthermore, if they had loved each other they would be her glory and her crown, and she, accepting them for ever as her children, would pray to the divine Goodness to infuse into their souls the abundance of graces that the Lord had infused into her own soul.

Besides this she told all present, with an authority deriving from love, that they should always long and pray for the reform and good estate of God's Holy Church and the Vicar of Christ. She told them that always, but especially during the previous seven years, she had carried such a wish in her heart and had never omitted, at least in those seven years, to pray to the divine Majesty and Goodness for this end. She confessed frankly that to obtain this grace she had had to suffer many pains and maladies, and that she was suffering the bitterest pains for that cause as she spoke.

She went on to say that as Satan had obtained permission from God to oppress Job's body with many pains and illnesses, so he seemed to have obtained licence to torment and crucify her body with many different kinds of afflictions. So true is this, that from the soles of her feet to the crown of her head no part of her body was unaffected, for each member suffered its own pain; some of her members, indeed, were afflicted by several pains at once, as anyone looking at her could see quite plainly, even though she said nothing about them.

She also said, "It seems to me, beloved ones, that my Heavenly Bridegroom has decided quite firmly that in and through this strong and ardent desire of mine, my soul, after the pains that His Goodness has given me, shall be taken out of its tomb of darkness and return to the place it came from."

The same witnesses relate in their writings that Catherine's pains seemed to them to be so horrible and unbearable that no one could have endured them except through a special grace from God; and they marvelled how she could bear them so calmly and with such apparent unconcern.

As they stood there marvelling and weeping grievously, she went on: "Dearest children, you must not let yourselves give way to grief if I die; on the contrary, you must be happy and rejoice with me that I am leaving a place of pain and going to find rest in an ocean of peace, in eternal God. I give you my word: after my death I shall be more use to you than I have ever been or ever could be while I was with you in this life of darkness and misery. Nevertheless, I leave life and death and all things in the hands of my Heavenly Bridegroom. If He sees that I can be of assistance to someone and wills that I should go on living in labour and pain, I am ready for the honour of His Name and the good of souls to endure torments and even death itself, a hundred times a day if it were possible. If on the other hand it is His pleasure that I should die, be certain of this, dearest children, that I have given my life for Holy Church, and this, I believe, as the result of an exceptional grace that the Lord has granted me."

Then, one by one, she called those present up to her, and told them what to do after her death. She asked them to refer everything to me and to look upon me as her representative. Some she sent off to be religious, others to the hermit's life, others again to the priesthood. Then, as head of the women, especially those belonging to the Sisters of Penance of St. Dominic, she appointed Alessia. Thus she arranged everything in detail, as the Holy Spirit led her to do; and experience has shown that all that she ordained was sound.

At this point she asked them all to forgive her, saying, "Beloved ones, although it is true that I have longed and thirsted continually for your salvation, at the same time I must confess that frequently, as I know, I have failed in my duty towards you, either because I have not been a good example of spiritual light and virtue and good works, as I should and could have been if I had been a true handmaid and bride of Jesus Christ, or because I have not been as careful as I should have been about your material needs. For this I ask each and all of you to forgive me and have sympathy with me, and humbly beg each one of you, yet again, to persevere along the path of virtue to the end. By so doing, as I have already said, you will be my joy and crown." And with this she ended her speech.

Calling her confessor, she made a general confession, although she had always confessed every day; and she asked humbly for the Holy Eucharist and the other sacraments, and was given them as she wished at the proper times. Then she asked to be given the plenary indulgence that had been granted her by the two Supreme Pontiffs, Gregory XI and Urban VI. Then she entered upon her agony, and a bitter conflict with the age-old Adversary, which the people present could see from her words and gestures; for sometimes she would be silent; then she would say something in reply to him; or she would laugh, as though she was amused at what he said, and sometimes she would become angry with him.

They noted one thing in especial which they passed on to me; I believe God willed it so. At one point, after being quiet for a while as though she had heard some sort of reproach, Catherine broke out into these words, with a joyful smile on her face: "Vainglory, never, but true glory and in praise of God, yes." Not without reason did divine Providence will that this should be known, for there were many men and women who believed that, lovable though she was, and showered though she was with graces by the Lord, she nevertheless sought popularity, or at least was self-satisfied about her gifts, and that this was why she was so fond of being with people. I myself have often heard it said of her, "What does she want to go traipsing about for? She is a woman! If she wants to serve God, why doesn't she stay at home?" But some of these people have already been dealt with.[1]

---

1. See Part II, Chapter 5.

"Vainglory, never," she said, "but true glory and in praise of God, yes!" As though to say, I have not travelled or done anything else out of vainglory; but everything I have done has been in praise and glory of the Saviour's Name.

I heard her confessions, both particular and general, very often indeed, and I weighed all her actions scrupulously, and I can state and affirm that all she did was done at God's command and under divine inspiration. Not only did Catherine not think about being popular, she did not even think about human beings at all unless she was praying for their salvation or labouring to procure their good. No one who did not know her personally can possibly realize how free her soul was from human passions, even those often found in persons of great virtue. In her the Apostle's saying seemed to be fulfilled: "Our conversation is in heaven." Catherine could never for a single moment forget the thing uppermost in her mind, or renounce the fervour of her charity: for this reason there was no room in her soul for vainglory or any other irrational appetite.

Let us take up the thread of our discourse again.

After a long agony, having won her victory, she regained her strength, and once again she made her general confession, which is usually made publicly, wisely asking for absolution and for another plenary indulgence—in this, I think, following the teaching and example of Martin, Jerome and Augustine, who teach the faithful that no Christian who wills to be perfect should pass into the other life without tears of repentance and sincere contrition for the sins he has committed. Augustine, for instance, had the Seven Penitential Psalms written out and hung up on the wall of his bedroom during his final illness, so that he could always have them before his eyes; and reading them continually as he lay in bed, he wept copiously and incessantly. Before Jerome breathed his last he made a public confession of his sins and failings. Martin on the first onset of death showed his disciples by his own example that the Christian should die in sackcloth and be laid on ashes as a sign of repentance. Our holy virgin, desirous of imitating these saints as closely as possible, showed great contrition in not being satisfied with asking once only for absolution of her sins and the attendant punishment.

At this point, as I have been told by those present at the time, she suddenly lost all her strength; but despite this she continued to give holy advice to the children, both present and absent, whom she had generated in Christ. At this last moment she remembered me too, and said, "In all your doubts and needs turn to Friar Raimondo, and tell him not to be discouraged or lose heart, whatever happens, for I shall always be with him to save him from any danger; and when he does anything he shouldn't I shall tell him, and see that he mends his ways and improves." They told me that she said this many times, for as long as she could speak.

Realizing that the moment of death was approaching she said, "Lord, I commend my spirit into your hands!" And with these words that holy soul was freed from the bonds of the flesh, as she had for so long desired, and was inseparably united for all eternity with the Heavenly Bridegroom she had loved so greatly. It was the year of the Lord 1380, the twenty-ninth day of April, a Sunday, about the hour of Terce.

I was in Genoa. At that moment her spirit told me nearly all the words I have written above, which she wanted to be passed on to me— may my witness be the Truth that can neither deceive nor be deceived. But my blind heart did not at the time understand whence they came, even though they clearly grasped their sound and meaning.

I was in Genoa, then, as Provincial of the province,[2] and the time was approaching for the General Chapter in Bologna, at which the Master General of the Order was to be elected. With other friars and priests I was preparing to leave the city to take ship to Pisa, and so, with God's help, to Bologna; which we did.

---

2. Raymond was elected Provincial of the province of Lombardy in May 1379, and General of the Order at the Chapter held in Bologna on May 12th, 1380, succeeding Friar Elia of Toulouse, who had been deposed from office for his adherence to the anti-Pope Clement VII.

Having hired a little boat, we awaited a suitable moment to set sail; but the moment did not seem to want to come. On the morning that the virgin ascended into heaven the Friars Preachers were celebrating the feast of St. Peter the Martyr; I therefore had gone down to the Church, and, unworthy though I was, said Mass. Then I went back into the dormitory to pack my bag. As I passed in front of the image of the glorious Virgin, I stopped there for a moment to say the Hail Mary, as is our custom. Suddenly there was a voice, though there was no sound in the air; the words sounded not in my bodily ears but in my mind, and I heard them more clearly than if they had come from the mouth of someone standing only a yard away. This is the only way I can think of describing the voice, if voice it can be called, since there was no sound attached to it. However that may be, these words resounded distinctly in my mind: "Fear not: I am here for your sake; I am in heaven for your sake. I will protect you and defend you. Go on your way in confidence, and do not lose heart: I am here for your sake." To tell the truth, on hearing this I was highly perplexed, and wondered what this comfort and promise of being safe could be.

For a moment the only thing I could think of was that the person who had spoken to me was Mary, the Mother of God, whom I had just addressed; but as soon as I reflected on my own unworthiness I did not dare to believe this. In fact, I was afraid that it might be a way of acquainting me with some misfortune that was about to befall me and so I commended myself to the Mother of mercy, who is always ready to comfort the afflicted, asking her to use this promise of help to make me more prepared to endure with resolution whatever was to come. I was in fact half-afraid that, having preached the crusade in the city against the schismatics, I might be about to come across them on the voyage, for I knew that they would be only too glad to do me and my companions some injury. Worried by these thoughts, I was unable to fathom the mystery that the most merciful Lord had performed through His bride to rally me from my faint-heartedness, for the virgin had quite clearly realized this and the Lord her Heavenly Bridegroom of course knew more about it still.

In recounting these things I find more cause for shame than for vanity, but I state them frankly despite my own shame, so as not to dim in any way the glory of the Heavenly Bridegroom and his holy bride, whose goodness so kindly comforted me.

For the rest, so that it will not be imagined that I was the only person to have Catherine's death revealed from a distance, I am obliged to describe a vision that a lady in Rome had at the very moment when the virgin was passing from this life. She herself told me about it in a solemn and devout way, and I take what she said seriously, for I had known the state of her conscience and her way of life intimately for more than twenty years before these things took place. For this lady used to confess to me, and always asked my advice in matters of conscience. I can therefore record her story with the utmost conviction.

There was then in Rome at the time of the holy virgin's death a certain lady, Semia by name, who was the mother of five sons. Though not of noble birth she was by no means of the people, for many of her relatives were amongst the most well-to-do in the city. Since before her husband had died and for the considerable time that had elapsed since his death she had given herself to the service of God, and what with her pilgrimages, her visits to the Roman churches, and her prayers, she had wholly dedicated herself to this kind of life and had been leading it for a long time. No matter what the season of the year was, she always stayed up all night, with only the briefest period of rest to recuperate for the fatigues of the next day's pilgrimages.

When the holy virgin came to Rome, Semia learned through me and others of the excellence of her virtues and at once went to see her, and as soon as she had begun to taste the pleasure of talking to Catherine she told me and the others who had talked to her about the virgin that we had not given her any idea of even half of her perfections. Semia ended by becoming a close companion of Catherine's and was often in the house with her; but because of her pilgrimages, and because she also had to look after her sons, she sometimes spent several days without seeing her and that was why in this case she did not know that Catherine was so ill.

On the eve of the holy virgin's death, Semia got up as usual to pray, and when day dawned and she ended her prayers she realized that it was Sunday and that she would have to be up early if she was not to miss High Mass, especially as she was alone in the house and had to do the cooking. So when she laid her head on the pillow it was with the intention of having a short sleep and then getting up at once.

As frequently happens when the mind is preoccupied, even while she was asleep she was thinking about getting up; and while, still asleep, she was thinking, "You must get up at once so that you can do the cooking first and then go off to Church in good time," a graceful child of about eight or ten years of age appeared to her and said, "I don't want you to wake up and get up until you have seen what I want you to see." Although she found pleasure in gazing at the child, because of her wish to go to Mass she answered, "Let me get up, dear child, for today I must go to Mass." But the boy said, "Don't get up until you have seen the marvels I have to show you from God." And he began to pull her, as it seemed to her, by the skirt and took her into an open place where there seemed to be an oratory or church, in the centre of which was a closed silver tabernacle most beautiful to behold. Then the boy said to her, "Wait a moment, and you will see what is inside that tabernacle."

At that moment another boy just as graceful as the first appeared carrying a ladder, which he leaned up against the silver tabernacle, then climbed up it, and, as it seemed to the lady, opened the tabernacle with a golden key. Whereupon there immediately appeared a little girl of rare beauty: she was dressed in shining white and resplendent with necklaces, and on her head she had three crowns one on top of the other, each more beautiful than the last. The lowest one was made of silver, and was as white as snow; the middle one of gold and silver mixed, and it gave out a ruddy glow, like red cloth interwoven with gold thread; the top one was made of pure gold and was decked out with gems and precious stones.

When the devout lady saw this girl adorned with all this finery she wondered who she was, and after looking in her face again and again she finally discovered that her features were those of the virgin Catherine of Siena; but as she knew that Catherine was many years older than the girl in the tabernacle she thought she must be someone else. The boy who had first appeared to her asked her if she recognized the person she was looking at, and she replied, "The face is certainly that of Catherine of Siena, but their ages are different." While she was looking at her, still in a state of doubt, the girl in the tabernacle said to the two little boys, with a smile, "You see, she doesn't recognize me."

Four more boys appeared carrying a couch that looked like a bridal bed, covered with precious stuffs, purple in hue; they placed it near the tabernacle, ran nimbly up the ladder, took the crowned girl by the hand and laid her upon the bridal bed. The girl said, "First let me go up to the person who is looking at me and cannot recognize me," and, half-flying, she came up to her and said, "Semia, don't you recognize me? I am Catherine of Siena, as you can tell by my face." "Are you my spiritual mother Catherine?" asked Semia. And Catherine answered, "Yes, I am; but ponder carefully on what you have seen, and what you are about to see now."

Having said this, she was placed on the bridal bed by the six boys and immediately began to rise high into the air. As Semia was watching her go, a throne suddenly appeared in heaven and upon it a king crowned and loaded with gems, holding an open book in his right hand. Meanwhile the boys were lifting the virgin on the bridal bed higher and higher, until they finally arrived at the step in front of the throne, at the feet of the person sitting there. Here they laid the bed down, and the virgin immediately got up, threw herself at the king's feet and worshipped him. The king said, "Welcome to you, Catherine, my most beloved bride and daughter." At the king's command the girl raised her head and read in the open book for as long a time as it takes to say the Our Father. Then she got up and remained standing by the throne to await the queen, who, as it seemed to Semia, was approaching the king accompanied by a great following of virgins. On the queen's approach, the virgin suddenly got down from the step and, falling upon her knees, revered her. The lady of heaven went up to her and taking her by the hand said, "Welcome to you, my most beloved daughter Catherine," and raising her up bestowed upon her the kiss of peace. Whereupon Catherine again revered the empress of heaven and at her command joined the other virgins, from each of them with great joy receiving the kiss of peace.

While these things were happening, Semia began to shout out loud, "O our Lady, O Mother of Our Lord Jesus Christ, intercede for us!" and "O holy Mary Magdalene, O Saint Catherine, O St. Agnes, St. Margaret, pray for us!" She told me that although all this was going on in heaven she could see the details as clearly as though she had been at the foot of a few steps and these things were going on at the top. She added that she had clearly seen not only the most blessed Mother of God but all the others quite distinctly and so had called them all by their names, each of them bearing the sign of her particular form of martyrdom: Catherine with the wheel; Margaret with the dragon under her feet; Agatha with her breasts cut off; and so on. In the end all the virgins applauded the virgin Catherine, who was placed amongst them and crowned with glory.

When Semia woke up the sun was already high and it was about the hour of Terce. She was greatly upset at this, both because she had missed Mass and also on account of her sons' dinner, which she had still to get ready. At the same time she began to reflect upon the extraordinary vision she had seen. She had been very busy during the previous few days and although she knew that Catherine was not well she had not gone to see her because she knew that the virgin always managed to get over her illnesses, however severe they were. For this reason she never imagined that she might be dead, and was inclined to think that during her vision Catherine had been in one of her usual ecstasies and had received great revelations from the Lord in it.

As it was so late, Semia was afraid she would be unable to get to any Mass that day, and began to suspect that the vision had been a trick of the Devil's to make her miss Mass on a Sunday, against the law of the Church. This made her hurry up, and, having put the cooking pot on the fire, she ran to the parish church, saying in her heart, "If I am too late for Mass, it will mean that the vision came from the Devil; if I am not too late, it will be thanks to the merits of mother Catherine."

When she got to the church she found them singing the Offertory, which comes immediately after the Gospel, and she was most upset. "Woe is me!" she exclaimed. "The Devil has deceived me."

She went off home as fast as she could so that she would at least be in time to get the dinner ready, and could have her mind free to set about finding another church where she might hear Mass right through.

While she was in the kitchen she heard a bell start ringing for Mass: it was coming from a convent near her home. Delighted at this, she hastily got ready so as to be there in time: on the table, washed and cut, she left the cabbages she intended to put in the pot when she got back and went off, locking the front door so that no one could get in.

When she got to the convent church she found that Mass was just beginning and said to herself, delightedly, "It wasn't the Devil deceiving me after all." She was a little afraid that her sons, who were no longer young, might get annoyed when they found that their meal was not ready, but she decided to leave everything in God's hands and at least enjoy the satisfaction of hearing the whole of Mass. At the same time she begged the Saviour, if the vision had truly come from Him, to save her from any grumbling from her sons, who were so particular that she was very much afraid of them. And so she heard High Mass to the end.

On her way home she found her sons coming down the street to meet her. "Mother," they shouted, "it's late! We're in a hurry for our dinner!" "Just wait a little while, dear sons," she answered, "everything will be ready in a trice." She ran off towards the house, and, finding it all locked up as she had left it, opened the door. And she was about to set about finishing all she had to do when she found that in fact everything had been done: that is to say, the cabbage and meat and everything else had been so well prepared that she and her sons would be able to sit down to table at once. Absolutely amazed, she realized that she must have been miraculously heard by the Lord, and she decided that as soon as dinner was over she would go and see Catherine, whom she imagined to be still alive, and tell her all about it.

In a state of high delight she called her sons, who were not far away, to the table; and during the meal she kept thinking of that marvellous vision, now confirmed by two miracles. Her sons, who were quite in the dark about everything, could do nothing but praise the dinner, which was better than usual; but all she could do was to go on thinking in her heart of what she had seen and still saw, and, as she later said to me, she kept exclaiming to herself, "O dear mother, you came into my house with the door locked to do my cooking for me. Now I know truly that you are a saint and a true handmaid of Christ."

Far from suspecting that the virgin was dead, when her sons had finished eating she went to her house to see her and knocked at the door as usual, but got no answer. Some women outside said that Catherine had gone to church and that there was no one at home. Believing them, Semia returned home. The truth was, however, that all the people who were in the house, weeping over their spiritual mother who had left them behind as orphans in this wicked world, were keeping her death a secret so that there should be no crowds or disturbance in the house. They also wanted to get advice on how to carry out the last rites. And so they had sent some of their own number out and then closed the door behind them as though there was no one in. In this way the others in the house could be left alone to their grief and could also arrange what was to be done in peace.

They finally came to the decision that the virgin's body should be carried to the church of the Friars Preachers, known to the people as the church of Santa Maria della Minerva, the following morning, and that the last rites should be performed there in the way the Lord would decide. Thus everything was done to keep Catherine's death quiet, and what had been decided in the house was carried out secretly; but despite all this her Heavenly Bridegroom divulged what had happened in a way beyond belief.

No sooner had the virgin's body been removed to the church than the news spread throughout Rome, and immediately there was a great rush of people to the church. It was a general scramble, with everyone wanting to touch the dead person's clothes and feet; and the holy virgin's sons and daughters, and the Friars as well, began to be afraid that the clothes and body would be torn to pieces. So they laid the corpse behind the iron railings in St. Dominic's chapel in the church.

What happened after that will be related in the next chapter.

While all this was going on, Semia happened to come into this part of the town, and, seeing the tumult, asked what it was all about. She was told that Catherine of Siena was dead, and that her body was in the church, and that was why everybody was trying to get in.

When she heard this she broke into bitter tears and rushed forward towards where the virgin's body lay, shouting to her spiritual daughters, who were grouped round the coffin, "You wicked women, why didn't you tell me that my sweetest mother was dead? Why didn't you call me when she was dying?" They tried to apologize but she interrupted them: "What time did she die?" They answered, "She gave up her spirit to the Creator yesterday, and it was at about the hour of Terce." Then Semia, clawing at her face, shrieked out, "I saw her! I saw my dearest mother leaving her body, and I saw her being carried up into heaven by the angels with three shining crowns of precious stones on her head and wearing a white dress! Now I know that the Lord sent one of his angels to me and let me see my mother's end, and kept Mass waiting for me and, what's more, gave me miraculous help in the kitchen. O, Mother, Mother, why didn't I realize during that vision that you were passing from the world?"

And then she told the sons and daughters who were standing round guarding the holy body all about the vision she had had.

I end the chapter.

CHAPTER FIVE

The Miracles

———————————— • ————————————

WHEN Catherine's earthly pilgrimage had ended and she had received her reward, the divine Power that had always accompanied her did not cease revealing the merits of her sanctity to the faithful.

As I have said, without any previous warning or invitation, in fact in spite of the attempt to conceal what had happened, the whole Roman populace came thronging to the church where the holy body was lying in its coffin, so that they could devoutly kiss the feet and hands and commend themselves to the virgin's prayers. There was such a crush that it became necessary to move the coffin and put it behind the iron railings in St. Dominic's Chapel.

Many people had such faith in Catherine's merits that they began to bring the sick and infirm to her, begging the Lord to cure them through the virgin's merits. They were not disappointed; and I feel obliged to relate what I have found written down about this matter, and to recount what I know.

Well, then, while the corpse was still in the church, a nun of the Third Order of St. Francis, Domenica by name—she was a native of Bergamo in Lombardy but was living in Rome—who had been suffering for some time from a serious complaint in one of her arms—she had not been able to use it for six months in fact and it was almost entirely wasted away—went to the church but could not get near it because of the crowd there. So she was obliged to give her veil to somebody else to touch the virgin's body with it and then give it back to her. When she got it back she put it on her arm and it was immediately cured.

At this she began to shout to the crowd, "Look! By the virgin's merits I am cured of an incurable complaint that had plysed all my arm!" When the news spread there was great excitement, and crowds of people came running up carrying their sick, so that they might at least touch the hem of Catherine's garments.

Amongst them there was a four-year-old boy, the sinews of whose neck had contracted so that he had to keep his head bent to one side. When he got into the presence of the holy body they touched the affected part with one of the virgin's hands and wrapped his neck up in a veil belonging to her. The boy at once began to get better, and after a short while straightened his head, absolutely cured.

Meanwhile, as a result of all these prodigies and miracles, for the space of three days it was impossible to get the corpse buried. During these three days there was such an endless stream of people that a Master of Sacred Theology who went up into the pulpit to deliver a panegyric on the virgin could not obtain silence and was unable to make himself heard. A lot of people heard him say these words, however: "Catherine has no need of our sermons, for she is a sermon in herself and can make herself known by herself," and he climbed down without finishing, or rather without even beginning his discourse.

In the meantime the miracles were increasing and multiplying.

There was for instance Lucio di Cannarola, who had been attacked by plysis in one of his legs from the thigh downwards, with the result that he could hardly move, even with the help of a crutch. Hearing of the miracles being performed by the Most High through the virgin Catherine, he dragged himself laboriously to the church and with the assistance of the people already there managed to reach the place where the virgin's body was lying. Very devoutly he placed one of the virgin's hands against the plysed thigh and shin and at once felt an improvement. Before he left he was completely cured. On seeing this marvellous event, those present gave thanks to Almighty God, who is always admirable in His saints.

A girl called Ratozola, who was suffering from a horrible leprosy of the face, her nose and upper lip being a ghastly, stinking, gangrenous mass, hearing of what was happening went to the church. When she tried to force her way to the sacred body she kept on being pushed back by those around her, but by dint of angry persistence she finally managed to get through. Eager for the grace she so ardently longed for, she put the affected parts to the virgin's hands, feet and even her face. Immediately she felt better, and in a short while she was cured of the leprosy. There was not the slightest sign of it left on her face.

Another Roman citizen, Ciprio by name, and his wife Lella had a daughter who had fallen into a consumption as a child and no kind of treatment had been able to cure her. When her parents heard of the miracles the holy virgin was performing, they commended themselves to her devoutly and got their daughter to touch a veil and some beads that had been in contact with Catherine's body. Wonderful! They had almost given up hope that the girl would ever get better, but as soon as she touched these things she was restored to health.

But that is not all. While the holy body was lying there still unburied, a Roman citizen, Antonio di Lello di Pietro, finding himself near the Church of the Prince of the Apostles, heard of the miracles that were taking place as a result of the merits of the holy virgin. This man, through over-exertion at his work, had succumbed to a complaint that made walking difficult for him. The doctors had been unable to do anything about it.

Hearing of the fame of these miracles, he devoutly commended himself to the virgin, and promised a votive offering if he got better. As soon as he had made this promise he found himself cured: he felt no inconvenience any more, and going on his way with a brisk and eager step he visited the mortal remains of his liberator and fulfilled the promise he had made, and he kept on telling anyone who would listen to him all about the grace he had received.

A pious Roman woman named Paola, who had been quite a close friend of Catherine's, in fact had been her servant, or rather hostess—for she had taken her into her own home with all her followers—had at the time when the holy virgin died been suffering for four months from gout and acute pains in her sides. As the treatment required for her complaints was the opposite in each case, one needing aperients, the other astringents, the aforesaid matron was in a bad way and had already sensed the approach of death.

When the holy virgin died this lady kept on asking for something that had touched her holy body. One evening it was found possible to satisfy her and the next morning she got up out of bed: she had been lying there for four months, and she got up and walked about as easily as though she had never been ill. She herself told me the whole story on my return to Rome.

These miracles, and many others that have been forgotten through carelessness on the part of the writers, were performed by the Almighty Lord through His bride before her body was carried to the grave—which, as has been said, had had to be put off for three days because of the crowds.

But when the corpse was laid in the tomb the power of God did not cease restoring the sick to health; in fact, in a way it increased.

A Roman named Giovanni di Neri had a little son who could not stand up on his feet and so could not learn to walk. On hearing of the fame of all these miracles Giovanni made a vow to God and the holy virgin Catherine if they would cure the little boy.

When the boy was carried to her tomb, as soon as he was put over it his feet and legs grew strong and he began to stand up straight and walk as though there had never been anything wrong with him.

A certain Giovanni di Tozzo had a horrible eye complaint and one of his eyes was always running. He made a vow to the holy virgin Catherine of Siena and was at once completely cured. He went to her tomb, described the grace he had received, and left the customary offering of wax candles there.

The same thing happened to a woman who was on a pilgrimage from Germany, whose name the people present, making a list of these miracles, forgot to take down. She too had had some serious trouble with her eyes for some time: she could hardly see at all and had lost all hope of ever getting better. Commending herself devoutly to the holy virgin and making a vow, in a short time, without any help from medicines, she got her sight back. When she went to Catherine's tomb she could see it as clearly as if there had never been anything wrong with her eyes.

Another lady, a Roman this time called Maria, was afflicted with such a serious head complaint that in spite of undergoing every possible kind of treatment she had finally lost the sight of one eye. As a result of this she had been so overcome by misery and shame that she had locked herself up in her house and refused to come out. Hearing of the holy virgin's miracles, she commended herself to her and made a promise.

The next night, in a dream, Catherine appeared to this lady's servant and said, "Tell the lady Maria to throw all her medicines away and go to Mass every morning. She will be cured." As soon as the maid told her this she gladly agreed, and went to Mass. The pain stopped at once and she began to be able to see again. Then, by persevering in this practice, she soon got back her original health and sight.

Reader, I beg you to consider what the virgin was doing in this particular case. She was imitating her Heavenly Bridegroom, or, to speak more correctly, in this work her Heavenly Bridegroom was making her like unto Himself; for He was not satisfied with curing the body of this person who had called upon His bride: He also willed to give medicine to her soul. Catherine could certainly have granted her the grace of having her eyes cured after her prayers and promises as she had done in other cases; she willed, however, to reward her with more than she had asked for. In the same way the Saviour did not cure the body without curing the soul too, for as in the case of one who came to Him asking for bodily health, He first forgave him his sins, saying, "Be of good heart, son, thy sins are forgiven thee." (*Matt.* 9:2).

A youth named Giacomo, the son of a Roman citizen called Pietro di Niccolo, was in bed for many months with a serious illness. No medicine brought any improvement and he seemed to be approaching his end. All hope of saving him having gone, a certain pious woman, Ceccola Carteria, consecrated him to the holy virgin Catherine and at once he got his strength back; he began to get better and in a short time was cured.

Another Roman woman, Cilia di Petruccio, who was bowed down by illness despite all the doctors tried to do, also found herself *in extremis*. The doctors themselves, having lost all hope of saving her, said that she was bound to die. But she turned devoutly to the holy virgin Catherine of Siena and at once began to get better. From that moment she continued to improve, until in a few days she had quite recovered her old health.

The noblewoman Giovanna degli Ilperini, who had been intimately acquainted with the holy virgin, seeing her miracles, conceived a still greater faith in her sanctity and urged all the sick people she knew to commend themselves devoutly to her. This led to many more being restored to health.

One of this noblewoman's children was amusing himself one day by running carelessly along the unprotected balcony in front of the house when he fell right down to the ground before his mother's eyes. When she saw this it seemed to her that he must inevitably die or at least suffer some permanent injury. Whereupon she shouted out in a loud voice, "Holy Catherine of Siena, I commend my son to you!" And a wonderful thing happened. Although the height of the house, the child's condition and the fall naturally made it seem as though he was likely to die, nothing of the sort happened and the little boy got up from his fall as sound and lively as ever. His mother rushed down as fast as she could, and when she found that he was all right, she gave devout and humble thanks to Almighty God and His bride Catherine, praising the virgin's sanctity to everyone she came across.

Another woman, Bona di Giovanni, a servant who mostly did washing, once, when she was washing clothes on the edge of the Tiber, happened to have to wash a piece of bedclothing made of linen and cotton-wool, of the kind normally known as a quilt. Rather thoughtlessly, she let this quilt sink slowly into the water, until it became so heavy that it was pulled out of her hands and swept away by the current. She was upset at the thought of losing it, for being poor she would not have been able to pay for the loss; so she tried to get it back, but in doing so she leaned over too far and she too began to be carried away by the current.

In such a situation the only help remaining to her could be from God, and while she was thinking of turning to Him there came into her mind all the tales of the prodigies and miracles being performed at that time in Rome by the holy virgin. Invoking her, she exclaimed, "O holy virgin, Catherine of Siena, save me from this great danger!" The virgin's help could not have been more prompt: the woman immediately felt herself lifted up above the waves, and then, as though they had stopped flowing, was able to reach the bank with the quilt, without the help of any human being at all. This absolutely amazed her and she was quite unable to understand however she had managed to get out of such danger, except by admitting that she must have been miraculously aided and saved by Catherine's merits.

All these and many other miracles the Lord performed in witness to the holy virgin His bride before my return to Rome—and when I came back it was with an unbearable burden, I being by then Master General of the Order of Friars Preachers. It was then that my Friars and the nuns, the holy virgin's sons and daughters in Christ, told me all the things that I have written down so far. But after my arrival a miracle took place of which I myself was partly a witness and which I must by no means omit.

I was in Rome, then, having moved the holy virgin's body on the day that she had foretold many years earlier, when I fell ill and had need of a doctor. The doctor lived near my Friars' monastery and was a very dear friend. He was Dr. Giacomo, of Santa Maria Rotonda.

He came to see me and prescribed the treatment, and told me that a young Roman, Niccolo—Cola, for short—the stepson of an eminent citizen named Cinzio Tancancini, was quite seriously ill with a throat complaint that the doctors call quinzy. My doctor friend did not see how he could be cured and despaired of his getting better. Later I learned that the boy had been at the end of his tether and that his death had been expected hourly. Alessia, Catherine's companion, hearing about this and not forgetting that Cinzio and his family had been very devoted to the holy virgin and very dear friends of hers, hurried off to see the young man, who was already in his last agony, taking with her one of the virgin's teeth, which she had kept as a great treasure. When she found that the invalid was on the point of death, for his throat was gradually being constricted, she put the tooth near it: immediately there was a loud noise as though a stone had fallen, and the abscess burst. The invalid began to lift his head up and to spit out mouthfuls of matter and in a very short time he was perfectly all right, giving thanks to God and the holy virgin, by the virtue of whose tooth he had been, this time at least, snatched from the jaws of death.

Niccolo (Cola) gave a public account of the miracle, and everyone, especially the doctor, marvelled, for he realized better than anyone else what condition the invalid had been in and how close he had been to death.

On one occasion, when I was preaching the word of God to the people and describing the great things that the Lord had done through His bride, I was telling the story of this miracle when Niccolo himself got up in the middle of the congregation and said in a loud voice, "Sir, that's the truth! I am the person to whom the virgin did that miracle."

To these signs and miracles which I have here recounted, you must know, reader, that many were added which were never written down; but they were made known by the tokens, that is to say, the waxen images which were placed above the tomb in great numbers, during the time when I myself was there personally; but the unbridled greed, not to say malevolence, of some brigands (I do not know whether they were foreigners, for Rome is always full of these, or native Romans) did not allow these images to remain there long. For they were all taken away secretly in a short time by thieves, who without doubt have been punished already, or will shortly be punished.

Accusing myself before God, His Angels and all the faithful, I confess that many men and women came to me who had received all manner of graces and miracles through the merits of the holy virgin, but they must remain lost in oblivion, more as a result of my negligence than anything else. I had not in fact been asked to put them down in writing; nevertheless, I went so far as to entrust them to a professional scribe, but he, alas, was not at all careful about them.

Nevertheless, I do remember one thing which, as it will help slightly to remedy this position, I shall not omit to relate.

At the time when Queen Joanna had sent Rinaldo of the Orsini family against Rome with a great following of armed men to take the Supreme Pontiff Urban VI prisoner or drive him out or kill him, the Romans remained staunchly loyal to the Pope, and many of them, especially amongst the people, were taken prisoner by the enemy; some were tied to trees and left to die a most cruel death, others were led off in chains to the camp, there to await ransom.

I was told by some of these that all who invoked the virgin were miraculously freed from their chains and with no help except from God returned safely to Rome. One of them told me that no sooner had he called upon Catherine than he found himself free from the cords with which the enemy had bound him to a tree and that on his way back to Rome, praying to the virgin all the time, he came upon no difficulty of any kind. He told me all this very devoutly, and added that there were others who had received the same grace through the merits of the holy virgin Catherine.

I can recollect hearing tales of many more miracles, but even my memory is growing old and I cannot remember them all clearly.

I beg the reader to gather these flowers and fruits devoutly for his own benefit, and not to get annoyed over the length of this book or its crude style; I likewise beg him to avoid all detractors, the lukewarm, the irreligious, and the malevolent, like the plague.

Here I should end this book, if I had not still to say a few words about Catherine's patience, which is a thing more highly esteemed by the Church Militant than miracles in its saints; as St. Gregory so rightly says, it is greater than prodigies and miracles. For this reason I shall describe it in a separate chapter—with Catherine's help, and if I be granted the power to do so by her Heavenly Bridegroom, who with the Father and the Holy Spirit lives and reigns world without end. Amen.

CHAPTER SIX

Epilogue: Catherine's Patience

---•---

T HE First Truth, who assumed human flesh for our salvation, said
  that those who keep the word of God in hearts that are pure and
good shall bear fruit with patience. St. Gregory, too, says in his book
of Dialogues, "I believe that the virtue of patience is greater than marvels and miracles."[1] The Apostle James, again, in his Epistle, says that
patience hath a perfect work, (*James* 1:4) not because it is the greatest
or the queen of virtues but because it is inseparable from charity, which,
as the Apostle says, is the greatest virtue, never coming to an end or
falling away. (*1 Cor.* 13). Without charity none of the other virtues are
any use to man. The same Apostle says in his description of it that it is
patient and kind, has no envy in it, is not provoked to anger and does
not seek its own interests. (*1 Cor.* 13:4–5).

And so when our most holy Mother Church examines the lives
of saintly people before inscribing their names in the catalogue of the
blessed, her first concern is never with any miracles they may have performed, for two reasons: first, because many evil men have worked,
and still go on working, marvels that seem to be miracles but are not
so—as Pharaoh's magicians did in the past, and as in the course of time

---

1. Bk. I, Chap. 12.

the Magician and Anti-Christ with all their followers will do; secondly, because there have been times when people have worked miracles, even by divine power, and then been damned, like Judas and others, of whom it is said in the Gospels that on the Day of Judgement they will say to the Lord, "Have we not performed miracles in thy name?" and He will reply, "Depart from me, all ye workers of iniquity." (*Luke* 13:27).

From this it is evident that in the prudent view of the learned, marvels and miracles have to be scrutinized most carefully, since of themselves they do not satisfy the Church Militant and do not prove that the person performing them has necessarily been predestined and admitted to eternal beatitude. But this does not mean that miracles are not a great sign of holiness, especially if they are performed after death. Though even these do not supply any absolute proof of holiness, for miracles can in fact take place at the grave of someone who is not a saint, to reward the faith of those who believe that the person concerned is a saint; but if the Lord makes these happen, it is not because of the presumed sanctity but for the glory of His Name, so that the believers shall not be disappointed in their desires.

Thus, when our most holy Mother Church, who is guided by the Holy Spirit, tries to ascertain as far as is possible in this life the true worth of the saints, she looks at their lives, that is to say, at what they did while they were on earth. Her Bridegroom teaches her to do this when He says, "By their fruits you shall know them"—*i.e.* by their works—and goes on, "A good tree cannot bring forth evil fruit." (*Matt.* 7:16; 7:18). The good fruit means the works of charity towards God and our neighbour, in which, as the Saviour Himself says, is to be found all the Law and the Prophets. But as these works are pleasing to God, so they are displeasing to the Devil, who adopts every method he can to prevent them, either directly himself or through people in the world.

Therefore, if holy people want to persevere in the good—for without perseverance there can be no final crown—they must have patience, through which they remain firmly established in the love of God and the neighbour despite every kind of persecution. The Saviour in fact told the disciples that in patience they would possess their souls, (*Luke* 21:19) and the Apostle laid down the first condition of charity by saying, "Charity is patient." (*1 Cor.* 13:4).

For this reason, then, in the canonization of the saints, their works are considered more attentively than their miracles, and amongst their works most regard is given to patience, as the virtue that gives the best guarantee of charity and sanctity.

I have said this because all that I have written has been with the intention of doing as much as I can to draw the attention of Holy Church and her rulers to Catherine's holiness. Thus it is absolutely necessary that I should add this present chapter on the subject of her patience; then no one will be able to have any reasonable doubts about her sanctity.

However, as this holy virgin's life was absolutely interwoven with patience throughout, it is essential that I should make this bird's eye view of her whole life as short as I can, especially having in mind those readers who easily get bored, and find an hour spent reading about religious matters more like twenty-four, whereas when they are reading a romance or other such nonsense the time simply flies by for them.

In this brief discussion of Catherine's patience I shall proceed in a highly orderly fashion, since order precludes longwindedness and leads to brevity.

Those acquainted with the properties of the virtues will know that the virtue of patience is exercised in the things that are contrary to man—as the name itself implies, for the word "patience" comes from *patior*. The things that man generally finds repugnant can be divided into two kinds, corresponding to the two substances in him: some are contrary to the body, others to the soul. In the things that are contrary to the interests of the soul patience is never virtuous but always weakness, as the Apostle says ironically when he writes to the Corinthians, "For you gladly suffer the foolish: whereas yourselves are wise." (*2 Cor.* 11:19). It is in the things that are contrary to the interests of the body that the virtue of patience is exercised—and by the body is meant everything we feel during our earthly pilgrimage, as we shall see more clearly from what follows.

According to the philosophers, the goods that man can possess in this life are of three kinds, and concern pleasure, use and honour. In the temporary or continual privation of these is to be found the virtue of patience. The pleasurable goods are the life and health of the body, delights of food and clothing, and everything that is attractive to the flesh, including the pleasures of the senses. The useful goods are wealth in all its aspects—houses, fields, money, animals, entertainments—and whatever else derives from these—large families and servants, and all the other things that help people in this world. The honourable goods are those that make a man respected in the eyes of others—good name and reputation, friendship, love of study, and all the things that tend to encourage the virtues. Of these goods some are unlawful, and these there is no need to discuss; others are by nature obstacles to the perfection of the virtues, and it is necessary to be on guard against them, or rather to despise them; some are lawful and necessary to human life and privation of these is to be borne with patience. We shall see this very clearly when in due course we come to describe each of this holy virgin's actions in turn.

Now, with the Lord's help, let us begin to summarize what we have said about the perfection of patience in Catherine.

Good reader, she knew that the possession of patience would have been no use to her if she had not first put far from her all unlawful things, above all the pleasures of the senses; so, before she reached the age at which she could be troubled by them, she wisely and firmly cut them out. She was helped to do this by an inspiration from heaven and a surprizing vision.

When she was six years old in fact, she saw the Lord in pontifical attire, with the crown of the Supreme Pontiff on His head, sitting on a most beautiful throne situated above the church of the Friars Preachers and accompanied by Peter, Paul, and John the Evangelist. The Lord looked at her out of gentle eyes, blessed her with His right hand, and filled her soul with such perfect love that she immediately abandoned her childish way of life, gave herself entirely to penitence and prayer, and made such progress that a year later, at the age of seven, having matured her plan through prayer, she made a vow of perpetual virginity before the image of the blessed Virgin. This was described at length in the second and third chapters of Part One.

Then this excellent child, realizing that for her to preserve the state of virginity abstinence would be necessary, not to say essential, began to practise this from her most tender years, and with the passage of time brought it to a state of marvellous perfection. This we have dealt with in the third chapter of Part One and also again in the sixth, when we explained how in childhood she began to go without meat very often and then when she got to a certain age stopped eating altogether. And so with wine: she watered it down so much that it hardly had any of its colour left. When she was fifteen she gave up wine altogether and nearly every kind of food, living entirely on bread and uncooked vegetables. Finally, at the age of twenty she gave up bread too, sustaining her body with nothing but raw vegetables. And she went on like this until Almighty God granted her a new, miraculous way of living, that is to say, on nothing at all, which, if I remember correctly, she began to do when she was about twenty-five or six. I have described all this in great detail in the fifth chapter of Part Two, where I explained how and why she reached this condition and, I hope, gave a satisfactory answer to the sceptics who complained about her way of living.

Now that we have seen the beginnings of her purity and abstinence, which destroyed all the pleasures of the flesh as being unlawful, let us go on to speak of this holy virgin's patience.

Good reader, you must know that a great part of her patience was exercised in the privation of the honourable goods, although she suffered bodily illnesses and the hazards of a violent death. But all this was a source of happiness to her, as will be seen, whereas she was greatly afflicted by the privation of the honourable goods.

Who was there in her own house who did not worry her to death from her earliest days by depriving her of one honourable good or another? First there were her mother and brothers who wanted to marry her off when she was still a girl and adopted every means they could think of to deprive her of all good, until in the end they even stopped her from having a room of her own and made her do all the dirty work in the kitchen, so that she should not be able to pray or meditate or perform any act of speculative or contemplative virtue. The patience she showed during this time of persecution, and the spirit with which she put up with it, have been described at length in the fourth chapter of Part One. In a way that was truly marvellous and by means that were wonderful too she stood firm in her intention to remain a virgin. Then she was delighted to do all the housework, and never allowed it or the lack of a room of her own to prevent her from praying; in fact it was then that she would commend herself to the Lord! Until finally she overcame the persecution and her persecutors, as is explained in the aforesaid chapter.

After this, when the age-old Enemy tried to break the austerity of her discipline and vigils and prevent her from lying down on that plank bed, he goaded her mother Lapa against her to the point of frenzy, but Catherine, strong in patience, and armed with extraordinary prudence, managed to placate her mother's fury and go on with her austerities, as can be read in the sixth chapter of Part One.

There is no space to speak at length of all the other obstacles that the Devil raised up to deprive her of continual prayer, her mortification of her body and concern for the needs of her neighbours; I shall therefore confine myself to summarizing what I have said and point out where descriptions of these things are to be found in this book.

From the beginning the age-old Enemy adopted every method he could to keep the holy virgin from the embraces of her Heavenly Bridegroom, then to take her from Him, and finally to hinder her from enjoying them, at least for a time; but she hurled him down with her fervent enthusiasm, defeated him with the wisdom of her behaviour, and reduced him to confusion by the constancy of her virtue.

The Enemy in his malice first tried to unsettle her from her holy decision when he made use of her married sister, and for the sake of a greater good the Lord permitted Catherine to be led away by vanity about her hair and clothes, as is to be read in the fourth chapter of Part One. Then he used force upon her by way of her brothers and her mother, who wanted to force her to take a husband, as is described in the same chapter. In the end he put her to the proof himself, afflicting her with brazen temptations and visual delusions, as I recently discovered amongst the writings of the virgin's own secretaries, these things happening before Catherine received the habit of the holy society mentioned in the seventh chapter of Part One.

These writings relate that one day, when Catherine was praying before an image of the crucified Jesus, the Devil appeared to her holding a silk dress in his hand, and tried to put it on her. The virgin treated him with derision and disdain, and turning to the Crucified One made the sign of the cross; but after he had vanished she was seized with such a strong temptation to indulge in fine clothes that it quite disturbed her mind. Then, suddenly remembering her vow of virginity, she said to her Bridegroom, "O my most sweet Bridegroom, you know that I have never wanted any husband but you; come to my aid, so that in your holy name I may overcome these temptations. I do not ask for them to be taken away, but that in your mercy you will enable me to emerge victorious."

When she had said this the queen of virgins, the Mother of God, appeared to her, and it seemed to her that she took a most beautiful garment out of the side of her crucified Son and began with her own hands to embroider it with the most splendid gems, and she put it upon her, saying, "Remember, daughter, that the garments that come from the side of my Son are above all others in beauty and charm." Whereupon all temptation left her and she felt comforted, and her fervour was such that she was able to overcome all three obstacles, each of which had been designed to shake her in her holy intention.

This wise advice thus enabled her to foil those who wanted to lead her astray. First of all, without lessening her penances, she cleverly pacified her mother Lapa, who had been complaining about the austerities of her life, as I have explained more than once. Then, with the same cleverness, she won her battle with her confessor and her other advisers, who in their ignorance had tried to get her to take food, as is described in the fifth chapter of Part Two. Lastly, perfect in her obedience to God, she yet showed marvellous wisdom in soothing her superiors, and others who tried to stop her from going to certain places where by divine revelation she had been ordered to go, and from doing things that the Lord had commanded her to do. With what patience she had to arm herself, no pen or tongue can describe.

I have not forgotten all the innumerable insults that were inflicted upon her at this time by the very people who should have comforted her, but I think it more desirable to keep quiet about these than to mention them here. I also know that she triumphed over them all by being wise and patient.

However, though the Devil had not managed to make her renounce her intention he tried to prevent it from taking effect for a while at least, either directly through his own efforts or indirectly through others. He immediately tried to distract her from her disciplines and mortifications by getting Lapa to take her off to the baths; but Catherine managed to invent a more severe kind of penance than she practised at home by patiently remaining for a long time in the boiling waters, as is described in the seventh chapter of Part One. As I said in that chapter, this could not possibly have happened except as the result of a miracle, for it is incredible that she should ever have managed to endure this without being mortally or at least very seriously scalded. Then the Devil made use of tactless superiors, or priors who hadn't the faintest idea what they were doing, all of whom kept on trying to stop Catherine from going to confession and communion and from performing all the other acts to which her piety prompted her. They were like animals, condemning the light, while they themselves were in darkness; claiming to be able to judge mountain heights, when they were down in the depths of the valleys! This I described in the fifth chapter of Part Two.

There, however, I did not mention something that brings out the greatness of Catherine's patience better than anything else. I shall mention this now, even though it may bring a blush to the cheeks of certain religious. It is better to make it known than to hide the gifts that the Holy Spirit granted our virgin! From this incident readers may derive both fear and love; fear, on hearing of the sins of those who offended her; love, at the wonderful sight of the virtue of patience. And so readers themselves will learn to eschew evil and do good, and to be strong in patience.

Before I had the good fortune to know the holy virgin, it was difficult for her to perform any act of devotion in public without being criticized, opposed and persecuted, especially by those who should have done just the opposite and protected and encouraged her. But it must not be thought surprising, as I said in the fifth chapter of Part Two, if devout people fall into the state of envy more violently than people in the world: it simply means that they have not succeeded in rooting self-love out of their hearts. In this connection I mentioned the case of Pacomius's monks, who said that they would leave the monastery if Macarius was not made to go, because they could not emulate his austerities.

Well, then, something similar happened in our own case, for some of the Sisters of Penance of St. Dominic, seeing that young Catherine was outstripping them in austerity, wisdom, devotion, prayer and contemplation, allowed themselves to be taken in by that fomenter of envy, the old Serpent, and began to say evil things about the way she was behaving both in public and in private. So they and the superiors of the Order finally came to the conclusion that the virgin should be reprimanded. There were some who imagined they had reached a high state of perfection—and how determined they were to show it!—and were unable to deny what everyone else knew to be true; so, like the Scribes and the Pharisees, they simply said that Catherine was performing miracles through Beelzebub, the prince of devils.

These women, like true daughters of Eve, infected Adam and made him fall into the same error, Adam being in this case some of the superiors and fathers of the Order of Preachers, who succeeded in keeping Catherine out of their meetings and deprived her of Holy Communion and confession and a confessor; but she endured all these things patiently without complaint, as though the insults were not directed against her at all. No one can claim to have ever heard her break out into words of complaint or resentment. She believed that everything was being done with a right intention for her own good, and that she was under an obligation to pray for all these people, not as persecutors but as extraordinary and beloved benefactors.

When she was allowed to receive communion, they tried to make her get up straight away and leave the church—which it was in fact impossible for her to do, since she received communion with such devotion that her spirit was rapt out of her senses and her body remained without feeling for several hours, as is described in the second and last chapters of Part Two. Sometimes those who were led astray by the nuns were so incensed with her that when they came upon her in an ecstasy they would lift her up by force, insensible as she was, and throw her out of the church as though she was dirt; where her companions, with the midday sun beating down upon them, would stay watching over her with tears in their eyes until she returned to her senses.

I have even had it told me that while she was in ecstasy some of these people got so vexed with her that they actually took to kicking her; but from her mouth there never issued any word of complaint about these offences and outrages. She herself never said a word about them or anything else of a similar kind, except to excuse those who had done them.

The more insults she got the more perfect became her patience; but her Heavenly Bridegroom, who is the most just of judges, rose up against her tormentors and punished them severely.

My predecessor as her confessor and other reliable persons told me when I first got to know the virgin that one day a certain woman got into a temper and gave her a kick while she was in ecstasy; on her return home this woman died all of a sudden without receiving the Sacraments of the Church.

Another wretch[2]—and it would have been better if he had never been born—who had done the same thing and more than once had also lent a hand in dragging the virgin roughly out of the church, was punished so severely that I can hardly bring myself to describe it.

This wretched fellow, whom I knew very well, nursed a great hatred against the virgin, and I have been told by responsible people that as well as the deeds mentioned above he once even planned to kill her, and only failed because he could not find her where he was looking for her. Catherine herself was quite unaware of all this, but her Heavenly Bridegroom, who knows all things, had His revenge for all this wickedness. After a few days, in fact, the fellow went off somewhere else, changed from the sane person he had always been, went into a frenzy and became a maniac. Night and day he kept howling, "For the love of God, help me! The executioner is coming to cut my head off!" The people in the house tried to get him not to be afraid, but from what he went on doing and saying they realized that nothing was to be done about him. He was quite mad, and they had to keep a close watch on him all the time, for he had made it quite clear that he intended to try to kill himself. After several days he seemed to come back to his senses, and they stopped watching him, but one night he departed secretly from the castle like another Judas, hid himself in a wood and hanged

2. Some of Catherine's modern biographers identify this unfortunate religious with another person who conceived the wrong kind of love for the holy virgin, as described by the anonymous follower who wrote the "Miracoli"; but it seems far more likely, judging by the documents in the St. Dominic archives, that there were in fact two cases of suicide, one the result of the wrong kind of love and the other of hatred. In Friar Simone's deposition, mention is made of "a certain Friar Pietro di maestro Lando, who one day after dinner, having said grace with the other friars, left the choir and went down into the body of the church and with brazen impudence pricked her [Catherine] with a needle all over her body; but even this did not awaken her [from her ecstasy]. But when she returned to her senses she could feel that she had been hurt. This friar was later for his sins—though not for this one—imprisoned, and in the end was obliged to leave the Order for leading an undisciplined life; and he died outside the Order." Friar Pietro was in the monastery in the January of 1375 and the "Miracoli" were written between May and October 1374.

himself. To speak more carefully, in point of fact he strangled himself, since he attached the rope not to the top of the tree but to the trunk; then he proceeded to sit down on the ground with the other end of the rope fastened round his neck and was throttled.

I was told this by the person who found him afterwards and brought the body home. He was not buried in holy ground but simply put on a manure heap, as he deserved.

From all this readers will be able to appreciate how great this virgin's patience was, and how greatly the Most High appreciated this if He was prepared to revenge insults against her in such a way.

The honourable goods rightly include one's good name, and holy friendship. This obliges me to come to certain very grave trials that Catherine had to endure in the matter of these goods. They will give further proof of her incompble patience, which could be better described as fortitude or the highest charity, as we said in the fourth chapter of Part Two.

All the holy Doctors agree that a virgin's good name is a sensitive thing and maidenly modesty a very delicate matter, and that nothing is more unbearable for a virgin than the stigma of shame and nothing more upsetting than the charge of impurity. For this reason the Lord willed that His Mother, the Queen of Virgins, should have a putative husband, and when He was affixed to the cross He entrusted His Virgin Mother to the virgin John. Any virgin, therefore, who can endure this kind of defamation patiently, shows that she possesses the virtue of patience more clearly than she would in enduring any torture, however violent, inflicted upon her body. I shall therefore now give a summary of the three matters concerning this subject which occur in the fourth chapter of Part Two, the first being marvellous, the second more marvellous, and the third the most marvellous of all.

The first thing discussed there is the matter of a certain woman named Cecca who caught leprosy and had to go into hospital. She was destitute of everything, even help, for no one would go near her for fear of catching her disease. The holy virgin, however, when she heard about this, went off to her jubilantly and offered to help her and wait on her and find her everything she needed. And she kept her promise.

All this attention was too much for the poor woman: she got too big for her boots and began to scold and insult her benefactress, and even tried to provoke her; but the virgin, armed with great patience, remained unmoved.

Meanwhile from frequent contact with the leper woman the virgin's own hands became infected with the disease, but this did not prevent her from going on looking after her, for she would rather have been absolutely covered with leprosy than give up the job of looking after her tormentor. She did not leave her until she had buried her herself. Whereupon the leprosy disappeared miraculously from her hands.

Charity, which is patient and kind, taught her to suffer all these things and triumph over them.

Then there is the story of a certain Palmarina who like herself wore the habit of the Sisters of Penance. This woman, after persecuting and maligning the virgin with a fierce and obstinate hatred, first of all fell ill and then for her sins gradually declined towards the death of the body, and all but suffered the death of her soul too, only managing to avoid eternal damnation because of the prayers of the woman she hated.

On this occasion the Lord worked to marvellous effect, for whereas the sinner's heart grew harder and harder for lack of divine grace, the virgin's on the other hand was inflamed by the infusion of heavenly charity, and the more obstinate the one became, the more ardent grew the other. In the end perfect holy charity triumphed, and she who had grown hard through lack of charity was vanquished. By fervent and persevering prayer, the virgin Catherine triumphed over all the old Enemy's efforts to render Palmarina insensitive; her heart and lips were filled with such grace that she was able to save the woman's ail-but damned soul. The Lord looked so kindly upon what the virgin had done that it may be said that Palmarina's soul was saved through the merits of her prayers.

All this was accomplished through the perfect patience with which charity had moulded Catherine's soul, as is said in the already mentioned fourth chapter of Part Two.

In the first of these two actions, then, this holy virgin showed herself very patient; in the second, both patient and marvellous; in the third, which we are about to recall, she revealed herself as a marvellous miracle of patience.

As we have said in the latter part of the aforesaid chapter, there was in Siena a certain old woman who professed the same religious state as the holy virgin and who, according to the city's custom, whereby masculine names are changed into feminine ones, was called Andrea. She had a cancer of the breast in such an advanced and dangerous state that no one could go near her except by stuffing up their noses, and it was difficult to find anyone to look after her.

As soon as the virgin got to know about this, she hurried to look after Andrea for the love of Christ: neither the horrible smell nor the thought of possible infection prevented her from visiting the sick woman quite freely and unperturbed, and she carefully looked after her, unbandaging the affected part, cleaning it of matter, washing it and bandaging it up again. When, as inevitably happened, she felt herself being overcome by a feeling of nausea, she bent down, like the perfect master of her own flesh that she was, and put her face to the sore until her body almost failed her.

But as the Devil had entered into Palmarina, so now he entered into Andrea, who began to nurse suspicions about her conduct and then to gossip about her, until she finally spread crazy lies about her character to the Sisters, saying that this most pure of virgins had surrendered her virginity to sensual gratification. When Catherine got to know about this—and it caused her more suffering than can be imagined—nevertheless, having established her own innocence in the eyes of the Sisters, and with hot tears called upon her Heavenly Bridegroom to help her, she still went on giving the sick woman her aid, until through waiting upon her and helping her with loving care, strong in patience, she succeeded in triumphing over the wicked woman.

By the merits of her patience and in witness to her sanctity, this infamous woman saw her transfigured one day in front of her, surrounded by a great light: Catherine's face was truly transformed into that of an angel, and Andrea, as she said herself, was so contented in her soul by this that she finally acknowledged how unjust she had been. Whereupon, she begged the virgin with tears in her eyes to forgive her, and called together the people to whom she had slandered her. Sobbing bitterly, she told them the truth, took back the foul lies she had uttered against her, and said that Catherine was not only pure and virginal but a genuine saint. Thus Satan, having imagined that he was going to sully the virgin's good name, found to his own despite that he had only increased it.

All this was done by the Lord, acting through the virtue of patience. From now onwards the virgin's fame began to spread abroad, until it finally reached the Apostolic throne and the ears of most of the cardinals.

In this episode there was one occurrence that should not be forgotten. On one occasion when the virgin was helping Andrea, she was unbandaging the stinking sore, and perhaps because of the machinations of the Enemy of the human race her stomach could not endure it. Growing angry with herself, she said, "By the living God, my Heavenly Bridegroom, for love of whom I serve this my sister, what you find so repugnant will now enter into your bowels!" With these words, having thoroughly washed the affected part, she collected all the water and pus in a bowl and drank the lot.

The following night the Lord appeared to her and told her that by that action she had won the victory over herself, and He went on, "Since you have done such violence to yourself as to drink that loathsome drink out of love for me, I shall give you a marvellous drink that will make you admirable in the eyes of all human beings." When He had finished saying these words He as it seemed to her drew her mouth to His side, saying, "Drink as much as you want of this ineffably sweet drink from my side, daughter; satiate your soul, and the body which you despised for my sake."

From that moment Catherine's stomach had no more need of

food, nor could it digest any. Let no one marvel at this, for, having approached the fountain of life, she had drunk to satiety a living drink that did away for ever with the need to eat. Thus began the marvellous fast described in the fifth chapter of Part Two, to which we also made reference a little earlier.

Behind all this was the virtue of patience, since the charity that filled the virgin's heart had planted the seed of life in a field fertile and excellent, and was bringing forth the fruit of patience: thirty-fold in the case of Cecca and Francesca the leper woman; sixtyfold in the second case, in what the Lord did to Palmarina through the holy virgin; a hundredfold and more in this final occurrence in which Andrea was concerned.

After this brief résumé of the events described in the course of this story, it becomes necessary to add a number of other facts not so far mentioned.

It fills one with amazement to realize how even Catherine's most intimate acquaintances did things to upset her and make her unhappy in one way or another. Satan, in fact, persecuted the virgin even through those dearest to her. She herself confessed to me that she suffered more from them than from the insults she received from strangers: nevertheless, she triumphed over them all with her amazing patience. I know that I have already said it several times, but I say it again now before the Church, that I was always more edified by this patience of hers than anything else I saw her do, or heard she had done, not excluding the most breathtaking miracles and wonders.

Catherine was like a rock, established by the Holy Spirit in such great charity that no storm of persecution could unsettle her. She was solidly based on that Rock of which it is said by Wisdom, "As everlasting foundations upon a solid rock, so the commandments of God in the heart of a holy woman." (*Ecclus.* 26:24). Her soul had become so firmly bound to the supreme Rock, Christ, based on its everlasting foundations, that the holy woman had God's laws written ineffaceably on her heart.

I have been told that one of our own people, led astray by the Devil, often used to hurl vituperations and shameful insults against Catherine even in the presence of her companions. The virgin was so patient that she was not in the least disturbed by this and gave no sign of being upset. She even told her companions not to answer him back or reprove him, and not to tell me what they had heard him say.

At the sight of such patience this fellow degenerated even further and in the end went to the length of robbing the virgin of some coins which she had been given as alms. The virgin did not allow this to shake her out of her customary charity, and asked us to keep quiet about it— for we knew all about it—and even forbade us to show any resentment against him for what he had done.

She nourished her fortitude in silence and in hope, and so conquered in all things, teaching us to do likewise in both word and deed.

In attempting to relate all the patience that she possessed and manifested in her bodily illnesses, the mind is confounded and the very pen drops from one's hand.

She suffered continually from pains in her sides, as we said at the beginning of the sixth chapter of Part Two, where the reason for these pains was explained—the freeing of her father Giacomo's soul from the pains of Purgatory. She also had a continual headache, to which was added a very fierce pain in the chest, which began when the Lord made her taste the pains of His Holy Passion, as is also described in the sixth chapter of Part Two. This pain in the chest never left her, and it was the most painful pain she had. Besides these afflictions, which were almost always well-nigh unendurable, she was constantly tormented by fever. Nevertheless, she never uttered a word of complaint, and never for a single minute showed that she was incommoded by them. On the contrary, she would welcome everyone who went to see her with a radiant face, and cheer them up, and when her few words did not suffice to raise their spirits and she had to undertake some labour for the good of their souls, not even all the aforesaid maladies could restrain her. She would get up out of bed and set about her business as though in perfect health. This we have seen in the seventh chapter of Part Two.

It is not easy to relate what she suffered at the hands of the Devil. We have already described in the second chapter of Part Two how she was frequently thrown into fires and emerged unscathed, according to the words of reliable witnesses who were present at the time.

I myself was present one day at what I am about to describe, when we were on our way back to Siena. Catherine was sitting on a donkey, and we were getting quite near the city when she was thrown from the saddle and fell headlong down a deep ravine. I called upon the Blessed Virgin, and then I saw Catherine laughing gaily as she lay there upon the ground, and she was saying that it was one of the "Pickpocket's" blows—*i.e.* the Devil's. She got back on the donkey and we went on our way, but when we had gone about the distance of a bowshot the Evil Spirit threw her again, and she finished up in the mud with the animal on top of her. Whereupon, with a smile, she said, "This donkey is warming the side that is always hurting me." Thus, freed for the moment from the pains in her side, she made fun of the Enemy. I lifted her up out of the mud where she was lying spreadeagled under the donkey, and we urged her not to get on its back again because we were in any case quite close to the city; so she continued on foot between two of us. But the old Enemy would not admit himself beaten, and he kept pulling her now one way, now another, and if we had not held on to her there is no knowing how many times she would not have fallen down. And all the time she was laughing at him, treating him with contempt and mocking him.

This deluding of the Devil led to great fruit for souls, as is recorded in chapter seven.

These and other molestations by devils, which tried her patience as she proceeded along the path of her earthly life, also if I am not mistaken made her, and showed her to us to be, a martyr, when by the virtue of charity they forced her to end her life in the midst of indescribable sufferings. These are described at length in the second chapter of Part Three.

Reader, remember St. Anthony, who, hungry for martyrdom, had his wish granted and was whipped by devils though not to death. Our holy virgin, however, beaten and whipped as she was, finally, after receiving her last blow from the devils, was taken out of this life. For those who understand these things, this was a clear proof of her sanctity.

To show her fortitude, and to silence the tongues of her calumniators, I am now obliged to relate something which shows how closely she resembled her Heavenly Bridegroom, at least in the matter of suffering. And because I am aware of some causes of her suffering that are not known to others, I feel obliged, for the glory of the incarnate Truth and His bride the virgin Catherine, to insert them here before bringing this chapter to an end, whatever may be said by those who have learned to speak with lying tongues.

In the year of the Lord 1375, as is related in the tenth chapter of Part Two, where we discussed this virgin's spirit of prophecy, the city of Florence, which for many reasons could count itself amongst the most beloved sons of the Holy Roman Church, either through the fault of church officials or through the pride of the Florentines joined forces with the sower of cockles, the Enemy of mankind, and the enemies of the Church and fought fiercely to destroy her temporal power.[3]

---

3. At this time a rumour spread through Florence that the Pope intended to take control of Tuscany through his Legates. Some of these rumours were encouraged by the wily Bernabo Visconti, Lord of Milan. With the talk of Papal betrayal growing every day, the Florentines became restless and a chance of open war came when Cardinal Guglielmo Noellet, the Legate in Bologna, refused to grant them any grain from the Church lands during a famine though they were supposed to be his allies. He told them, instead, that he would not be able to receive the soldier of fortune "Giovanni Aguto", who until then had been in the service of the Church against the Visconti and who by the truce had been permitted to make inroads into Tuscany with his soldiery, saying that he was no longer in his pay. Behind this the Florentines imagined they saw a betrayal because if he had wanted to he could easily have received him; and this became a certainty for them when they discovered Aguto coming down upon Florence with the intention of taking Prato by surprise and threatening to fire the crops. Whereupon the Florentines bought Aguto and his soldiery off and there was open war with the Church. Later they joined up with Visconti, and thus the Guelfs and the Ghibellines joined hands to ruin the Church itself.

Through this conspiracy the Roman Pontiff, who, it is said, had been head over sixty bishops' cities and ten thousand castles in Italy, lost nearly all of them, and practically nothing remained under his control.

While these invasions were going on, Pope Gregory XI of happy memory published very severe decrees against the Florentines, with the result that they were imprisoned throughout nearly all the world and their goods were confiscated by the controllers and governors of the lands where they carried on trade. They were therefore obliged to sue to the Holy Pontiff for peace, for this purpose seeking the services of certain persons whom they knew to be in the Pope's favour. They were told that the holy virgin was very highly regarded by the Pope because of the fame of her sanctity. Whereupon they ordered me to go and see the Supreme Pontiff on the virgin's behalf, to placate him; and then they actually got her to come to the outskirts of Florence.

The Priors of the city went to meet her and implored her passionately and repeatedly to go to Avignon in person and see the Pontiff and negotiate peace. Catherine, brimful of love of God and the neighbour and zealous for the good of the Church, set off for Avignon. I was there too and I acted as interpreter between them, the Pontiff speaking in Latin and she in Tuscan. I can testify before God and man that that benignant Pope left the matter of the peace to the virgin, saying, "So that you may see quite clearly that I want peace, I leave the matter entirely to you; but have the Church's honour at heart."

But some of the city's deceitful rulers only wished for peace in words, and secretly only wanted it to come when the Church had been reduced to such a state of poverty that she no longer had any temporal power left and would not be able to take vengeance on them. I got to know this later from what some of them told me, when they revealed what till then had been kept hidden. They acted like real hypocrites, for while they were making out to the people that they were doing all they could to make peace with the Pope and the Church of God, secretly they were doing all they could to prevent it; and this became quite clear in the trick they played upon the holy virgin.

When in fact they begged the holy virgin to take this journey and to take this load upon her shoulders, they promised her that she would be followed by their ambassadors, who would not make the slightest move except upon her orders or advice. But in their wickedness they lied. The ambassadors were sent off, but too late; so that the Pontiff, failing to see any sign of them, when he met Catherine said to her, "Believe me, Catherine, they have hoodwinked you, and they will do it again! They will not send them, and even if they do their coming won't mean a thing."

When the ambassadors arrived in Avignon the holy virgin summoned them to her—I was there at the time—and, after reminding them of the promise that the city priors and governors had made her, she told them that the Pontiff had left the matter of the peace to her and that this was a good omen, and that if they really wanted peace they could have it. Whereupon these people, closing their ears against the voice of peace like deaf adders, replied that they had no mandate to confer with her or to wait upon her decisions. At this she realized their wicked cunning, and was obliged to admit that the Supreme Pontiff had been a true prophet. Nevertheless, this did not stop her from begging that same judge not to treat them harshly, but to receive them with mercy, showing himself to be not so much a judge as a father.

After the Vicar of Jesus Christ had been persuaded by the virgin to return to his seat in Rome, and had arrived there, we too set off on our way back to Italy. Having done certain things for the good of souls in Tuscany, the virgin sent me to see the Pope in Rome, with a number of suggestions which if properly carried out would be to the advantage of the holy Church of God.

While I was thus sojourning in Rome, I was obliged to shoulder the burden of the priorship of the monastery in Rome,[4] which I had previously had to bear in the time of Urban V of happy memory. This meant that I was unable to go back to the virgin. But before my com-

---

4. Raymond was elected Prior of the Minerva again in March 1378.

ing to Rome I had had a long conversation with a citizen of Florence who was highly attached to God and Holy Church and devoted to the virgin: his name was Niccolo Soderini.[5]

We had been talking about Florentine affairs, especially about this trick, which had made it clear that they wanted to make peace only in word with Holy Church, whom they had so greatly offended, whilst their deeds were designed to ruin her. As I discussed this wickedness with him, the good fellow, wise and straightforward as he was, said to me, "And yet you can be quite certain that all the people of Florence and the best men in the city want peace; but there are a few wicked ones who for our sins govern the city and who are preventing it." "Isn't there any way of remedying this evil?" I asked him. "One could be found," he said, "if such and such citizens would take it upon themselves to defend God's cause. It would be sufficient for them to come to an agreement with the leaders of the Guelfs to take over the command from this minority, as being enemies of the common good. For there are not more than four of them, or six at the most."

I kept all this to myself until the virgin sent me to see the Vicar of Christ, when I told him what I had heard from this good man. He had told me these things in Siena; then he went back to Florence, and I, as I have said, went off to Rome.

When I had been in Rome several months, labouring to govern the monastery and preaching the word of God, one Sunday morning someone came to see me on behalf of the Supreme Pontiff and told me that His Holiness was expecting me to dinner. I obeyed the command, and after dinner the Pope called me to him and said, "I have had a letter telling me that if Catherine goes from Siena to Florence I shall have peace." I replied, "Not only Catherine but all and every one of us are ready at

---

5. Niccolo Soderini, a very religious man exceptionally devoted to Catherine, came from a distinguished family, but he was on the side of the populace, as a result of which he was Standard Bearer of Justice and one of the Priors of the Arts. He joined with friends in building a villa for Catherine on the seashore at S. Giorgio. This house he later occupied himself when his own was invaded and burned down during the rising of the Ciompi.

a word of command from you to go even to martyrdom!" "I don't want you to go," he said, "because they would treat you very badly. As for Catherine, I don't think anything would happen to her, partly because she is a woman and partly because they have a reverence for her. You see what Bulls it will be necessary to draw up, and tomorrow morning bring me a written account, because I want to get the business settled." The next morning everything was ready and I took the account to him. When the letters had been written I sent them off to the holy virgin, who, like the true daughter of obedience she was, immediately set off on her journey.

When she arrived in Florence she was received with great respect by a number of people who had remained faithful to God and Holy Church, and through Niccolo Soderini she was able to meet some honourable citizens whom she prevailed upon not to persist in war and discord with the Shepherd of their souls but to be reconciled as quickly as possible with him, for he was the Vicar of Jesus Christ.

Then, still through Soderini, she met representatives of the Guelf party, to whom she said, amongst other things, that if any of them wanted to prevent peace and concord between the Father and his sons the only thing to do was to relieve them of their posts, because they were not worth calling rulers but were destroying the city and the common good; nor must they have any qualms about removing a few citizens from their midst to liberate their city. She also said that peace was necessary not only for bodily and temporal reasons but still more for the sake of the salvation of souls, which could only be attained through this peace; in particular, because hands had been laid publicly and scandalously on the goods that belonged to the Roman Church for the perfecting of her rule. Even if the Church had been a mere private individual, before God and before any judge whatsoever she would have been entitled to the restitution of all they had taken from her or allowed others to take from her; and if through peace this debt could be honoured the result would be great good, both for their personal interests and for their souls. By these and other arguments, the above-mentioned representatives and a number of other worthy citizens were induced to beg the governors and priors to sue for peace, and to make it not in words but in deeds.

Some, however, resisted these suggestions, especially those who had been waging war against the Church, and who were eight in number; but the representatives of the Guelfs, having the power, relieved one of these eight and a few others of their offices.

This led to two sudden inter-related outbreaks, one caused by the people who had been dismissed, the other by certain evil-doers who rose up in revolt, clamouring for the deposition of others whom they did not like, endeavouring thus, against the commandment of God, to satisfy their own personal lust for revenge. This second outbreak did more harm than the first, and raised up a lot of people against the holy virgin; so many people were dismissed from office that the whole city rose up in protest. But the holy virgin was in no way to blame, in fact she grieved greatly over it, and said again and again that these people were doing wrong in being so quick to raise their hands against so many, and that what had been done for the sake of peace should not be manipulated in a partisan way to create civil war.

Those who had been deputed to direct the war continued to follow their own evil ways and went from bad to worse, collecting together armed men, rousing the people against those who had caused the dismissals and throwing the whole city into confusion. In fact the populace rose in revolt and threw the authors of the aforesaid reforms out of the city, seized their possessions, set fire to their houses and, as I was told, thrust daggers into some of them.

In the course of this uprising, the intentional work of men with no sense of responsibility, many innocent people suffered, and most of those who wanted peace were obliged to go into exile. Amongst these was the holy virgin, who had gone to Florence solely for the sake of peace, and whose advice from the beginning had been to deprive those who were opposed to peace of their positions. Her name was the first to be mentioned by the evildoers, and it was presented in such a bad light that the ignorant populace took to howling, "Let us seize her! Let us burn this infamous woman! Let us slay her!"

At this the people with whom she was staying sent her and her followers away, saying that they did not want to stand by and watch their house being burnt down on her account. Conscious of her own innocence and glad to suffer for the sake of Holy Church, she lost none of her constancy, and, smiling and comforting her friends, she imitated her Bridegroom and went off to a spot where there was a garden, and there, having fortified them somewhat, set herself to prayer.

Finally, while like Christ she was praying in the garden, the satellites of Satan came rushing in with sticks and daggers, shouting, "Where is this infamous woman? Where is she?" Hearing the shouts, the virgin, as though she had been invited to a wedding feast, made ready for the martyrdom she had so long desired and went forward to meet one of them, who with dagger unsheathed was shouting the most loudly of all. Smiling she knelt down and said to him, "I am Catherine; do what the Lord permits with me! But on behalf of the Almighty I order you not to touch any of the people with me!" At this that wicked man was so taken aback that he no longer had the strength to strike and was ashamed to find himself in her presence.

After having sought her out with such ferocious eagerness, now that he had her in front of him all he could do was drive her away, shouting, "Go away from me!" But, hungry for martyrdom, she replied, "I feel so well here! Where should I go to now? I am ready to suffer for Christ and His Church: this is what I have been longing and asking for so long! Must I go away now when I have found what I want? I offer myself as a living host to my Heavenly Bridegroom. If you are destined to be my executioner, do what you have to do and have no fear, for I shall not move a single step from here. But you must not touch any of my people!" But the Lord did not allow this ruffian to inflict his cruelty on the virgin, and he went off absolutely dumbfounded with the rest of his companions.

Meanwhile Catherine's spiritual sons and daughters had gathered round her and were congratulating each other that she had emerged unscathed from those impious hands. But she herself was miserable and said, weeping, "Unhappy that I am! I thought the Lord Almighty was to bring my glory to completion today, and that, as He had deigned to grant me the white rose of virginity, so He would also bestow upon me the red rose of martyrdom. What a delusion! And all because of my innumerable sins, which by God's just judgement have deprived me of so great a good. How blessed had my soul been had my blood been shed for love of Him who redeemed me with His blood!"

The tumult now began to die down, but the holy virgin and her companions were still not by any means safe; in point of fact, the inhabitants of the city had all been seized with fear as in the days of the martyrs and there was not one who would take Catherine in. Her spiritual sons and daughters therefore advised her to return to Siena, but she replied that she could not leave the district until the Father and his sons were reconciled: this was the order that had been given her by the Lord. Not daring to oppose her they found a good man, who feared God but nothing else, and he took her into his house with him and kept her hidden there so that she would escape the fury of the people and their rascally leaders. After a few days, when the tumult had died down, the virgin mother and her spiritual children left the city, but not the district, and took refuge in a solitary spot where only hermits usually live.[6]

The riot having by divine disposition ended, with all the rebels punished by the law and sent off to different places, the virgin set foot in Florence again but remained in hiding, since she seemed to be such a source of annoyance to the rulers; then she appeared in public again, until, on the death of Pope Gregory XI and the election of Pope Urban VI, she could embark on the peace negotiations with the Florentines again, peace being concluded, signed and proclaimed in the city itself.

Then the virgin said to her sons and daughters in Christ, "Now we can leave this city. By the grace of Christ I have now done what

---

6. Traditionally believed to be Vallombrosa, where Catherine had friends.

He and His Vicar ordered, for I leave those who had rebelled against the Church at peace and reconciled with their good Mother. So let us return to Siena whence we came." And so it was done.[7]

Thus Catherine, in the Name of the Lord, escaped from the hands of the impious and obtained the longed-for peace. This was not done by men or by means of men but solely by Jesus Christ, who, with the help of the angels of peace, effected invisibly what evil men, helped by the angels of Satan, aimed to prevent.

From this episode anyone with a head on his shoulders will see what patience Catherine had, when she was prepared to suffer death; will also realize what a fund of natural wisdom she had, that taught her how to behave in such desperate circumstances; and will not fail to observe with what unconquerable constancy she persevered, beating on the door of the King of Peace until she had obtained peace for Florence and the Church.

Now, good reader, if I have not wearied you, this same episode proves not only the virtue of her patience but also the splendour of her charity and her uninterrupted constancy.

And now we come to the last act of her patience, in the course of which, enduring for the love of Christ and His Holy Church a hard and bitter death, she equalled and surpassed the merits of the martyrs. The latter indeed were tormented by men, who sometimes grow gentle, or more kindly, or tired; whereas Catherine was tormented by devils, who are always the same and never lessen their cruelty. Some of the martyrs received their martyrdom quickly, and their death was not always so violent; whereas Catherine was tormented most acutely for thirteen weeks, from Sexagesima Sunday to the next to the last day of April; and as her pains increased daily, so with corresponding joy she bore them all most patiently, giving thanks to God and gladly offering her life to appease Christ and preserve Holy Church from scandal. And so nothing was lacking to her of the merits and sufferings of a perfect

---

7. July 1378.

martyrdom, as is described in the second chapter of Part Three and repeated in the third and fourth chapters.

From this it may be concluded that in heaven Catherine has gained the double crown, of martyrdom by desire and martyrdom by blood. For those who understand these things, this means that her canonization may be proceeded with most confidently and in the shortest possible time, as usually happens in the case of the canonization of saints in whom the strength of martyrdom is to be found, for in those there can be no doubt or argument as to whether they also possess patience. For the rest, the witnesses we have named in the first chapter of Part Three swear to the things narrated in the second and subsequent chapters of the same Part.

All things considered, it can be said that the name of this saint, virgin and martyr should be recorded by the Church Militant in the catalogue of the Saints—and may this be granted to me and her other sons and daughters by the Eternal Goodness, who, one in three and three in one, lives and reigns, world without end. Amen.

Spread the Faith with . . .

TAN·BOOKS

A Division of Saint Benedict Press, LLC

TAN books are powerful tools for evangelization. They lift the mind to God and change lives. Millions of readers have found in TAN books and booklets an effective way to teach and defend the Faith, soften hearts, and grow in prayer and holiness of life.

Throughout history the faithful have distributed Catholic literature and sacramentals to save souls. St. Francis de Sales passed out his own pamphlets to win back those who had abandoned the Faith. Countless others have distributed the Miraculous Medal to prompt conversions and inspire deeper devotion to God. Our customers use TAN books in that same spirit.

If you have been helped by this or another TAN title, share it with others. Become a TAN Missionary and share our life changing books and booklets with your family, friends and community. We'll help by providing special discounts for books and booklets purchased in quantity for purposes of evangelization. Write or call us for additional details.

**TAN Books
Attn: TAN Missionaries Department
PO Box 410487
Charlotte, NC 28241**

**Toll-free (800) 437-5876
missionaries@TANBooks.com**